D1606298

SAS
IN ITALY
1943-1945

SAS IN ITALY

1943-1945

RAIDERS IN ENEMY TERRITORY

MALCOLM TUDOR

FONTHILL

Fonthill Media Language Policy

Fonthill Media publishes in the international English language market. One language edition is published worldwide. As there are minor differences in spelling and presentation, especially with regard to American English and British English, a policy is necessary to define which form of English to use. The Fonthill Policy is to use the form of English native to the author. Malcolm Tudor was born and educated in Newtown; therefore British English has been adopted in this publication.

Fonthill Media Limited
Fonthill Media LLC
www.fonthillmedia.com
office@fonthillmedia.com

First published in the United Kingdom and the United States of America 2018

British Library Cataloguing in Publication Data:
A catalogue record for this book is available from the British Library

ISBN 978-1-78155-697-9

Typeset in 10.5pt on 13pt Sabon
Printed and bound in England

Song of the 2nd SAS Regiment (Reggio Emilia, 1945)

'The Boys Who Ride the Slipstream'

We're reckless parachutists,
At least that's what we're told.
But when action station's sounded,
Then we don't feel quite so bold.

We're the boys who ride the slipstream,
We're the heroes of the sky.
But we all know deep inside us,
It's an awful way to die.

Stand to the door, stand to the door,
And my poor old knees are trembling.
Up off the floor, up off the floor,
And I'm seeing scores of gremlins.

Red light on! Green light on!
Out through the door we go.
Fighting for breath, battered near to death,
Drifting down to earth below.

We're the boys who ride the slipstream,
We're the boys who jump for fame.
If our parachutes don't open,
Then we get there just the same.

There's a big court of inquiry,
And the packer gets the sack.
But all the juries in creation,
Can't fetch that poor chap back.

(Lyric written by men of the regiment on duty on the Cisa Pass, sung to the tune of a famous German marching song.)

Contents

Introduction

On 10 June 1940, the Fascist dictator Benito Mussolini came out on to the balcony of the Palazzo Venezia in Rome and announced to a vast crowd that Italy was now at war with Britain and France. Military bands played and black-shirted youths chanted 'Corsica, Tunis and Suez', the first gains expected for the new Roman Empire. From the other side of the Alps, Adolf Hitler telegraphed that he was deeply moved by the historic decision and assured Mussolini and King Victor Emmanuel of Germany's total support in the struggle that was to come.

Over the following three years, Allied and Axis armies fought a savage war of attrition across the Mediterranean and the deserts of North Africa. In the summer of 1941, the Special Air Service (SAS) emerged as the inspiration of David Stirling, a young officer serving in Egypt, and most of its raids were carried out in Libya, an Italian colony since 1911. The unconditional surrender of all German and Italian forces in North Africa on 12 and 13 May 1943 then opened the way for the invasion of Sicily and the Italian mainland.

It was during this time—the last two years of the Second World War—that the SAS exploded on to the Italian scene. Its operations came in two waves, separated by deployment in France. In the first phase, the SAS mounted island raids, took part in the invasion of the mainland, rescued escaped prisoners of war, and supported the Anzio landings; in the second phase, it helped to breach the Gothic Line and to secure the victory, this time in concert with the Italian Resistance movement.

The 2nd SAS Regiment was responsible for a majority of the operations, while the Special Raiding Squadron (SRS) (temporarily replacing the 1st SAS Regiment) was also in action during Operation Husky, the capture of Sicily; Operation Baytown, the attack across the Straits of Messina; and Operation Devon, the capture of Termoli.

When the war ended in Italy on 2 May 1945, over twenty main SAS operations had taken place. All of them are covered in this book:

Snapdragon (Pantelleria); Marigold (Sardinia); Buttercup (Lampedusa); Narcissus (Sicily); Husky (Sicily); Chestnut (Sicily); Speedwell (Tuscany); Slapstick (Taranto); Baytown (Calabria); Begonia (Marche and Abruzzo); Jonquil (Marche and Abruzzo); Devon (Termoli); Candytuft (Abruzzo); Maple—Thistledown (Abruzzo); Maple—Driftwood (Marche); Pomegranate (Umbria); Baobab (Marche); Sleepy Lad (Marche and Abruzzo); Galia (Tuscany); Canuck (Piedmont); Cold Comfort (Bolzano); Tombola (Reggio Emilia); and Blimey (Tuscany).

These operations are shown with their actual landing areas, which were not always those intended by military planners located in North Africa or in southern Italy. In July 1944, the Allied Force Headquarters (AFHQ) for the Mediterranean Theatre of Operations, which planned and directed ground, naval, and air operations, moved forward from Algiers to the Royal Palace of the Bourbons at Caserta, 19 miles from Naples in Campania.

The story of the SAS in Italy has remained largely unknown and it is a pleasure to shed light on what many members of the Regiment called the 'Italian Job', well before the film of the same name.

The accounts are woven through with the ethos of the SAS as we have come to know it since the Regiment's birth in North Africa, but they also show how the men responded successfully to the different conditions they found in Italy, which helped to ensure final victory.

1

David Stirling

In June 1943, Lt-Col. David Stirling was among a group of officers given permission by their Escape Committee to attempt to break out of Italy's highest security prison. Known as PG 5, and often referred to as the 'Italian Colditz', the camp at Gavi, in the province of Alessandria in Piedmont, was designed to accommodate more than 200 Allied servicemen. Based in a medieval fortress, overlooking the town and strategic road links, the prison was the destination for Allied prisoners of war from all over Italy who had made at least one previous escape attempt. The men took great pride in calling their new home 'the bad boys' camp' and in being categorised as dangerous, unruly, and riotous by the Italians.

I was in contact with one of the officers who took part in the escape attempt with David Stirling: Lt John Muir, a Scotsman in the Durham Light Infantry, who was wounded and captured by a German Panzer light infantry unit on the Libyan–Egyptian border near Fort Capuzzo in April 1941. He recalled that Stirling had already participated in an escape attempt with eleven other men in April 1943, and that once things had settled down, permission was granted to start the new scheme at the end of June. It involved lifting a metal platform in one of the toilets and digging into the unused dungeon that lay below the row of cells, with the intention of seeing where they could go.

It took about a month to remove the metal platform (by using razor blades to separate the metal from the concrete) and to dig down along the sewage pipe through the roof and into the dungeon. The prisoners were disappointed to find that its main walls were composed of the solid rock on which the fortress was built. A side wall had a bricked up doorway and they removed enough bricks to get through it and into a passageway, but then found that it led to another door and a walkway that was in constant use by the Italians. This only left the front wall of the dungeon. The men removed three heavy stones and started to tunnel under the courtyard of their cell compound towards the outer wall of the fortress, but they had only gone 7 or 8 feet when the Armistice between the Allies and the Italians was announced by the Camp Commandant on the evening of 8 September. Both he and the Senior Allied Officer, New Zealand Brig. George Clifton, made it clear that the prisoners were to remain in the camp until arrangements were made to hand them over to the Allies.

However, in the morning, the men were awoken by the sound of gunfire. The Italian ration party had been ambushed. Most were killed, with only a few making it back to the fortress, closely followed by a German SS unit that took over. Three days later, the prisoners were told to pack and to be ready to move in the morning.

Brig. Clifton, Col. Stirling, Lt Muir, and everyone else involved in earlier escape attempts quickly disappeared into the dungeon they had found; they heard the roll call next day and the marching out of the prisoners. The Germans rushed about with a great deal of shouting and hammering, which continued well into the evening and started up again early next morning. At about 3 p.m. on the third day, the hammering was outside the bricked-up doorway leading to the passage and the Italian area. The prisoners heard the voices of Germans in the corridor, but then the troops went away, only to return an hour later, knocking down the door into the dungeon.

The German captain was delighted that he had found all the missing prisoners, fifty-eight in all. He told Brig. Clifton that he had obtained a plan of the fortress and that this had helped him to find the hiding place. The captives were locked up, but allowed to collect some kit from their cells in the morning. The next day, they were marched out, loaded into buses, and driven away with a massive escort of German military police. The party stopped in Mantua, where the prisoners were bedded down for the night on the football pitch, with guards posted all around the terracing.

The following afternoon, the captives were taken to a railway siding and packed into three cattle trucks. Lt Muir was put in a wooden one, which he learned after the war was just as well, as the others were made of steel, which offered far less potential for escape. The train moved off at dusk. The captives began cutting a hole in the wooden truck and had just finished making it large enough to squeeze through when the train arrived in Verona, a journey of 23 miles. There they spent a fraught half hour holding a blanket over the opening as German guards walked up and down on the platform.

The men drew lots in pairs, and John Muir was matched with Hugh Baker, a Rhodesian serving with the Royal Air Force. Also paired were Lt James Riccomini of the Royal Army Service Corps (a future member of the SAS) and Lt Harold Andrew Peterson of the 2/13 Australian Infantry

Battalion. Muir and Baker jumped from the train just after it had left Verona, swam the River Adige, and crossed into Switzerland near Villa di Tirano on 12 October. Riccomini and Peterson jumped later, when the train was on the main line north of Rovereto (40-odd miles beyond Verona), and they fled into the hills above Trento. They too escaped to Switzerland, in early 1944, as we shall see. However, no such opportunity was afforded to David Stirling and the other captives in the steel wagons. They had the pleasure of witnessing the discomfort of the guards when finding an empty wagon, but were then moved to camps in Greater Germany and held there until liberated in the last weeks of the war. Stirling was destined to join the other prominent prisoners held in the actual Colditz, *Oflag IV-C* in Saxony. He was finally released in April 1945.

The introduction to the *SAS War Diary 1941–1945* (which has been available in book form from Extraordinary Editions since 2011) includes this tribute to the Colonel:

> During the North African Campaign there appeared in the newspapers a few occasional and rather vague stories about a British officer known to the Axis troops as the Phantom Major. He was an incredibly successful raider behind the enemy lines. His command destroyed hundreds, if not thousands, of enemy planes and vehicles. The information he supplied to the British General Staff in Cairo was invaluable, sometimes decisive. He was Major David Stirling of the Scots Guards, and of the old Scottish family of Stirling of Kier.
>
> It's now possible to tell a little more—but not yet all—about David Stirling and his merry men; about a man who, an awkward and sensitive boy of artistic tastes, made himself into a most desperate and successful soldier; a man who chafed under Regimental discipline but was the happy warrior, and more than a regiment himself, when he got loose in the desert with a handful of fighters, and a jeep to take them about.
>
> SAS was never a large outfit. Each party in its jeep consisted only of three to four men. But a moderate calculation is that the hunting of David Stirling and his lads and defence against his darting forays, immobilised at least 5,000 Axis troops of quality. They got him at last. He was caught by the Germans, escaped, and was subsequently recaptured by the Italians, having been betrayed to them by an Arab.

How was it that this 'happy warrior' ended up as a prisoner of war? David Stirling had sailed with 8 (Guards) Commando on HMS *Glenroy* in the convoy that left Scotland for the Middle East on 1 February 1941. He spent more and more time sleeping as the voyage went on, and his companions in the small cabin on deck, Carol Mather and Frank Usher, became seriously worried about him. Mather recalled: 'True, he was not entirely a fit man and suffered from headaches, but the sleeping sickness became so endemic that he became known to fellow officers as "the great sloth", and one wondered if he would last the pace'. The Commando went on to form part of the 2,000-man Brigade led by Lt-Col. Robert Laycock and called Layforce.

In June 1941, twenty-five-year-old Lt Stirling was in a hospital bed in the Scottish Military Hospital in Cairo, recuperating from injuries caused in a parachute accident. Together with his friend John Steel (Jock) Lewes, he had been experimenting at jumping from an old, borrowed Valencia bomber, using some parachutes acquired by chance. While receiving treatment, Stirling learnt from another friend—the novelist Evelyn Waugh—that Layforce was being disbanded owing to a shortage of manpower and the failure of large-scale amphibious operations. In response to the news, he drafted a memorandum entitled 'Case for the Retention of a Limited Number of Special Service Troops for Employment as Parachutists'.

Stirling wrote an account of this original plan in 1948 so that it could be used by the Staff College at Camberley:

> I argued the advantages of establishing a unit based on the principle of the fullest exploitation of surprise and of making the minimum demands on manpower and equipment. I argued that the application of this principle would mean in effect the employment of a sub-unit of five men to cover a target previously requiring four troops of a Commando, i.e., about 200 men. I sought to prove that, if an aerodrome or transport park was the objective of an operation, then the destruction of fifty aircraft or units of transport was more easily accomplished by a sub-unit of five men than by a force of 200 men. I further concluded that 200 properly selected, trained and equipped men, organised into sub-units of five should be able to attack at least thirty different objectives at the same time, on the same night, as compared to only one objective using the Commando technique; and that only twenty-five per cent success in the former was the equivalent to many times the maximum possible result in the latter.[1]

The men engaged in these tasks would have to be to be capable of arriving on operations by land, sea, or air. The unit would also need to be responsible for its own training and operational planning, and so its commander would have to be directly responsible to the Commander-in-Chief. Finally, 'to help sell the proposition', Stirling put forward a plan for the employment of the unit in the approaching offensive, Operation Crusader, which began in November 1941.

Stirling delivered his proposals to Middle East Headquarters by slipping under the perimeter wire and making for the office of Gen. Neil Ritchie, the Deputy Chief of Staff and a family friend. The general agreed to discuss the document with the Commander-in-Chief, Gen. Claude Auchinleck. Three days later, Stirling was summoned to a meeting and he found himself before Auchinleck, Ritchie, and Maj.-Gen. Arthur Smith, Chief of the General Staff. After some discussion, they agreed that the unit would be formed immediately and that Stirling should continue to plan the proposed operation with the Director of Military Operations.

Stirling was promoted to captain and given authority to recruit the unit from Layforce and, if this did not provide the number required, from forward formations in the desert. There was already a phantom body known as the SAS Brigade. It had been dreamt up by Col. Dudley Clarke, head of MI9's deception and escape organisation, part of 'A' Force, based in Cairo. Stirling recalled that Dudley Clarke welcomed the creation of a real parachute unit, 'which greatly assisted him in his game with the enemy. To humour him, we agreed to name our unit "L" Detachment, SAS Brigade'.

The first recruits created the iconic SAS beret and insignia. The cap badge of a flaming Excalibur was designed by Sgt Bob Tait, though his motto of 'Strike and Destroy' lost out to Stirling's suggestion of 'Who Dares Wins'. The first berets were snow white in colour, but they were soon replaced by the sand-coloured version. The unit's operational wings were devised by Lt Lewes, inspired by the outstretched wings of the symbolic Isis in the foyer of the famous Shepheard's Hotel in Cairo. Personnel who completed SAS parachute training were entitled to wear the wings on their shoulder, and after three missions behind enemy lines, they could place them above their left breast pocket.

The first parachute operation to Gazala and Timimi duly took place on 17 November 1941 (Operation Squatter), as outlined by Stirling and led by him, but, in his own words, it turned out to be 'a complete failure'. However, over the next four months, the detachment carried out twenty raids on enemy targets, mainly landing grounds. Between April and June 1942, successful attacks were made on seven landing grounds in Cyrenaica and against another two in Crete after a voyage by submarine. By July, all the most important German and Italian aerodromes within 300 miles of the forward area had been targeted at least once or twice, and even three or four times in a few cases. Once the Eighth Army was based at El Alamein, the SAS launched attacks from a forward base in the Siwa Oasis. Stirling related that the most important operation (codenamed Bigamy), a raid on Benghazi, was also 'the least successful', but shortly afterwards, he was promoted to Lt-Col. and 'L' Detachment was renamed the 1st SAS

Regiment and given an establishment of twenty-nine officers and 572 'other ranks'.

When the Axis forces resumed their offensive, Gen. Montgomery, the new Commander of Eighth Army, ordered the SAS to concentrate on disrupting supply systems and communications. By this time, the regiment had put almost 400 enemy aircraft out of action, a higher number than that achieved by the RAF. 'We were able to contribute quite importantly to Rommel's difficulties,' Stirling recalled.

The SAS then took part in the Allied pursuit of Axis forces through the desert for 1,600 miles after the decisive Second Battle of El Alamein (23 October to 11 November). By the middle of January 1943, Stirling wrote: 'We had shifted our activities westwards and were mounting patrols and continued raiding on enemy communications as far north as Sfax in Tunisia. Incidentally, this is where I was captured by a German Reconnaissance Unit.' The colonel managed to escape, but was recaptured next day. Rommel, in a letter to his wife, Lucie, in February, wrote that with Stirling's capture, 'The British lost the very able and adaptable commander of the desert group which had caused us more damage than any other British unit of equal size'. On 23 February, the field marshal was promoted to commander of a new Army Group Africa, but on 9 March, he left the continent for ever after the failure of his attack on the Eighth Army at Medenine. On 12 May, his successor, Gen. Hans-Jürgen von Arnim, surrendered all German forces, followed next day by the surrender of the Italian First Army under Marshal Giovanni Messe.

On 14 February, the *SAS War Diary 1941–1945* reported Stirling's capture on 24 January in Tunisia and stated that he was 'missing, believed prisoner of war'. After being briefly interrogated by Col. Mario Revetria, head of Italian Military Intelligence in Libya, the colonel was flown to Sicily. Together with other POWs, he was then held in the police barracks in the north-eastern district of central Rome known as the Castro Pretorio. Italian Military Intelligence introduced a spy into the prison in the guise of a POW called Capt. John Richards, who was in fact Theodore Schurch, twenty-four years old, of Anglo-Swiss parentage, a former member of the British Union of Fascists, and a driver in the Royal Army Service Corps. He had been captured by Axis forces at Tobruk in 1942. Schurch attempted to befriend Stirling and claimed subsequently to have discovered the name of his successor as Paddy Mayne through their conversations, though the colonel himself related that he had been warned by another prisoner that the supposed captain was a stool pigeon for the Italians. Schurch was captured by the British and executed in 1946 after being found guilty of nine charges of treachery and one of desertion with intent to join the enemy.

It was after his encounter with Schurch that David Stirling was sent to Camp 5 at Gavi, the medieval fortress and camp in Liguria for POWs deemed 'unruly or riotous' by the Italians.

At the time of his capture, the 1st SAS Regiment included the French SAS Squadron, the Greek Sacred Squadron, and the Special Boat Section, which had been absorbed in August 1942. However, by the early spring of 1943, Middle East Command had decided that the regiment should be reorganised, and at the beginning of April, four of its five squadrons were formed into the SRS, under Maj. Paddy Mayne; the fifth squadron was detached as the Special Boat Squadron, led by Capt. the Earl Jellicoe; the French Squadron returned to the United Kingdom and was split into two regiments; and the Greek Sacred Squadron was sent to Palestine.

The 2nd SAS Regiment was also raised at Philippeville (now Skikda) in Algeria by David Stirling's elder brother, William. Indeed, when asked what 'SAS' stood for, David Stirling would always reply 'Stirling and Stirling, naturally'. William 'Bill' Joseph Stirling was born on 9 May 1911 and educated at Ampleforth College, Yorkshire, and Trinity College, Cambridge, where he gained a BA degree in 1932. He was commissioned in the Scots Guards, became an instructor at the Special Training Centre at Lochailort in Scotland, and commanded 62 Commando before leading the 2nd SAS Regiment from 1943 to 1944 with the rank of lieutenant-colonel.

The Stirling brothers are the two most eminent of the many colourful characters that populate our story, as we shall see in the next chapter.

2

'Tanky' Challenor

On 4 June 1964, a decorated SAS wartime hero sat in the dock of Number One Court in the Old Bailey between two prison officers. Many notorious criminals had appeared in the same place and this defendant had frequently given evidence from the witness box as a detective sergeant at the West End Central Police Station, helping to send a large number of lawbreakers to prison. On this occasion, he felt that he had something marginally in common with a member of this criminal fraternity, the Rillington Place serial murderer, John Christie, reflecting: 'He was an ex-policeman and I was certainly a mass killer, although I had the blessing of the state at the time'.

Harold Gordon Challenor, former member of the Royal Army Medical Corps, 62 Commando, and 2nd SAS Regiment, holder of the Military Medal (MM) for gallantry in action, was accused of conspiring with three junior detectives to pervert the course of justice by making unlawful arrests and false statements and by fabricating evidence in planting pieces of brick on people demonstrating against a visit by the King and Queen of Greece. On the recommendation of medical experts, Challenor was being detained under the Mental Health Act in a locked ward at Netherne Mental Hospital in Surrey, where he was treated with drugs and electric shock therapy. Before the trial was able to proceed, the jury had to decide if he was fit to plead, which depended on whether or not at the time of the crime he was suffering from a defect of reason such as to make him unaware of the nature of the act or that he was doing wrong.

As a formidable array of medical experts appeared to give evidence, Challenor's head seemed bowed to the people in the public gallery, but in reality his eyes had been drawn to the gleaming, black shoes of one of the prison officers sitting beside him, and his thoughts returned to the period when he was a soldier in wartime Italy. Challenor had been a POW and doing his utmost to withstand the brutal interrogations of the German SS, who wanted details about the secret mission he had been parachuted into Italy to carry out. 'They too had worn shiny, black shoes,' he recalled. 'I relieved those moments of terror, memories of which still wake me in the night, sweating and shaking.' Challenor believed that the trial was part of a major plan that required him to be publicly disgraced before he could be sent on another clandestine mission.

Once again, he switched off and another incident came to mind from his cloak and dagger days with the SAS. This time he remembered a jeep attack on a German staff car in a French forest in September 1944. The car blew up and Challenor shot an enemy officer. He reflected: 'I felt no remorse, only a great sense of elation. I was only doing what I had been trained to do. It was just one more Kraut to my personal tally'.

Challenor had been preparing himself for a return to these wartime days for several months because an inner voice had been telling him that he was being recalled for duty and should stand by for a highly dangerous and secret assignment, which would require all his old wartime skills: how to carry out acts of demolition after being parachuted from a low-flying aircraft; how to kill silently with his bare hands (using a piece of wire or a razor-sharp dagger); and how to withstand the most brutal interrogation without breaking down and revealing anything important to the enemy.

Challenor's thoughts returned to the present and he found that the jury had needed less than a minute to find that he was unfit to plead. The judge ordered that he be detained in strict custody until Her Majesty's pleasure was known, which meant either a return to Netherne Mental Hospital or a transfer to Broadmoor. Challenor rose to his feet, took a glance at the rapidly emptying court, and followed the polished shoes of the prison officer down to the cells; once again, it occurred to him that he had to endure this public humiliation before he could take part in the hush-hush operation with his old wartime outfit, the SAS. As he sat in the van that was taking him to a temporary billet at Brixton prison, he repeated the mantra that had stood him in good stead during those times: 'Who Dares Wins'.

Once they arrived at the jail, Challenor took in the cell, the barred window, and the sense of brooding, unknown terror, and believed that he was back in the POW camp in wartime Italy. However, when he was escorted around the yard by a young prison officer, he gradually realised that he was in Brixton prison, which he had visited many times in an official capacity in order to interview prisoners.

Challenor asked himself what he would not give to be back with the lads on a sky drop behind the enemy lines: 'If only I could make a break for it! But the reality of my situation became apparent the more I thought about it. Where would I escape to? There were no friendly lines to strike for, no welcome back like before, certainly no hero's welcome. I had to take my medicine'.

Harold Gordon Challenor was born on 16 March 1922 in Bradley, near Wolverhampton, Staffordshire, the second of five children. Their domineering and often-violent father, Thomas, a steel worker and a soldier in the Staffordshire Regiment during the First World War, lost his job during the economic depression of the early 1930s and walked to the south of England to find employment. The family followed him to Caterham in Surrey, but over a period of less than three years, they had to make eight moonlight flits to avoid irate creditors before finally settling in Garston, near Watford, Hertfordshire.

The young Challenor was known to his family as Peter, to his army companions as Tanky, and to fellow policemen and most other people as Harry. At Leavesden village school, he was an able student and a fine sportsman, but at age fourteen in 1936, he was obliged by his father to find full-time employment and became an apprentice in the machine shop at Scammell Lorries. The young teenager left after only six months to join his father, who was now working as a nurse at the Leavesden Mental Hospital, located on the outskirts of Abbots Langley: 'Not to be near him,' he recalled, 'but in order to keep away from him: single men lived in.'

In his own words, Challenor 'itched for action', and once he was eighteen in March 1940, he volunteered to join the armed forces, but was turned down successively by the Royal Navy, owing to a hernia, and by the RAF, owing to lack of educational attainment. While waiting for his call-up papers to arrive, he left the hospital and drifted into a variety of jobs before becoming a driver and labourer for the de Havilland Aircraft Company, working on building a new airfield locally and then on extending another one near Liverpool.

On 30 April 1942, Challenor was finally called up, but his joy was short-lived when his nursing experience led to him being posted to the RAMC, rather than to a fighting unit. He was eventually sent as a reserve on attachment to the First Army, based outside Algiers, which had been created to command British and American land forces involved in the occupation of French North Africa.

One morning, two rakish-looking officers arrived at the base seeking recruits for 62 Commando; one of the pair was Randolph Churchill, the Prime Minister's son. Challenor volunteered immediately, but there was a catch: he was told that he had to remain a medical orderly. However, once the unit moved to the Commando Headquarters in Philippeville, he managed to wheedle his way into all the training activities, and his proficiency was assessed as high in every category. It was at this time that he lost his beret and replaced it with one from the Tank Corps, being promptly christened Tanky, a name which followed him throughout the war.

Challenor was strongly built, deep-chested, and over 5 feet 10 inches tall. A fellow police detective remarked that in his face you could see authority, determination, decisiveness, and ruthlessness. Challenor himself related that he was rough, tough, coarse, and often profane, saying: 'There was no doubt that I was the most aggressive medical orderly the Commandos ever had'. His repeated lobbying finally worked, and he was told that he could hand over his medical duties to another member of the corps and join a fighting formation. More extensive training followed and rumours began to circulate that 62 Commando was to be expanded and developed into an extremely elite unit. A period of rapid activity began as the commando was transformed into part of the 2nd SAS Regiment.

Tanky Challenor's itch for action was about to be met.

3

Island Raids

New recruit to the SAS, Harold 'Tanky' Challenor, first saw action on 30 May 1943 on the island of Sardinia in Operation Marigold, one of a series of small probing and reconnaissance missions launched as the Allies sought to advance from North Africa. He wrote later that Col. Bill Stirling 'must have had an odd sense of humour because he liked to name his sorties after flowers'.

The mission was in two parts: first, two men would be landed at a point on the coast in order to leave a notebook at a marked spot for collection by a secret agent; second, an attack would be carried out on a poorly-manned German guardhouse at a different location; one of the occupants would be taken away for interrogation, but the others would be killed.

The commanding officer was Capt. Roger James Allen Courtney of the Special Boat Section, with the rest of the party made up of two other members of the section, plus Capt. Patrick Dudgeon and seven 'other ranks' from the SAS. Capt. Courtney, known as 'Jumbo, in his early forties, had been a big game hunter and prospector in East Africa, and had travelled down almost the whole course of the White Nile from Lake Victoria to Egypt in a two-man canoe. He served as a sergeant in the Palestine Police Force, and on the outbreak of war in 1939, he returned to the United Kingdom and was commissioned in the King's Royal Rifle Corps. In 1940, Courtney joined 8 (Guards) Commando at the Combined Training Centre in Scotland and put forward the case for a seaborne raiding force, deploying a type of folding kayak that was manufactured by the American Folbot Company and was in use by civilians for sporting purposes.

At first, the officers involved in Combined Operations were highly sceptical over the use of the folbot, but after demonstrating the effectiveness of the concept by carrying out two mock raids on HMS *Glengyle*, an infantry landing craft at anchor in the River Clyde, Courtney was made commander of a new Folbot Section, with second in command

Robert Wilson and sixteen 'other ranks'. The design of the craft was adapted for military use by the addition of navigation aids, spray covers, bow and stern buoyancy bags, and inflatable tubes on the gunwales to add stability. On 1 February 1941, the section was part of the commando flotilla that left Arran to form 'Layforce' in the Middle East. In June, Lt Wilson and Marine Wally Hughes landed from a folbot on the coast of Italy and blew a goods train off the tracks. It was around this time that the unit was enlarged and renamed the Special Boat Section; it became part of the SAS in August 1942 and regained its independence as the Special Boat Squadron on 19 March 1943.

Capt. Patrick Dudgeon, Royal Corps of Signals, was born in Egypt to a Hampshire service family. At only twenty-three years old, he had already been awarded the Military Cross (MC) and Mentioned in Dispatches. Challenor recalled: 'He stood over six feet tall and was viewed as something of a Capt. Bligh character. Oddly enough it did not diminish the affection we held for him.... Charisma was not a word that was in common use then, but it certainly applied to him'. The captain's nickname was Toomai, inspired by the elephant handler in a short story by Rudyard Kipling, which had been popularised in the 1937 film *Elephant Boy*.

The small force engaged in Operation Marigold left Philippeville for Algiers at the end of May 1943 and boarded HMS *Maidstone*, the depot ship for a flotilla of submarines. After a restless night in hammocks, the men embarked on the submarine HMS *Safari* (P 211), captained by Lt-Cdr Barklie Lakin, one of the most successful British wartime commanders. The journey to Sardinia took five days on a circular route and the vessel was forced to remain under water during the long hours of daylight; as a result, the air became fetid and the bulkheads dripped with condensation, creating a claustrophobic atmosphere for the parachutists, who were unused to the confined space.

When the submarine reached the area for part one of the operation to be carried out, a periscope reconnaissance revealed a house and three pill boxes on the shore, but no defences for half a mile southward. Once night-time arrived, the submarine surfaced and Capt. Courtney and Sgt Thompson climbed into a folbot and paddled ashore. The sergeant kept watch on the boat while the captain headed inland; he saw a house with the lights on and heard voices and the barking of dogs, but by-passed it without anyone coming out, and placed the notebook in the appointed place; both men then returned to the submarine.

On the following day, HMS *Safari* reached the area where part two of the operation was to take place. A detailed periscope reconnaissance of the site was carried out from 8 a.m. to 3.30 p.m., and it revealed that only four German soldiers were moving in and out of the guardhouse. Capt.

Courtney decided that the best landing point would be a group of rocks, about 10 feet high, which should provide some cover for the boats from the guns ranged on the area.

At midnight, the submarine surfaced and the raiders got into their dinghies, but as soon as they started for the beach, things began to go wrong. There was a north-west current of about half a knot, which increased the length of the journey three-fold to one and a half hours, and when the men did reach the landing point, they were unable to disembark because they discovered jagged rocks hidden under the surface of the water; a lengthy detour was necessary, but fortunately 'there was no sound or movement from the shore'. As the landing was behind schedule, it was decided not to deflate the dinghies, thus ensuring that they would be ready when the time came to pull off, though this also made them easier to detect by the enemy.

When the attackers began to climb the steep cliff to the enemy guardhouse, their boots made a noise so loud on the loose shale that they began to worry that someone would hear them. Challenor recalled that when they were about a third of the way up the slope, 'Private Hughes dropped his gun and there was a clatter of steel on stone. I can still hear the clatter now; it seemed to echo along the beach like an avalanche. Seconds later machine guns and small arms fire opened up from all directions'. The enemy lit a ground flare and suddenly from pitch darkness 'it was Piccadilly with the lights on'. The raiders were exposed like ducks in a shooting gallery, but it soon became obvious that the enemy could not see them clearly from their elevated position, as most of the bullets went high over their heads.

Challenor was relieved to find that he had not been scared in his baptism of fire; on the contrary, he had been eagerly waiting to hear the order to charge the enemy. Capt. Courtney knew better and ordered the men to withhold their fire as it would give away their position; he told them to disperse and to make their way back to the boats. Challenor found himself in a dinghy with Sgt Fitzpatrick and two other men, and they began paddling frantically to escape the enemy fire. They were eventually able to pull away into the darkness and then to take a compass bearing on the rendezvous position for the submarine, though they had far exceeded the estimated time of arrival and were even discussing the prospects of rowing back to Algiers. Suddenly, 'a large shape like a surfaced whale loomed to port'. The crew of HMS *Safari* had turned a blind eye to their orders not to jeopardise the safety of the craft by remaining in the area longer than intended; Lt-Cdr Lakin had even been making arrangements to put a landing party ashore to help out.

As a sailor lent down to give Challenor a hand out of the dinghy, he asked jocularly: 'Well, where's your prisoner?' Challenor replied with a grin: 'Still sitting behind a bloody great machine gun'.

It seemed at first that all the other members of the party had returned too, but Capt. Dudgeon, who was the last man on board, revealed that his Special Boat Section companion in a folbot, a Sgt R. W. Loasby, was missing; later, it was discovered that he had survived and was being treated as a POW.

The submarine dived and made for open sea, but after a short time, the lieutenant-commander gave the order to stop engines and the vessel settled on the sea bed, with the occupants forbidden to speak or to make a noise. Once it became clear that there was no search underway by enemy shipping on the surface, the submarine set off for North Africa, arriving at the port of Bone in Algeria at 8.30 a.m. on 3 June.

Challenor reflected that the party had achieved very little in the raid, apart from leaving the message and discovering that the enemy was very much on the alert. However, this knowledge was tempered by the fact that it had given him great personal satisfaction. He recalled: 'I had faced the enemy for the first time and felt no fear. In fact, my only regret was that I had not had a chance to kill any of them.'

Once safely back in North Africa, the unit was sent for parachute training in Mascara. Three daylight drops from a Dakota at a height of 300 feet were deemed sufficient, and the men became entitled to wear their wings on their tunics and to claim 2 shillings a day extra pay. It was during this time that Challenor met his future commander for SAS operations in France, Roy Farran, whom he described as stocky, with a very strong face, cold, penetrating eyes, and a row of medals that were evidence of why he had become a legend among fighting soldiers. More intensive instruction followed back at Philippeville, with the emphasis on demolitions, weapons training, and endurance. At this point, Challenor succumbed to his first bout of malaria; he had refused to take anti-malarial tablets, even though mosquitos thrived in a nearby swamp and most of the regiment were afflicted at one time or other. He said later that he had thought that sheer willpower could defeat the attentions of the insects.

After several months, the atmosphere changed suddenly and Capt. Dudgeon, Challenor, and eleven other men were selected for training on sabotage operations on railways. Four days after the successful invasion of the Italian mainland in the south on 3 September 1943, Operation Speedwell would be under way.

In the meantime, the island raids by 2nd SAS continued. Another mission was to the small island of Pantelleria, located in a strategic position 25 miles nearer to Tunisia than to Sicily, which served as an enemy base for both aircraft and E-boats. It would have to be subdued as a prelude to the invasion of Sicily (Operation Husky) and could then act as a base for Allied aircraft.

The party left Malta at the end of May in the submarine HMS *Unshaken* (commanded by Lt John Whitton) in Operation Snapdragon. The raiding force consisted of Maj. John Geoffrey Appleyard, DSO, MC, Commanding Officer; Lt John Cochrane, who was a Canadian from the Toronto Scottish Regiment; two sergeants; and six parachutists. The youthful major had been chosen personally by Gen. Alexander for the task, and he already had a wealth of experience as a commando and as commander of the Small-Scale Raiding Force before joining the SAS. The party had orders to find suitable landing places for an invasion force, to obtain intelligence on the Italian troops' strength and dispositions, and to take a prisoner for interrogation.

After arriving off the island, a careful periscope reconnaissance was made and the base of a high cliff was eventually chosen as a suitable landing point for the mission. Shortly before midnight on 28 May, the raiders disembarked from two RAF rescue dinghies, left one man to guard the craft, and began to climb the volcanic rock face. After almost three quarters of an hour, they reached the top and the major ordered Lt Cochrane and two men to guard the route down, while he left with three companions to find a sentry to capture. The two parties then had to hide in the gorse from the relief guard, which marched past at a distance of a few yards.

According to Cochrane's recollection, Appleyard finally heard a sentry singing ''O Sole Mio' and decided to pounce: 'They crept silently up to him and then Geoff sprang for his throat. In the uncertain light he missed his hold and the sentry let out a scream of fear'. The sound alerted the next guard, who was 50 yards away, and he came running through the gorse to investigate. One of the parachutists tried to head him off, though only armed with a rubber truncheon meant to deal with the sentry who was to be captured, but he was cut down by a burst of automatic fire. Gunner Ernest Maxwell Herstell, aged twenty-seven, was a married man from Charlton-cum-Hardy, Manchester. Appleyard and his two remaining men fought off the rest of the guards on the cliff edge and then he gave the order 'Every man for himself'.

The two parties of SAS men began to climb back down the 100-yard-high cliff, but in the chaos, their prisoner was accidentally dropped, and he broke his neck on the rocks below. Despite machine-gun fire and illumination from signal lights, all the remaining men were able to reach the dinghies and to give the emergency signal to the submarine of two grenades thrown in the sea; the explosion brought the craft to the surface in a hurry and the raiders swiftly clambered on board for the return journey to Malta.

On 11 June, the island of Pantelleria was taken by the British in a landing by sea after a fierce naval and aerial bombardment; the Italian garrison of 12,000 men immediately surrendered. Prime Minister Winston Churchill noted in his wartime memoir that, according to sailors' stories, the only British casualty of the operation was a soldier bitten by a mule.

Another early mission to the islands displayed elements of farce. SAS Operation Buttercup (the third given that name during the war) was a raid on a radar station on Italy's southernmost island of Lampedusa, which is only 70 miles from Tunisia, but 127 miles from Sicily. The commanding officer was Lt Anthony 'Tony' Greville-Bell, aged twenty-three. The Royal Artillery officer was born in Sydney, Australia, but received his education in the United Kingdom at Blundell's School, Tiverton, in Devon.

The raiding party left their motor torpedo boats and took to canoes, but at a distance of about 300 yards from the shore, a green flare suddenly burst above their heads and machine-gun fire began to rain down on them from the cliff top; the men beat a hasty retreat. Greville-Bell related: 'It didn't occur to the planners that the radar station would pick us up as we approached'. He added: 'The thing about war is that you plan and plan, but the ones who win are the ones who are most able to overcome disasters, because nothing ever goes the way it's supposed to'. The lieutenant was another member of 2nd SAS who took part in Operation Speedwell in September 1943.

The Italian garrison on Lampedusa surrendered without resistance on 12 June 1943, when a party of Coldstream Guards was put ashore from the Royal Navy destroyer HMS *Lookout* in Operation Corkscrew. No enemy garrison now remained south of Sicily.

4

'Paddy' Mayne

The next stage in the story of the SAS in Italy is inevitably tied up with the formidable and charismatic figure of Robert Blair 'Paddy' Mayne. He was born to a Northern Irish Protestant family in Newtownards, County Down, on 11 January 1915. His father and mother, William and Margaret, owned a wine and grocery shop and lived in some style in a house called Mount Pleasant in the hills above the town. Blair, as he was usually known to family and friends, was the second youngest son of seven children. He attended Miss Brown's Lady School and then the local grammar school, Regent House, where he was liked by everyone and remembered as a tall and gangly boy who was quiet and modest, bookish, and keen on all types of sport.

When he left school, Mayne was articled to a solicitor in Newtownards and began to read law at Queen's University in Belfast. At the age of eighteen, he became captain of the Newtownards Rugby team. Three years later, he was Irish Universities' Heavyweight Boxing Champion, an impressive figure at 6 feet 3 inches tall and over 15 stone in weight. Mayne received the first of six caps playing rugby for Ireland in 1937, and in the following year, he was a forward in the British and Irish Lions Team that toured South Africa. His captain, Samuel Walker, recalled: 'He was quiet, soft-spoken and self-effacing off the field, but in the heat of a match he could be frightening. He was the toughest and strongest man I have ever known'. During the tour of South Africa, Mayne smashed up his companions' hotel rooms, picked fights with longshoremen, freed a convict from a working party, and left a formal dinner to go hunting antelope with new barroom friends.

In December 1938, as Britain prepared for war, Mayne applied to join the Army, although as a cadet in the Queen's University Belfast Contingent, Officer Training Corps, he had been assessed as 'unpromising material for a combat regiment, undisciplined, unruly and generally unreliable'. He clearly impressed the Selection Board, though, as on 27 March 1939, he was commissioned as a second-lieutenant in the 5th Light Anti-Aircraft Battery of the Royal Artillery. The battery was deployed to Egypt following the outbreak of war in September 1939, but Mayne did not go with them and he spent several frustrating months in Belfast. His longing for action led him to transfer to the Royal Ulster Rifles on 17 April 1940 and then to move successively to the Cameronians (Scottish Rifles) and finally to Number 11 (Scottish) Commando, where he felt at home.

The unit was based in Lamlash, the largest village on the Isle of Arran, and the men were billeted in local houses. The lessons in field craft were designed to teach them how to destroy things quickly. They were told that if raids were to be of real military value, the aim had to be to destroy anything important to the enemy's war effort—communications, transport, ships, docks, planes, weapons, ammunition, and food. Destruction could be achieved with fire, with sabotage, with booby traps, and with explosives.

During their four months on Arran, Mayne and his best friend, Eoin McGonigal, a Roman Catholic, ran the Commando shooting courses. The most effective personal weapons proved to be the short and light American Thompson M1 sub-machine gun, popularly known as the Tommy gun, and the British .303-calibre Bren light machine gun. It was gas-operated, air-cooled and shoulder-controlled, and had a fire rate of 500 rounds a minute. The gun was normally fired from the bipod, though it could also be mounted on a vehicle or on a tripod to act in an anti-aircraft capacity. It was recorded that Mayne was a great shot with the Thompson sub-machine gun and also with a Colt revolver.

On 31 January 1941, 11 (Scottish) Commando joined 7 Commando and 8 (Guards) Commando in embarking on three large Landing Ships (Infantry): HMS *Glenroy*, HMS *Glengyle*, and HMS *Glenearn*, which were originally built as merchantmen for the Far East run. The men paraded on deck for the arrival of Admiral of the Fleet and Director of Combined Operations, Sir Roger Keyes. He addressed the men with stirring words, but on grounds of security, he refrained from informing them of their future role or their destination.

Together with an escort, the ships set sail next day for a voyage of six weeks around the Cape of Good Hope, following a circuitous route to the Middle East to avoid the submarine menace. During the enforced confinement, gambling, drinking, and endless speculation became the harmless pastimes of the officers. On 7 March, the ships sailed up the Suez Canal to the Great Bitter Lake in Egypt, where they dropped anchor. Three days later, they were visited by Lt-Gen. John Fullerton Evetts, General Officer Commanding 6th Infantry Division, under whose command they were to serve. He told them that the commandos were to be brigaded into 'Layforce', under the leadership of Lt-Col. Robert Laycock. The men disembarked and were taken to basic tented accommodation in the Canal Zone.

Number 11 Commando subsequently moved to Kabrit, site of an RAF station, and now known as Kibrit. After desert training, they were transferred to Cyprus. On 9 June, the force took part in a raid to secure the lower reaches of the Litani River, in present-day Lebanon, part of Churchill's plan to advance into Syria and to remove the collaborationist Vichy French regime.

Though a bridgehead was eventually created, the Commanding Officer, Lt-Col. Richard Pedder, four other officers, and 127 men were killed. Mayne was mentioned in dispatches for his part in the operation, during which his troop captured an enemy headquarters and ninety soldiers. At the young age of twenty-four, Maj. Geoffrey Keyes, son of Sir Roger Keyes, was appointed the new CO of 11 Commando and promoted to acting lieutenant-colonel. Educated at Eton and Sandhurst, the Scots Greys' officer had already won the *Croix de Guerre* for service during the Norwegian Campaign. He was awarded the MC for his part in the Litani River raid and would also receive a posthumous Victoria Cross for leading the failed attempt to assassinate Rommel (Operation Flipper) on 17–18 November 1941.

By July, the commando was back in Cyprus on garrison duty. It is said that, one night, Mayne ran amok with a rifle and bayonet and chased everyone out of the mess, including his new CO. When the commando moved back to Kabrit in Egypt, there was an even more serious incident. Mayne's youngest brother, Douglas, recalled: 'Blair and Eoin McGonigal were playing chess together. Perhaps it was regarded as inappropriate for them to be playing chess on a mess night, but according to Blair the manner in which Keyes, the Commanding Officer, approached them was asking for trouble'. Mayne rose from the table and knocked Keyes down; he was immediately placed under close confinement, with the threat of an imminent court-martial.

David Stirling related that Mayne's temperament and moods made him a difficult subordinate, describing him as quick-tempered, audacious, and vigorous in action, but not one who took kindly to being thwarted, frustrated, or crossed in any way. To add to the problem, Mayne had a dislike of anyone in authority who came from a privileged background. During a conversation one evening in the mess at Kabrit, Stirling told Mayne about his frustrated ambition of becoming a professional artist, and the Ulsterman replied that he had always wanted to be a writer. In retrospect, Stirling suggested that there was no outlet for Mayne's creative energy and that it got repressed to an intolerable level, leading to 'some of his heavy drinking bouts in an attempt to open the closed door'. This frustration explained at least some of his violent acts and his black moods. Among its positive effects, it also explained his astonishing intuition and inspiration in battle.

Stirling had gone to see Mayne when he was recruiting for his new detachment and found that he was initially 'very suspicious'. However, once Stirling told Mayne what he was up to, he could see that he was becoming extremely responsive, recalling: 'After half an hour or so, he committed himself to come and join me. It wasn't because by joining me he got out of prison, it was because he wanted to. The SAS was something that he'd been dreaming about'. Stirling, though, did feel the need to make a deal with Mayne that 'This Commanding Officer isn't for hitting', an undertaking, he thought, that was given slightly reluctantly but was always kept.

Mayne played a prominent part in many of the SAS raids in North Africa from November 1941 to December 1942. For his gallantry during the first of these—an attack on the airfield at Tamet in northern Libya on 14 December 1941—he was awarded the Distinguished Service Order (DSO), though Stirling wrote later: 'Paddy was brilliantly successful but he pushed ruthlessness to the point of callousness'—referring to the mowing down of around thirty German and Italian pilots, who were talking, drinking, and playing cards in the officers' mess. Over the months, Mayne was successively promoted from lieutenant to captain to major; in the second half of 1942, he was also given his own 'A' Squadron of SAS veterans, and led them in raids on Tripoli and El Agheila.

However, by the end of 1942, the war in the desert was nearing its dramatic conclusion. The Allies had landed in French North Africa on 8 November in Operation Torch. Two days later, Hitler ordered the invasion of the unoccupied zone of France, while sending Panzer and infantry divisions to Tunis. The two sides first clashed on 17 November, beginning the Battle for Tunisia, which ended with the Axis surrender on 12–13 May 1943.

Special operations were no longer being prioritised, and before his capture David Stirling had been planning to send Mayne's Squadron to the Lebanon for ski training and possible deployment in Iran, an action which in the event was rendered unnecessary by enemy reverses on the field of battle. Through using the British informer known as Capt. John Richards, real name Theodore Schurch, Italian Military Intelligence had also learned from the captive Stirling in Rome that he intended Mayne to be his successor. Stirling related later: 'Paddy was hugely brave. I do not think he could ever have commanded an ordinary regular regiment, but he was exactly the man I wanted to succeed me in command of 1 SAS'.

Paddy Mayne was summoned to Middle East Headquarters in Cairo to discuss the future of the SAS at a time when some in authority favoured disbanding the Regiment altogether. In the capital, he belatedly heard of the death of his father, William, on 10 January 1943, and he became bitterly disillusioned when his request to return home on compassionate leave was rejected out of hand. Mayne had also developed a grudge against a well-known broadcaster and war correspondent, accusing him of reporting 'on the thunder of tanks and big battles' from the lounge of a Cairo hotel. He set off in a vain attempt to find the man, smashing up several restaurants in the process; as a finale, he threw the Provost Marshal and two Military Policemen down the steps of Shepheard's Hotel. Mayne was promptly rearrested and detained in the British Army's Qasr El Nil barracks overlooking the River Nile.

However, higher authority intervened and Mayne was soon set free. He was eventually given command of a successor unit to the 1st SAS Regiment, known as the SRS. The force was given a new role as assault troops in preparation for the invasion of the island of Sicily and they began training in Palestine, which at the time was under the British Mandate.

Mayne chose the officers and senior non-commissioned officers and they in turn selected the rest of their own sections; most of the men were in their late teens and twenties. After learning that the eventual target would be coastal batteries, the recruits carried out endless night exercises involving mock landing craft. One of the officers, Lt Derrick Harrison of No. 3 Troop recalled: 'During these manoeuvres I remember that Paddy usually started out after us, but always managed to get there before us'. His main mantra was: 'Every man has to be his own saviour and has to be totally self-sufficient'.

At the Casablanca Conference in January 1943, Prime Minister Churchill and President Roosevelt had agreed to invade Sicily after the capture of Tunisia. Italy would be the first European country upon which Allied soldiers would land. Operation Husky, the operational codename for the capture of Sicily, was planned as the first large-scale amphibious landing. The appointed day was 10 July.

5

The Capture of Sicily

On 5 July 1943, the men of Paddy Mayne's SRS embarked on their mother ships, HMS *Ulster Monarch* and HMT *Dunera*, at Port Said in Egypt for a new mission. The destination remained a mystery until a copy of the *Soldier's Guide to Sicily* was given out to every man. The stirring foreword to the twenty-page booklet was written by the Commander-in-Chief of the Mediterranean Theatre, United States Gen. Dwight D. Eisenhower:

> We are about to engage in the second phase of the operations which began with the invasion of North Africa.
>
> We have defeated the enemies' forces on the south shore of the Mediterranean and captured his army intact.
>
> The French in North Africa, for whom the yoke of Axis domination has been lifted, are now our loyal allies.
>
> However, this is NOT enough. Our untiring pressure on the enemy must be maintained, and as this book falls into your hands we are about to pursue the invasion and occupation of enemy territory.
>
> The successful conclusion of these operations will NOT only strike closer to the heart of Axis, but also will remove the last threat to the free sea lanes of the Mediterranean.
>
> Remember that this time it is indeed enemy territory which we are attacking, and as such we must expect extremely difficult fighting.
>
> But we have learned to work smoothly alongside one another as a team, and many of you who will be in the first ranks of this force know full well the power of our Allied air and naval forces and the real meaning of air and naval supremacy.
>
> The task is difficult, but your skill, courage and devotion to duty will be successful in driving our enemies closer to disaster and leading us towards victory and the liberation of Europe and Asia.

At this time, the establishment of the SRS ran to eighteen officers and 262 'other ranks'. The Headquarters consisted of Maj. Mayne, Commander; Maj. Lea, Second in Command; Capt. Francis, Administrative Officer; Capt. Gunn, Medical Officer; Capt. Melot, Intelligence Officer; Capt. Muirhead, Commander of the twenty-eight-man Mortar Platoon; and the new Padre, Capt. Robert Lunt. No. 1 Troop was led by Maj. Fraser, with Capt. Wilson and Lieutenants Riley and Wiseman as section commanders; Capt. Poat commanded No. 2 Troop, with section commanders of Capt. Marsh and Lieutenants Davis and Harrison; and No. 3 Troop was led by Capt. Barnby, with Capt. Lepine and Lieutenants Gurmin and Tonkin as section commanders. A small detachment of Royal Engineers was also attached to the Squadron.

The unit's role in the invasion was revealed in a series of briefings over four days at sea, making use of intelligence reports, aerial photographs, and maps. The primary mission was to capture and destroy a coastal battery at Capo Murro di Porco (Cape of the Pig's Snout) in order to ensure the safe landing of the Eighth Army of Gen. Sir Bernard Law Montgomery just a few hours later. The main Allied landings were to take place along 75 miles of coastline to the east and west of Cape Passero, the extreme south-eastern tip of the island. In the initial assault, nearly 3,000 ships and landing craft would carry 160,000 men, 14,000 vehicles, 600 tanks, and 1,800 guns into battle. Admiral of the Fleet Sir Andrew Cunningham, who was in charge of naval operations and responsible for 3,266 surface craft, sent this message to the personnel before the armada embarked: 'Our primary duty is to place this vast expedition ashore in the minimum time and subsequently to maintain our military and air forces as they drive relentlessly forward into enemy territory. In the light of this duty great risks must and are to be accepted'.

On the morning of 9 September, ships from east and west converged south of Malta, ready to steam to the beaches of the Mediterranean's largest island. By noon, a fresh and unseasonal north-west wind had sprung up and by evening there was a heavy swell, making landings hazardous. At 8 p.m., Admiral Cunningham reported: 'Weather not favourable, but operation proceeding'. He recalled that it was too late for postponement, but considerable anxiety was felt, particularly for the small-craft convoys. In the event, they were delayed, became scattered, and many ships arrived late, but no great harm resulted. The Admiral recalled that the apparently unfavourable factors 'had the effect of making the weary Italians, who had been alert for many nights, turn thankfully in their beds, saying: "Tonight at any rate they can't come." But they came'.

The Eighth Army's Order of Battle provided for a HQ of two corps, the XIII, commanded by Lt-Gen. Miles Dempsey, and the XXX, commanded by Lt-Gen. Sir Oliver Leese. In the initial wave were the 1st Canadian and the 5th, 50th, and 51st Divisions, part of the 1st Airborne Division, the 231st Infantry Brigade, the 4th and 23rd Armoured Brigades, and three commandos. In Gen. Dempsey's own words, the SRS was 'lent' to his XIII Corps for this operation, and was then due to return to the Middle East, but went on to undertake three more successful missions in Italy.

The Eighth Army was to be landed by the Eastern Naval Task Force, led by Vice-Admiral Sir Bertram Ramsay. Its assault area, to the east of the American beaches, was divided into smaller sectors to provide for the landing of the three main components of the task force, which originated in the United Kingdom, the Middle East, and Tunisia. The assault beaches were codenamed, from north to south, Acid North, Acid Centre, Acid South, Bark East, Bark South, and Bark West. The SAS target, the guns of Capo Murro di Porco, was at the northern tip of the area designated as Acid North, and the landing force for the sector was the British 5th Infantry Division, with the 50th Division coming ashore in Acid Centre, just to the south.

On the night of 9 July 1943, the two vessels carrying the SRS, the former ferry on the Belfast to Liverpool run, HMS *Ulster Monarch*, and the troopship HMT *Dunera* hove to off the imposing headland. Bombers from the RAF flew overhead on raids to soften up the site's defences. As well as the coastal battery, the intelligence service had identified a barracks, underground bunkers, and a heavily fortified farmhouse, known as Damerio after the tenants.

The first landing craft left the blacked-out ships at around 1 a.m. on 10 September in raging seas. The strong winds at times exceeded force seven, which meant speeds of more than 40 mph and gigantic waves. Some of the sections had to board landing assault craft suspended over the side by davits, using a plank that swayed dangerously. Other men boarded via oiling doors lower down on the ships' sides, as the assault craft rocked up and down in the swell.

Navigation by the pilots on the landing craft was helped by loudspeaker signals from a gunboat close inshore and also from help provided by an SAS parachutist already on the island. Jack Nixon had landed two days earlier from a destroyer, together with five men from the Combined Operations Pilotage Parties (COPPs). They began to signal with torch flashes from a small, sandy cove at the allotted time and remained hidden from the Italians.

As the landing craft neared the shore, the men suddenly heard desperate cries emerging out of the darkness. An armada of gliders had been released from US Army Air Force (USAAF) Douglas C-47 Skytrains to carry the men and equipment of the 1st Air Landing Brigade (made up of the Border

Regiment, the South Staffordshire Regiment, and the Royal Engineers) to the Ponte Grande bridge, south of Syracuse, in Operation Ladbroke. However, owing to the atrocious weather conditions, many of the gliders fell short of their target and ditched in the sea. Some of the pilots on the landing craft were able to pluck drowning men from the water, but a general rescue operation would have compromised the main task, and most had to be left to their fate. Mayne wrote later to a friend that 'it was a terrible thing to have to do'. A total of 252 men from the 1st Air Landing Brigade and the Glider Pilot Regiment were lost at sea from sixty-nine gliders, and only twenty of the planes actually landed on Sicily.

By 3.15 a.m., all the raiders had disembarked on to a small beach and clambered over rocky outcrops at the base of the cliff. They were surprised to find that the area had not been mined and that there was no enemy fire. The men had brought scaling ladders, expecting that the headland would be difficult to climb, but many of them were able to use a set of steps cut into the rock face by the Italian soldiers to provide access to the beach.

Capt. Alex Muirhead's 3-inch mortar platoon led the attack on the battery. Their first shot of a smoke or phosphorous round (normally used for sighting purposes) hit the main cordite dump, igniting it, and causing an intense explosion. The enemy finally reacted and red and green trails of tracer and heavy bursts of small arms fire began to fill the air.

Lt John 'Johnny' Wiseman and his section of No. 1 Troop were given the task of making straight for the battery, while the other two troops came in from the flanks and rear. The lieutenant, aged twenty-seven, was from Kingston upon Thames, and educated at St Paul's School and Pembroke College, Cambridge, where he studied French and German. On graduation, he worked for the family's optical instrument business, until joining the Army on the outbreak of war and serving as a trooper with the North Somerset Yeomanry in the campaign against the Vichy French in the Lebanon. Wiseman eventually joined the Duke of Cornwall's Light Infantry and was selected for officer training in Cairo, where he made contact with David Stirling and volunteered for the SAS, taking part in the major raids against enemy airfields across North Africa.

After the area had been raked with mortar fire by Alex Muirhead's platoon, the men cut through coils of barbed wire forming the perimeter fence. 'The Italian gun-crew were in the dugouts under the guns,' Wiseman recalled. 'It was just a matter of winkling them out. They were too shell-shocked or scared to offer resistance.' When Maj. Mayne arrived, the prisoners were being brought out.

'Get your men off the site,' he said to the lieutenant. 'The Royal Engineers are ready to blow the guns.'

'Sorry, sir,' Wiseman mumbled. 'I've lost my false teeth.'

'Don't be so bloody silly,' Mayne roared.

Wiseman recalled: 'It was true, but by good luck I found them, God knows how, in the dark.' He was subsequently awarded the MC for his 'determination, initiative, leadership and personal bravery'.

A barracks and a command post were attacked with mortars and then three large underground bunkers were cleared one by one. Sgt Reg Seekings recalled: 'The blood was running high and we were in a real killing mood. Then up the steps comes a little girl. It set me back, I can tell you. She looked just like my young sister that I'd left in hospital'. Albert Reginald 'Reg' Seekings was one of the original members of 'L' Detachment SAS Brigade and took part in their first disastrous operation, the parachute drop in the Gazala area. He was born in Stuntney, near Ely, on 19 March 1920, and left school at the age of fourteen to work with his father, a tenant farmer. Although almost blind in one eye, Seekings was a fine boxer, and at the age of eighteen, he joined the Cambridgeshire Regiment (Territorial Army). In 1940, along with his younger brother, he volunteered for 7 Commando (part of Layforce, commanded by Lt-Col. Robert Laycock) and saw action with them before they were disbanded, after which he joined 'L' Detachment. He was awarded the Distinguished Conduct Medal (DCM) in North Africa in November 1942.

Some more civilians followed, and finally three disoriented airborne soldiers, who had been captured by the Italians, were persuaded to emerge from another bunker. By 5 a.m., the coastal defence battery had been destroyed. It comprised four 6-inch coastal defence guns and three 20-mm light anti-aircraft guns, together with a range finder and several heavy machine guns. Fifty or sixty Italians were killed or wounded and another fifty had been taken prisoner.

Mayne gave the order to fire a green star rocket to signal to the invasion force that the coast was clear. Youthful Lt Peter Davis recalled: 'The great fleet, just visible on the horizon, began to steam towards the shore. We watched them with pride, for we realised that it was only by our achievements that they were now able to approach so close to the land'. The sun had risen and the men gathered on the headland to see the fleet arrive. But suddenly there was a mighty explosion from inland and heavy shells began to rain down, causing the waves to erupt in the path of the leading ships; another battery, located over 2 miles inland, had joined the fight.

Mayne sent No. 1 Troop and No. 2 Troop north-westwards to attack the battery and No. 3 Troop to take the fortified farmhouse identified by intelligence. The defenders of the building were low-grade Italian infantry, who proved eager to surrender. The fleet began to return fire on the battery, until an urgent message was sent by the squadron to desist as they made their way up the Della Maddalena peninsula. As the raiders advanced on the gun emplacements, they neutralised groups of snipers, and enemy strong points, including an anti-aircraft site of five guns after the mortar detachment had blown up its ammunition dump.

Sgt Seeking's section came upon a group of Italians waving a white flag, but, as soon as they approached to round them up, the men fell flat and a machine gun opened fire from a nearby pillbox, killing one of the SAS troops. Cpl Geoffrey Caton, aged twenty-two, from Preston in Lancashire, had been with Mayne since commando days in Galashiels. The sergeant charged the pillbox, throwing grenades and killing the occupants with his revolver; he then gathered his section and, with coolness and determination, led the advance and wiped out a mortar post.

As they approached the main coastal battery, Mayne, who was accompanied by Sgt-Maj. Graham Rose, another of the SAS originals, suddenly swung round and fired his Colt .45 revolver twice, killing an Italian who was about to drill Rose in the back. Reg Seekings heard him mutter: 'Mr Rose, be more careful!'

No. 1 Troop was entrusted with outflanking machine-gun posts and mortar positions that were protecting the battery. Acting Lance-Sergeant Charles Dalziel, who had served with the Scots Guards, led a sub-section on the left flank with distinction. Mayne's recommendation for the award of MM (granted to the sergeant on 21 October 1943) concluded: 'With great determination he killed and routed a party of enemy many times as large as his sub-section without casualties to himself'.

Lt Peter Davis remembered the actual capture of the battery as 'a very light-hearted affair with the men soon realising they were up against a poorly trained and ill-disciplined enemy who had trouble shooting straight'. When the SAS stormed the guns, they found the Italians waiting for them with their arms in the air and smiles on their faces. After the mortar detachment had blown up an ammunition dump and the gun emplacements had been destroyed, the doors to a food store were broken open and the SAS men sat down to breakfast, which they shared with their captives. 'Such was our first morning on Sicily and for many of us the first taste of action,' said Davis. 'And a very pleasant form of fighting it was.' The sun had risen and the raiders relaxed on the headland as they watched the vast armada of ships and landing craft that filled the horizon.

The men of the SRS then took the main road to the city of Syracuse; on the way, they came across more snipers and defended farms, which were speedily neutralised. In the morning, the troops met up with forward elements of the 5th Infantry Division and were able to hand over their prisoners and march across the bridge targeted by the glider landing. The column was attacked by a lone enemy bomber, but only one man dived for cover; he was immediately marked for return to his parent unit.

The next day, 12 July, with the 5th Infantry Division taking over, the weary SAS men marched to the harbour in Syracuse and returned to the *Ulster Monarch*. In less than thirty-six hours, they had captured or destroyed eighteen large guns, four mortars, three rangefinders, and numerous machine guns and small arms; they had also taken over 500 prisoners and killed or wounded around 200 more. The squadron had lost Cpl Caton, while two other men had sustained injuries. The actions lasted for eighteen hours and covered a distance of about 24 miles; on their dangerous journey inland, the men had been outnumbered on most occasions by at least fifty to one. As a dramatic finale to their enterprise, the night's sleep was disturbed by a heavy attack on the harbour by German and Italian planes.

On 21 October 1943, several members of the squadron received awards 'in recognition of gallant and distinguished services in Sicily'. Maj. Mayne was awarded a Bar to his DSO; Harry Poat (promoted to acting major and appointed second in command of the squadron on 8 August 1943) was given the MC, as was Lt Johnny Wiseman; and seven men received the MM: Sgt Reg Seekings, Lance-Sergeants Sillito and Frame, Cpl Dalziel, Lance-Corporal Jones, and Privates Noble and Skinner. The squadron had admirably demonstrated the qualities set out in Gen. Eisenhower's exhortation of 'skill, courage and devotion'.

On 12 July, however, there was little time for celebration, as in the afternoon, the men were told that that they were to go into action immediately, again using the assault landing craft, but this time in broad daylight. The target was to be one of Italy's main ports, the naval base of Augusta, 11 miles north of Syracuse. The area was garrisoned by the Hermann Göring Panzer Division, as well as by Fascist forces, but the task was said to be a mopping-up operation. As a result, the men were only issued with half the normal ammunition and rations, and they began to look at the mission as a piece of cake.

It was a balmy summer's evening as the *Ulster Monarch* approached the harbour, escorted by the destroyers HMS *Kanaris*, HMS *Nubian*, and HMS *Tetcott*. The captain of a light cruiser which was on station in the bay, Capt. William Wellclose Davis of HMS *Mauritius*, signalled: '*Ulster Monarch*, what the hell are you doing here?' When Lt-Cdr Thompson replied that he was about to land troops, he was warned against carrying out the operation, on the grounds that the enemy strength was unknown. When the commander said that he intended carrying out his orders as planned, Capt. Davis of the *Mauritius* promised to follow them in and to provide any necessary support.

As the whole squadron was on board the *Ulster Monarch*, the men had to be landed in two waves from the six assault landing craft. Augusta appeared strangely quiet and peaceful in the evening sunshine as the

Ulster Monarch hove to about 300 yards offshore, but as the landing craft began to be lowered, the enemy unleashed a shattering barrage. Coastal defence batteries on the surrounding hills shelled the ship and its escorts with 6-inch guns, while light anti-aircraft batteries and machine gunners fired at the invaders from positions around the bay.

As soon as the doors of the landing craft opened, the men ran forward with their weapons above their heads. Johnny Wiseman remembered: 'No quay, straight into the sea up to our necks in water. With tracer coming at you, you muttered, "I hope that one doesn't quite reach me."' There were two fatalities during the landings: Cpl John Bentley and Private George Shaw, two of the squadron's three medics; eight men were also wounded at Augusta.

The official *SAS Diary 1941–1945* noted: 'This part of the operation was carried out very successfully against the Navy's advice in broad daylight under heavy machine gun fire from the northern peninsula, and coastal defence fire from the west, splendidly counteracted by machine gun fire from the landing craft and by guns of *Ulster Monarch* and supporting ships'.

The men in the first wave of No. 3 Troop crossed the bridge out of the old town and advanced along the railway line. They captured the station and followed the tracks towards a crossroads a mile away, where they were due to link up with troops from the 17th Infantry Brigade of the 5th Infantry Division. However, the advance was stopped in its tracks by fierce opposition from Germans equipped with artillery and three light tanks, as well as mortars and machine guns. The other two troops fanned out through the ruined streets of the town, and there was heavy house-to-house fighting as German troops put up a determined resistance from well-entrenched positions in a maze of ancient buildings. They were cleared by lobbing in grenades, kicking in the doors, and spraying the rooms with heavy bursts of machine-gun fire; few prisoners were taken.

Mayne eventually pulled No. 3 Troop back, under the cover of Alex Muirhead's mortar section, and ordered the squadron to take up defensive positions around the local citadel, the Castello Svevo (Hohenstaufen Castle, built *c.* 1232), which dominates the old town, as it appeared that the Germans were planning a counterattack using armour. Lt Peter Davis recalled that the night was peaceful: '[Until] Suddenly at about four in the morning we sat up with a jerk. Again, we caught the faint sound—tanks moving along the road. The noise reached us in waves, sometimes loud and sometimes almost inaudible according to the vagaries of the mind'. The men prepared for the attack, but gradually the sounds began to recede, and as dawn broke, they learned that the Germans had pulled out as forward elements of 17th Infantry Brigade began arriving in the area.

In the morning, the men of the SRS had a party. Cpl William 'Kit' Kennedy donned a top hat and played a pianola that had been pulled on to the main street. Across the town, many of his comrades helped themselves to items from the deserted buildings and swigged bottles of wine. Mayne took his explosives expert, Canadian-born Sgt William Anthony 'Bill' Deakins, to blow a safe on the first floor of a bank, but the haul only consisted of a gold ring, a brooch, and six silver spoons, all of which were handed to the sergeant for his trouble. Officers from the 17th Infantry Brigade were now flooding into the town and they were appalled at what seemed to them to be the anarchy unfolding before their eyes, but when they demanded to know who was in command, they were pointed to the tall figure of Paddy Mayne pushing a pram crammed with wine bottles along the street.

Mayne's Bar to his DSO was gazetted on 21 October 1943. The citation read:

> On 10 July 1943 and on 12 July 1943, Major R. B. Mayne carried out two successful operations, the first the capture and destruction of a Coastal Defence battery on Capo Murro di Porco, the outcome of which was vital to the safe landing of XIII Corps. By nightfall, Special Raiding Squadron had captured three additional batteries and 450 prisoners, as well as killing 200 to 300 Italians.
>
> The second operation was the capture and holding of the town of Augusta. The landing was carried out in daylight, a most hazardous combined operation. By the audacity displayed, the Italians were forced from their positions and masses of valuable stores and equipment were saved from enemy destruction. In both of these operations it was Major Mayne's courage, determination and superb leadership which proved the key to success. He personally led his men from the landing craft in the face of heavy machine gun fire. By this action, he succeeded in forcing his way to ground where it was possible to form up and sum up the enemy's defences. [1]

Shortly after this action, the *Ulster Monarch* was sent back to the Middle East and the men of the SRS went to a camp near Augusta to enjoy some well-earned leave.

The British Eighth Army under Gen. Montgomery advanced along the eastern coast, while the American 7th Army under Gen. Patton moved westwards towards Palermo. When the two armies joined up at Messina on 17 August, the Germans were in full retreat across the Straits to the Italian mainland, though they succeeded in evacuating 100,000 of their troops. After the initial surprise, the enemy fought stubbornly, but the capture of the island only took thirty-eight days.

6

Roy Farran

Alongside the SRS, a new detachment of the 2nd SAS Regiment took part in Operation Husky, the capture of Sicily, under the command of the eccentric and charismatic Roy Alexander Farran. He was born on 2 January 1921 to an Irish Roman Catholic family living in India, where his father was serving as a warrant officer in the RAF. After attending the elite Bishops Cotton School in Shimla, the young man travelled to England and eventually graduated from the Royal Military College, Sandhurst. He was commissioned in the 3rd Carabiniers (Prince of Wales's Dragoon Guards) as a second-lieutenant and assigned to the 51st Training Regiment.

Farran was then posted on attachment to the 3rd The King's Own Hussars in Egypt and first saw action during the closing stages of the Battle of Sidi Barrani, which was part of Operation Compass, the successful British counteroffensive against Italian Forces, which drove them over the border and out of Cyrenaica, the north-eastern region of Libya. The Hussars were then deployed to the island of Crete, and in May 1941, Farran was captured after being wounded in the right arm and both legs when leading a force of light tanks in a counterattack against German forces. He was awarded his first MC for gallantry in action during this period.

Farran was evacuated to Greece by plane and eventually escaped under the perimeter wire of an Athenian POW hospital where he was receiving treatment. With the help of Greek civilians, he was able to hire a fishing boat and to set course for Egypt with a crew of three other Allied escapers, a Pole, and ten Greeks. After a fraught nine-day journey, during which they nearly ran out of drinking water, the party was picked up by Royal Navy destroyer HMS *Jackal*, 40 miles north of Alexandria. Farran was awarded a Bar to his MC for his actions.

In January 1942, he was appointed to the 7th Armoured Division as Intelligence Officer and *aide-de-camp* to the new commander, Maj.-Gen.

John 'Jock' Campbell, holder of the Victoria Cross. On 26 February, Farran was driving the commander in his staff car back to Alexandria after an inspection tour when it skidded from side to side for 200 yards on a newly laid clay surface and overturned. The general was killed, Farran was thrown out the vehicle, and the two other occupants (the general's servant and driver) were rendered unconscious.

After courts of enquiry were held, Farran was reappointed Divisional Intelligence Officer. On 27 May 1942, German and Italian troops launched their great summer offensive and he was given command of a small composite force to defend the beleaguered headquarters, which was eventually obliged to cross the border back into Egypt. In the first week of July, two aircraft were seen approaching the camp and Farran was convinced that they were 'Bostons' (Douglas A-20 Havocs) and shouted: 'Don't run. It's all right. They're ours!' Too late he saw the black crosses on their wings. Both planes unleashed a basket of butterfly bombs and before he could throw himself flat, he had been hit in the arm, the only person in the camp to be wounded.

On 19 July, Farran was put on a train for Cairo and final embarkation on a hospital ship to South Africa. Following six weeks' rest and recuperation in Natal, he boarded a troopship bound for Liverpool. After a month of sick leave in the United Kingdom, Farran appeared before a Medical Board and persuaded them to upgrade his status to 'A' category. His one wish was to get back to the regiment, recalling: 'I wrote to solicit help from any Generals I knew, but it was easier to get into England than to get out of it'. He was posted to three separate units, all of which were bound for the Middle East, but at the last minute, their sailing orders were cancelled. After 'wandering from one unit to another all over England', Farran at last found himself with a draft bound for North Africa in February 1943.

The newcomers arrived at the Armoured Corps transit camp in Algiers in March. Farran languished there for several weeks, visiting Allied Force HQ every day in a fruitless quest for transfer to the Eighth Army. However, one day he met a former colleague, Alexander James 'Sandy' Scratchley, a one-time jockey and bloodstock breeder, and now a member of the 2nd SAS Regiment. Farran related: 'I told him that I had an introduction from General Willoughby Norrie and was it possible that there might be a vacancy for another officer. He promised to take me up for an interview with Bill Stirling at AFHQ the next day'.

Together with another officer called Tyser, Farran went for what turned out to be a very unconventional meeting. He recalled that Bill Stirling was a mountain of a man, who radiated an encouraging aura of confidence. He shook them warmly by the hand, asked some embarrassing questions, and offered a fortnight's trial. They jumped at the opportunity and immediately felt part of the team, particularly as the interview was followed by an invitation to lunch, rather than by the usual abrupt dismissal.

Two days later, Farran was on a course with the Parachute Battalion at Mascara, on the border with Morocco. After five days of hard physical training on the ground, followed by five drops over forty-eight hours, he received his wings and was sent to the 2nd SAS regimental base at Philippeville. He described it as 'a pleasant, tented camp pitched alongside a wonderful beach. Behind were the towering hills of the Jebel, covered with thick green cork forest'. The discovery of the danger of contracting malaria from the voracious mosquitos in the nearby swamp was to come.

Farran's seniority led to his appointment as second in command to Sandy Scratchley in a new squadron that was training for a landing codenamed Operation Narcissus (which was in support of Operation Husky, the capture of Sicily). About two weeks before the start of the mission, Bill Stirling revealed that they were to go ahead of the Highland Division to seize a lighthouse believed to house an artillery observation post, which posed a threat to the landings on the assault beaches around Cape Passero (I have a special interest in this sector, codenamed Bark South, as my father, Sgt Kenneth Winston Tudor, was one of the soldiers due to disembark from landing craft with the Royal Corps of Signals hours later).

While Scratchley went to Sousse in north-eastern Tunisia to liaise with the Highland Division and to arrange the reception of the rest of the squadron, Farran took them up to Djelli for a dress rehearsal of a landing. It was the first time that any of them had seen an actual landing craft, having made do with a model made out of sandbags on the beaches at Philippeville, but the first part of exercise went exactly to plan. The men left their mother ship, the former passenger ferry HMS *Royal Scotsman*, captured a small island in a mock attack, and fired Very lights to signal success, but then found that the Navy had forgotten to pick them up; they sat on the deserted island for a whole day, desperately sending signals, until someone in Djelli remembered them.

About a week before the operation, the squadron moved into Tunisia by road and set up camp in an olive grove at M'saken, near Sousse, with the Highland Division all around them. The SAS began rigorous training, but malaria struck and the force was reduced from forty-five to thirteen within two days. Farran noted that recurrences of the disease continued to bedevil the squadron in France and Italy over a year later and that they had to insist upon mepacrine tablets for operational groups right up to the end of the war.

Among those afflicted was Scratchley, and on the last day, he had to drop out and hand command of the mission to Farran. In the evening, the squadron embarked at the French naval base of Sousse in the *Royal Scotsman* for the journey to Sicily, part of a vast armada. On the following afternoon, Farran also developed the symptoms of malaria, and his Russian second in command, Boris Samarine, obtained a large dose of quinine from the doctor to treat him and he went into a deep sleep, which lasted eleven hours. At 3 a.m., Samarine shook Farran awake and reported that the rest of the men were already on board the landing craft; he threw on his equipment and staggered out of the cabin to join them.

The landing craft followed a small launch with a red taillight and lurched up and down in choppy seas until it met calmer waters nearer the landing point north of a narrow sandbar joining the lighthouse to the shore; however, 5 yards out, the vessel snagged on a rock and ground to a standstill. The men waded ashore with their weapons above their heads and crawled up a slope to the lighthouse, which appeared white and gleaming in the moonlight.

Farran saw three shadowy figures run out of the front door and disappear around the back. He recalled: 'We took the last few yards in a rush, fingers on our Tommy guns, ready to fire. I kicked open the front door to find the house deserted, although the uneaten meal on the table showed that the occupants had only recently left'. While they were searching the rooms and outhouses, the first wave of Highlanders opened fire from their beach on the left and Italians farther back replied with periodic mortar fire. As odd bullets began to shatter the glass of the lighthouse, Farran went outside and fired his Very pistol to signal success. A thorough search of the island revealed 'three terrified little Italians, crouching in holes in the ground, and an abandoned machine gun'.

At dawn, the SAS men targeted scattered enemy machine-gun posts firing at Highlanders coming ashore from landing craft. Randolph Churchill, the Prime Minister's son and liaison officer with the Highland Division, walked up through the bullets and told Farran to take the squadron to Bizerta in northern Tunisia as soon as he could find a ship as they might be required to reinforce forces around Syracuse.

At around 10 a.m., the parachutists left the beached landing craft to be salvaged and hitched a lift on another boat back to the *Royal Scotsman*. When the men returned to North Africa, they heard that the Highland Division had already advanced inland and taken the town of Pachino. Farran reflected: 'At last we had a firm foothold on European soil'.

Farran's mission was followed two days later by the first 2nd SAS Regiment parachute drop, when two parties of ten men each were landed on 12 July in the north of the island in Operation Chestnut. The first group was led by Maj. Philip Hugh Pinckney and the men were tasked with cutting the main railway line between Messina and Catania and with attacking roads and telephone lines elsewhere in the north-east. The second group, under Capt. Roy Harvey Bridgman-Evans, whose parent unit was the Royal Regiment of Artillery, was to destroy a strategic enemy headquarters located on a high mountain (931 metres) in the centre of the island at Enna (said by the Roman historian Livy to be impregnable) and to attack convoys moving south to counter the Allied invasion.

Pinckney's party was scattered on landing and the men lost much of their equipment, including their radios. The plane that brought the parachutists also failed to return to base and crew and passengers were lost, including the officer supervising the drop, Maj. John Geoffrey Appleyard, former commander of the Small-Scale Raiding Force.

Bridgman-Evans' group landed too near centres of population and a search began by the enemy to round them up. The captain was captured on 14 July, but he eventually escaped to France from Fort Bismarck Camp, Strasbourg, Germany (Alsace was annexed in 1940), and then travelled to Spain, which allowed his return to the United Kingdom; he was awarded the MC on 17 February 1944.

To compound the disaster for Operation Chestnut, planes bringing in planned reinforcements on 13 July failed to make contact with either party owing to the loss of their radio equipment and they returned to base without result. The official report on the mission concluded: 'The value of damage and disorganisation inflicted on the enemy was not proportionate to the number of men, amount of equipment, and planes used'. However, important lessons were learned for future parachute operations. Most of the men eventually made their way back through the enemy lines or were overrun by advancing Allied forces and lived to fight another day.

In the months between the capture of Sicily and the invasion of the Italian mainland, Bill Stirling sent Roy Farran to Alexandria to seek recruits for the SAS from among the forces of Middle East Command, which involved him making a round trip of 3,500 miles (the last leg of the return by plane from Tripoli). He recalled that though he ultimately failed in his official object, he had a very pleasant holiday.

Soon after returning from Egypt, Farran was given command of a new squadron equipped with jeeps manning twin Vickers aircraft machine guns. While the unit was still forming, it was thrown into frantic preparations in support of an operation by the 1st Airborne Division, which was codenamed Slapstick. Its target was Taranto, described by Churchill as a first-class port, capable of serving a whole army. The squadron embarked on an American cruiser at Bizerta for the voyage to Italy and prepared to take part in a large-scale landing on a hostile shore.

7

The Invasion of the Mainland

While the 2nd SAS Regiment was bound for the southern port of Taranto in the heel of Italy, the SRS had already landed on the toe at Bagnara Calabra, a fishing port surrounded by terraces of vines on steep slopes. The town is 15 miles north-east of Reggio, where the main Eighth Army landings had taken place the day before. The task was to open the way for the invasion force by preventing the enemy destroying bridges and installations. The German troops defending Bagnara were both able and experienced, some being veterans from the North African and Russian campaigns.

On this occasion, the squadron was to revert to landing under the cover of darkness. The force of 245 men belatedly left the eastern Sicilian port of Risposto on the evening of 3 September after the assault craft suffered a number of mishaps. Landfall from a large American Landing Craft (Infantry) and the four remaining Landing Craft (Assault) took place at 4.45 a.m. on 4 September. The *SAS War Diary 1941–1945* noted: 'Had our landing taken place at 02.00 hours as intended, the whole position would have been cleared with far fewer casualties'. Instead, dawn was breaking as the action got under way.

The landing was unopposed, and at first, the men feared that this could be because the beach was mined. But this thought soon evaporated as Maj. Paddy Mayne leapt on to the beach and they followed without mishap. However, he soon realised that they had been dropped on the wrong beach; this turned out to be provident, as the right beach had been heavily mined.

As the men reached the outskirts of the town, they found that it was virtually deserted, but hundreds of residents gradually emerged from caves and tunnels on the surrounding hillside and greeted them as liberators. As a section of No. 1 Troop advanced towards the centre of the town, they were amazed to see a company of German engineers marching round a bend in the main road about 40 yards behind them, with their rifles on their shoulders, seemingly unaware of the landing. The troop's Bren gunner opened fire immediately. Five of the enemy were wounded and another twenty-eight were captured. The *SAS War Diary 1941–1945* recorded: 'Prisoners questioned stated that they were completely taken by surprise and were unaware of a landing until we engaged them'.

Germans opened fire from a ridge with machine guns and mortars on two other sections of No. 1 Troop, killing two men and wounding several others. Private Richard Higham, a young Lancastrian, launched a one-man rescue mission for the injured men, for which he was to receive the MM. In recommending Higham for the award, Mayne wrote:

> During operations at Bagnara on 4 September 1943, while crossing a road that was swept by machine gun fire, three men were wounded and fell in the middle of the road unable to move. Several attempts were made to reach the wounded but the heavy enemy machine gun fire drove them back. Private Higham, however, using a small gutter, crawled up the road, and although each time he appeared, heavy fire was brought down on him, he brought the wounded back one by one.[1]

No. 2 Troop moved south through the town and on to the main road. After one section took up defensive positions around a blown bridge, another split into smaller groups to attempt to push into the terraced hills above the town. However, they faced determined opposition from Germans well dug in above them. Mayne left his HQ in the town centre to join the troop and to issue fresh orders. He grabbed a captured MP 40 machine gun and shot three Germans manning a machine-gun post, which had been holding up the advance up a ravine. Meanwhile, No. 3 Troop took the railway station and secured the tunnels. The battle raged for the rest of the day, but by nightfall, the opposition was largely silenced. The mortar unit attached to the HQ Troop had fired over 300 rounds on 4–5 September. Over the course of the morning on the second day, a cruiser in the bay cleared the remaining Germans from the hills, and troops from the 15th Infantry Brigade began to flood into the town. Meanwhile, Mayne's batman, Cpl Corps, carried out a demolition at the Post Office, but failed to open the safe.

Five men from the SRS were killed during the operation at Bagnara; seventeen more were wounded; and the enemy suffered eighty-two casualties. By capturing and holding the town and the surrounding area, the squadron enabled Eighth Army to continue their advance up the toe of the Italian mainland unhindered. After the two days of hard fighting, the squadron was withdrawn to Sicily on the afternoon of 5 September for rest and recuperation and to prepare for the next assignment, Operation

Devon, the capture of Termoli, a fishing port and a pretty resort with a long, sandy beach and attractive old buildings in the region of Molise.

In October, the SRS formed part of a 1,000-man Special Service Brigade—together with No. 3 (Army) Commando and No. 40 (Royal Marine) Commando. The objectives of the operation were to seize the valuable harbour and to impede German resistance to the advance of the British 78th Infantry Division (nicknamed the Battleaxe Division) up the coastline, and in so doing also remove an outlier of the German winter line. The mission to take the port on the Adriatic Coast from the Germans would rely on speed and surprise. It was held by a German battlegroup of about 600 men, mainly a platoon from the 1st Parachute Division, which also had a battalion dug in along the River Biferno, just south of Termoli, but the garrison also included a section of railway engineers and other rear echelon troops.

The operation was timed to begin at 2.45 a.m. on 3 October. The SRS of 207 men left in the convoy from Manfredonia, south of Termoli, in an American Landing Craft (Infantry) at noon on 2 October. Troops of No. 3 (Army) Commando made a successful landing on the beach and signalled to the men of the Raiding Squadron and No. 40 (Royal Marine) Commando to begin disembarking from the landing craft at the mouth of the River Biferno. By dawn on 3 October, all the units had moved off the narrow beach and begun their advance on the port and surrounding countryside. The Royal Marines took the railway station after some fierce fighting as the men of the Raiding Squadron began to push down towards two strategic bridges across the river, where they were due to be met by forward elements of the British 78th Infantry Division.

The German commanders were taken completely by surprise, but were not slow in reacting. After hearing that the invasion force only consisted of about a 1,000 men and that they were mainly parachutists armed with light weapons, Field Marshal Albert Kesselring issued orders to his troops to 'recapture Termoli at all costs and to drive the British into the sea'. Two battlegroups of the 16th Panzer Division, which was refitting and reorganising after suffered badly at the hands of the Allies in the Salerno bridgehead, were quickly drafted to fill the breach and sent on a 75-mile trek over the mountains. They would arrive on the outskirts of the town on the night of 4–5 October.

Early after the landing on 3 October, 'B' section of No. 3 Troop, led by Lt John Tonkin, was sent in a south-easterly direction along the road between Termoli and Campomarino to try to capture and hold one of two bridges over the river until the arrival of the 78th Infantry Division. The section captured several Germans and raked a convoy of five trucks with mortar fire, but such was the speed of their advance that they overtook a strong force of retreating Germans from the 1st Parachute Division. After a fierce firefight, the section took refuge in a ditch, and it soon became evident that they were completely outmanned and outgunned. Lt Tonkin gave the order 'Every man for himself', as they tried to fight their way out. Lance-Bombardier Joseph William Fassam, a twenty-three-year-old from Salisbury in Wiltshire, was cut down in the attempt, but six others escaped in the chaos; Lt Tonkin and twenty-one men were captured. The lieutenant was subsequently wined and dined by a leading German general before being told by a major returning him to prison that he faced the prospect of summary execution under Hitler's notorious Commando Order. However, the lieutenant managed to escape and to return to the squadron on 18 October.

Meanwhile, men of 'A' Section of the same troop arrived on the scene and were also engaged by a large force of enemy troops. Among the squadron's wounded was the Intelligence Officer, Capt. Bob Melot, a Belgian former aviator, and by far the unit's oldest man at fifty-four. After this fierce firefight, the section continued to move down the ditch and on towards the bridge. The remaining men from No. 3 Troop travelled along the Campomarino road and made contact with advance elements of the British 11th Infantry Brigade from the 78th Infantry Division as planned. 'C' Section also linked up with another group of marines from No. 40 Commando and together they carried out reconnaissance in the San Giacomo degli Schiavoni area.

Parachutists from No. 1 Troop began their own advance on Campomarino and they were joined by men from No. 3 Commando in neutralising a series of defended farmhouses. Ten Germans were killed and another fourteen were wounded; only one man from the Raiding Squadron suffered injuries. Members of the troop continued down the road to Larino and one of the bridges, only to find that it had been recently demolished by the enemy.

Meanwhile, No. 2 Troop had taken up positions on rising ground near the port, and together with mortar crews from No. 40 Commando, scattered a group of 200 Germans attempting to move to the south along a spur known as the Difesa Grande. The Raiding Squadron HQ Troop crossed paths with a party of forty Germans, and, together with another section of marines, killed some and captured the rest after a firefight.

On the evening of 3 October, the squadron was relieved by units of the 11th Infantry Brigade and ordered to move into Termoli. The men took shelter in requisitioned houses and deserted monastery buildings and began to plan for another embarkation. However, the next day was spent in reinforcing defensive positions around the town as rumours began to circulate that the Germans were planning a counter-attack. This became a reality at first light on 5 October: the harbour was bombed and tanks and infantry from the 16th Panzer Division advanced from the south. The intensity of the fighting can be gauged by the story of Capt. (later Lt-Col.) John Anthony 'Tony' Marsh, commander of a section of No. 2 Troop, who was awarded the DSO for his actions at Termoli.

Tony Marsh joined the Officers' Training Corps (OTC) at school, qualified for the King's Hundred of elite riflemen at Bisley, and eventually enrolled as a private in the Artists Rifles. He was commissioned in the Duke of Cornwall's Light Infantry on the outbreak of war and, during this period, was credited with nearly burning down the Officers' Mess, though the circumstances remain far from clear. Marsh was posted to his regiment in Egypt in 1942, but arrived just after the Battle of Bir-el-Harmat, and, finding no battalion to join, transferred to the 1st SAS Regiment. The award of the DSO was gazetted on 27 January 1944, and Mayne's recommendation read:

> Captain Marsh, with fifty-six men, was holding a front of one mile on the right flank of the sector west of Termoli. At mid-day on 5 October 1943, his positions were subjected to very heavy and accurate shelling and mortar fire, at the height of which, his position was further weakened by the transfer of one of his sections to another sector. At this time the enemy was developing a determined counter-attack on his left flank. Despite the intensity of enemy fire he held fast and with his own fire pinned down groups of the enemy infantry which attempted to infiltrate into his position. Later in the afternoon several of his men were badly wounded, while some distance away on his right flank his remaining other section was being gradually forced back. Although by this time Captain Marsh's position had become untenable, he refused to move until he was able to communicate his intention to the troops on his left. Meanwhile, with his few remaining men, he succeeded in beating off further attacks on his position by German Infantry. Striking north to join up with his right hand section he came across two wounded men. From them he learned that he was completely cut off, but pushed on, taking the wounded men with him, until finally pinned down by machine gun fire. He eventually succeeded in evacuating all the wounded men to our own lines under cover of darkness although only 150 yards from an enemy post.
>
> Throughout, Captain Marsh showed great coolness and determination. His high standard of courage and complete disregard for personal safety throughout the Operation played a decisive part in saving a very dangerous situation.[2]

Tony Marsh was also mentioned in dispatches twice for service with the 1st SAS Regiment in north-western Europe and remained in the Army until 1957, when he retired to Bermuda, becoming commander of the local artillery militia and subsequently of the Bermuda Regiment, which amalgamated the island's forces.

In the middle of Termoli on the early afternoon of 5 October 1943, Paddy Mayne learnt that the German forces had broken through in the cemetery area with tanks, artillery, and mortar sections. At the time, he was playing a game of snooker with the commander of No. 1 Troop, Maj. William 'Bill' Fraser, the Medical Officer, Capt. Philip Gunn, and Sgt Pat Riley. Though shells were falling close enough to shake the ground, Mayne insisted on finishing the game. 'Like Drake and bowls', reflected Riley. Paddy Mayne then gave the order: 'Get the cooks, bottle-washers, everybody, up there at once!'

Lt Johnny Wiseman's section of No. 1 Troop was taking a rest in the garden of the monastery after returning from a brisk engagement with Germans north of the town when Mayne's batman arrived with the message: 'He wants you back in line. We've run into a lot of trouble'. Reg Seekings recalled that they quickly loaded up a commandeered truck in a narrow side street that was being ranged by German mortars: 'We were just kicking the tail-gate down, the section were getting aboard, when this bloody shell landed right in the middle of the truck. It blew us to hell. We were carrying detonators for the "78" 2-lb. grenades in our packs—you never loaded the grenades till you needed. Mine was the only one not to explode'. The sergeant was picked up and thrown backwards by the force of the blast, but emerged unscathed apart from a split fingernail.

Lt Johnny Wiseman also miraculously survived. He was sitting in the cab beside the driver and had bent down to talk to the messenger from Paddy Mayne when the shell dropped: 'There wasn't a living soul beside me,' he recalled. 'The fellow I was talking to disappeared. The driver was sitting unwounded but dead. Part of the top of the truck had gone right through my Sergeant, right through him. I just got out of the truck, just like that. Untouched.' Maj. Bill Fraser was picked up by the force of the blast and lay bleeding on top of Parachutist Douglas Monteith, who had not been hurt at all. Eighteen men were killed or died subsequently of their wounds. A family of three or four women who lived in the street and had been doing the troops' washing were also blown apart and their young son had to be put out of his misery owing to his mortal wounds.

Lt Wiseman subsequently went up the clock tower in the centre of Termoli, which had housed a German artillery observation post and was blamed by many for directing the fatal shell. He recalled: 'Someone had undoubtedly been there, but I don't think that was the reason. It was just a lucky shell. One of those things'. The lieutenant reported to Paddy Mayne, who simply said: 'I hear from the Company Sgt-Maj. that you've had one or two casualties'.

'I haven't got a section any more,' Wiseman replied.

'Right. You join up with my unit at Headquarters,' the major said. Next day, Johnny Wiseman was promoted to acting captain.

Riley recalled that when Paddy Mayne came up and saw the carnage 'he was silent, very silent. He just told us to get the rest up to the cemetery straight away'. After the loss of most of the section, their comrades stayed awake all night and got drunk, but the memory of the tragedy would haunt them always.

Once on the front line, Paddy Mayne found a detachment from an infantry battalion cowering under the relentless enemy assault and got them to fire their heavy mortars, with devastating results. As members of the HQ Troop were entering Termoli later, they crossed paths with a group of forty Germans going up a ravine. Mayne killed a mortar crew with a grenade and attacked the rest with repeated bursts of a Bren gun used like a carbine. Over twelve of the enemy were killed and the rest were captured with the aid of troops from No. 40 Commando.

Elsewhere, the Raiding Squadron was facing repeated mortar fire and infantry attacks along the forward defensive line on a ridge overlooking the railway line, near the Sinarca torrent, to the west of the town. Maj. Harry Poat led sections from No. 1 and No. 2 Troop in the area and they were reinforced by men from 3 Commando and by some units of the 78th Division.

Thirty men from No. 2 and No. 3 Troops, deploying two anti-tank guns, were also supporting a detachment from 2nd SAS Regiment, the first time that both regiments had fought alongside one another. After a patrol at Castelnuovo, Roy Farran's men had been ordered to return to Bari, where the unit was being restructured. Two of their sister squadrons were detached for operations Jonquil and Begonia to assist with the rescue of escaped prisoners of war and they commandeered a two-masted schooner and four fishing boats to take them up to a new base at Termoli. Farran was ordered to make speed to the port with his jeeps 'with the object of requisitioning a good house near the harbour for the main party'.

The 78th Infantry Division was heading for Termoli at the same time, to link up with the Special Service Brigade, and so Farran's jeeps of 'D' Squadron joined their columns. North of San Severo, they were attacked for the first time by enemy aircraft. German Messerschmitt 109s swooped down on the packed convoys and set several trucks on fire.

Farran drove into the town with his force unscathed on the afternoon of 3 October and was able to see the SAS flotilla arrive. He related that for most of the following day Termoli was quiet. The 78th Division was taking over from the commandos and everything seemed normal. The SAS settled in their new billet, which he described as 'a rather slummy building near the harbour where we waited for our tiny fleet to arrive', and where they were entertained by their comrades in the 1st SAS Regiment. Meanwhile, the first parties were landed farther up the coast to help with rescuing escaped POWs.

Next morning, reports came in about a strong enemy counterattack and shells began to rain down on the town, wounding several civilians outside the house taken over by the SAS. The bombardment grew heavier as the hours passed, but the detachment felt that as far as they were concerned the battle was somebody else's affair. Farran recalled that all he did was to improve the security of their billet with sacks of corn: 'The regular infantry with several tanks had arrived in Termoli and I could not see where we could fit in with our twenty-odd men. It may have been a weak view, but we had had a good run from Taranto and were supposed to be resting'. Several times during the day, Focke-Wulfs hit shipping, clogging the harbour, including one of the SAS fishing boats, which was sunk. Farran dived in the sea to save one man, but forgot to remove his German jackboots and had to be rescued himself.

The shellfire had become even more intense by morning and Farran sent Lt Peter Jackson to obtain intelligence from Brigade HQ. The result was unsettling. The lieutenant reported that '78th Division was fighting off fierce counter-attacks between the bridge and the brickworks, that whole units were fleeing in panic from the village, and that the Commandos had been called back into the line to hold Termoli itself'. When the bombardment was at its height during the afternoon, Capt. Alexander James 'Sandy' Scratchley, a former steeplechase jockey who had recruited Farran for the SAS earlier in the year, arrived at the detachment's billet. Farran related: 'He quite rightly reprimanded me for sitting idle like a rat in a hole while Termoli was in acute danger of falling to the enemy. I sheepishly collected twenty men with six Bren guns and followed him down to the Commando headquarters'.

The 2nd SAS Regiment's position was initially on a crest at right angles to the coast, about a mile north of the town. The Germans soon advanced on their left and seized the cemetery, forcing the parachutists to withdraw to the last ridge before the railway goods yard. They deployed a 2-inch mortar as well as the six Bren guns and covered a 1,000-yard front between the sea and positions held by the thirty men with two anti-tank guns from the 1st SAS.

Despite heavy mortar bomb and sniper fire, only one of Farran's men was wounded, and they held their position for three days. The nights were bitterly cold and the men were short of rations. Farran recalled: 'It was the only pure infantry battle I fought in the war and I never want to fight another'. On the third day, the 38th (Irish) Brigade landed in the harbour and the London Irish Rifles Battalion moved up to carry out a counterattack. Both regiments of the SAS provided covering fire while the infantry advanced and hundreds of Germans fled back down the beach.

At dusk on 5 October, Termoli had been in danger of being retaken by the Germans, as their forces had penetrated to a point less than a mile south-west of the port. But instead of pressing the attack during the night, they began to withdraw. The *SAS War Diary 1941–1945* reported:

> It is a good sign that, although the fighting of 5 October was an all-out attempt to regain Termoli through the cemetery and down the railway, and the enemy forces had ample forces and heavy support to smash our light forces which were there, he was unable to do so. It seems as if their troops were without the morale to advance far—again through fear of being cut off, to which they had been subjected since Sicily—and the attack was abandoned when the threat to the town was greatest.

It was fairly quiet during the night of 5–6 October, until at 5 a.m., the Germans began a final determined counterattack on the British forces. In his orders for the day, Paddy Mayne told his troops: 'We came here to take this place. We've taken it and we're staying. What we have, we hold on to'. Over the course of the morning, two men from 'C' Section of No. 1 Troop were killed by mortar fire when manning an anti-tank gun behind a large haystack: Capt. Alexander Melville 'Sandy' Wilson, aged twenty-two, from Aberdeen, and thirty-one-year-old Lance-Bombardier Robert Scherzinger, a Londoner.

The squadron's mortar detachment fired the closing shots of the duel at around 3 p.m. as men from the 38th (Irish) Infantry Brigade and fifteen Sherman tanks of the Canadian *Régiment de Trois Rivières* began to clear the ridge and put the enemy to flight.

In total, twenty-one men from the SRS were killed at Termoli, twenty-four were wounded, and twenty-three were taken prisoner. The 16th Panzer Division lost fifty-six men killed and seventy-three missing, and also had 246 wounded. In a dispatch on the fall of Termoli, Field Marshal Kesselring blamed 'the toughness of the enemy's defence, his skilful exploitation of the terrain and German problems in moving their armour and self-propelled equipment over the very arduous mountain roads'.

As dusk fell on the evening of 6 October, the men of SRS, No. 3 (Army) Commando, and No. 40 (Royal Marine) Commando were stood down. For the squadron, it was to be the end of their war in Italy. During the campaign, thirty men had been killed in action, fifty-four were wounded, and twenty-two had been taken prisoner. Before leaving to return to Britain to prepare for the D-Day invasion, the squadron received visits from Gen. Montgomery and, on 10 October, from Lt-Gen. Miles Dempsey, the Commander of XIII Corps. Pat Riley recalled that during the final battles in Termoli, Gen. Dempsey had arrived and spoken to them: 'I never saw anything like it. There he was with the red band round his head. A General right up in the front line'.

It was to be the general's farewell to the squadron. He told them:

> It is just three months since we landed in Sicily and during that time you have carried out four successful operations. You were originally only lent to me for the first operation, that of Capo Murro di Porco. That was a brilliant operation, brilliantly planned and brilliantly carried out. Your orders were to capture and destroy a coastal battery, but you did more. I left it entirely up to you what do did after that and you went on to capture two more batteries and a very large number of prisoners, an excellent piece of work. No one then could have foretold that things would have turned out as they have. You were to have returned to the Middle East after that operation but then you went on to take Augusta. You had no time for careful planning, but still you were highly successful.
>
> Then came Bagnara and finally Termoli; the landing at Termoli completely upset the Germans' schedule and the balance of their forces by introducing a threat to the north of Rome. They were obliged to bring to the east coast the 16th Panzer Division that was in reserve in the Naples area. They had orders, which have since come into our hands, to recapture Termoli at all costs and drive the British into the sea. These orders, thanks to you, they were unable to carry out. It had another effect though, it eased pressure on the American 5th Army, and, as you have probably heard, they are now advancing. When I first saw you at Az-zib and told you that you were going to work with XIIIth Corps I was very impressed by you and everything that I saw. When I told you that you had a coastal battery to destroy I was convinced that it was the right sort of job for you. In all my military career, and in my time I have commanded many units, I have never met a unit in which I had such confidence as I have in yours, and I mean that.[3]

On 12 October, the SRS boarded American Landing Craft 179 for a journey to Molfetta and the first stage of their voyage to Glasgow. After a period of leave, the men joined Paddy Mayne at a new training base on the Lanfine Estate, near Darvel in Ayrshire. The label of SRS was jettisoned and the unit reverted to its name of 1st SAS Regiment. The two regiments were joined by new French battalions and a Belgian squadron, and grew rapidly to brigade strength. Mayne was promoted to the rank of lieutenant-colonel on 7 April 1944 and served with great distinction in north-western Europe for the rest of the war.

8

Operation Speedwell One

Reflecting the scope of the ambition of the commanders of the 2nd SAS Regiment, on the late afternoon of 7 September 1943 two Armstrong Whitworth Albemarle transport aircraft took off from Kairouan in Tunisia carrying men over 500 miles to the north of Italy. Operation Speedwell was designed to disrupt enemy rail communications across the northern Apennine passes in order to reduce the flow of German reinforcements to the south, where the first Allied landings had just begun.

Lt-Col. Bill Stirling, commander of the regiment, recalled that the Germans had been holding their Armoured Reserve of four divisions well to the north and that owing to a shortage of petrol and spare tank tracks they were relying on the excellent Italian railway system to get them quickly to wherever the landings took place. SAS parties were to attack these lines in order to deny their use to the enemy during the weeks following the landings. As a result, by the time that the German Armoured Reserve began to arrive on the battlefield by road, the Allied forces would already be well established and able to defeat them.

Planning for the operation began in the middle of August with proposals to drop two squadrons of men. However, lack of air transport and competing priorities meant that only four officers and nine men were parachuted in two sticks (the number of troops due to drop on one drop zone in a single run) to attack targets north of Florence and La Spezia. The parties were known as Group One and Group Two, or for convenience, Speedwell One and Speedwell Two.

Capt. Philip Hugh Pinckney briefed the two groups on 5 September, two days before the operation began; age twenty-eight, he came from Hungerford in Berkshire and was educated at Eton and Trinity College, Cambridge. He had wide experience with the Royal Artillery and No. 12 Commando before joining the SAS in March 1943 and taking part in Operation Chestnut. At the time of the new operation, the captain was suffering from a back injury and took part against medical advice.

The plan involved the men parachuting by night on to mountain sides deep inside enemy territory without a ground reception party, radios, or detailed local knowledge. The means of exfiltration were also extremely hazy: reliance was placed on a swift advance by Allied forces (ensuring 'contact in a week') rather than on the more likely prospect of the necessity of marching through enemy territory towards Allied armies in the south, a distance of over 500 miles at the time. In addition, the parachutists were unaware that Italy had changed sides or that the Germans had turned on their former ally; the SAS men had orders to avoid contact with civilians and to move by night, and they would only become aware of the new developments after two weeks, when forced by hunger to approach local farmers for food.

When leaving Tunisia on 7 September, the parachutists wore blue-grey US Army overalls on top of their uniforms, because at a distance they were thought to resemble Wehrmacht clothing. They had obtained a variety of Allied and foreign weapons from the armoury and carried heavy packs containing ammunition, explosives, and rations. Every man was issued with plentiful amounts of lire in banknotes to pay any civilians who might provide food and shelter, while the officers also received a supply of gold sovereigns, nicknamed the Knights of Saint George, which were only to be used in the last resort.

Capt. Pinckney led Group One, destined for the area north of Florence, with the well-connected Australian Lt Anthony Greville-Bell, veteran of the ill-fated Operation Buttercup, as second in command. The other members of the group were Sgt George 'Bepe' Daniels, from Ilkeston in Derbyshire; Sgt Joseph 'Tim' Robinson; L/Sgt Horace 'Stokey' Stokes, from Birmingham; Cpl Peter Tomasso, who lived in Scotland but was born in Italy; and Parachutist Leonard 'Len' William Curtis, a Londoner.

Their plane took off at 6.30 p.m. and reached the drop zone after five and a half hours. No flak was encountered when crossing the coast. It was a high drop at 7,000 feet and the prevailing wind of 20–25 mph ensured that the parachutists drifted away from one another; as they dropped, they heard the air raid siren sounding in the village of Castiglione. Visibility was poor and there was a ground mist.

Lt Greville-Bell made a bad landing in rocks on the mountainside and received injuries to his back and to his ribs, subsequently discovering that two were broken; his helmet saved his head. He found the two containers and awaited the arrival of his companions. One light panier, also containing valuable supplies, had drifted away and was never found.

All the men appeared at the rendezvous except Capt. Pinckney, and he also failed to make contact with Lt Greville-Bell as required in the operational orders. Cpl Tomasso related that the captain landed about 300 yards away from him, out of sight, round the side of a hill, and called him by name; he replied and waited for him to arrive, but never saw him again. Horace Stokes wrote later: 'We all got together, except for the Captain, and against orders spent an hour and a half looking for him. There is no doubt at all in my mind that his back gave way when he landed'. It is believed that Capt. Pinckney was captured and shot by Italian *Carabinieri*, despite being in uniform, and that he was then buried at Baigno. On 22 February 1945, the captain was reburied and now rests in the Florence War Cemetery.

After waiting for two hours, the rest of the group hid the parachutes and containers and proceeded up the mountainside south of Castiglione. They were challenged by a sentry guarding a hydro-electric plant on a lake, and altered course slightly, reaching the top of the mountain at 4 a.m. Greville-Bell was hardly able to breathe owing to his injuries. He recalled that he began to use syrettes of morphine: 'I was able to march almost normally for three hours after each dose and almost without conscious pain, but could not think straight and became rather querulous'.

The lieutenant decided to split the group into two sabotage parties, instead of the three planned, since he was not certain that he would be able to continue due to his injuries. In the morning, a truckload of Germans arrived and searched the drop zone. Meanwhile, the raiders lay up in a wood and split the meagre supplies they had. Each party took 160 lb of plastic explosive, 4½ lb of cheese, two tins of sardines, and some biscuits and tea.

On the evening of 8 September, as the raiders were splitting up into their sabotage parties, a message on the secret armistice and surrender concluded five days earlier was breaking into a music programme on Italian radio. In a recorded speech at 7.43 p.m., Marshal Pietro Badoglio said:

> The Italian Government, recognizing the impossibility of continuing the unequal struggle against the overwhelming power of the enemy, with the object of avoiding further and more grievous harm to the nation, has requested an armistice from General Eisenhower, Commander-in-Chief of the Anglo-American Allied forces. The request has been granted, consequently all hostile acts against the Anglo-American forces on the part of the Italian forces must cease everywhere; they will, however, react to possible attack from any other quarter.[1]

At dusk, the men of Group One of the Speedwell mission moved off in their different parties. Greville-Bell took Sgt Daniels and Cpl Tomasso with him, temporarily handing over command to the sergeant as he was unable to think clearly. Sgt Robinson led Sgt Stokes and Parachutist Curtis towards their target of the Bologna–Prato railway line. Sgt Daniels, nicknamed Bepe, tall and slim, with blue eyes and a light moustache, was born in Derby and brought up in Ilkeston. He came from a poor background, his father was the local rag and bone man, and times were hard. His mother used to say: 'We have no silver spoons in our family, and if we did have they'd be down the pawn brokers by now'. Daniels had been chosen to train new recruits in 1st SAS and fulfilled the same role in 2nd SAS after a spell with Popski's Private Army on jeep operations. He was known to be capable, tough, and resourceful.

Greville-Bell's party crossed the mountain and lay up south-west of a second lake. Next day, he was in great pain and felt exhausted after marching for 2 miles, and decided that another night's rest was required; if he was not able to keep up, he would send Daniels and Tomasso on without him. However, on the fourth day, his ribs felt better and were beginning to knit, even though they made a nasty grating noise every time he fell, and he decided to carry on. The terrain was broken and precipitous and progress was very slow, though there was plenty of cover in the woods.

On the fifth day, the lieutenant felt well enough to resume command. In the early morning, the men crept past silent farmhouses in the mountains above a road junction south of Porretta. A large German armoured column swept across and took the road east. The raiders moved south, parallel with the road and the railway, and chose an unguarded tunnel for demolition on the Pistoia–Bologna single-line track. On day six, the SAS men fixed a charge 150 yards inside the tunnel, using a fog signal igniter, and retreated up the mountainside. Cpl Tomasso recalled:

> We had only just stopped when we heard a train coming at a decent speed, roughly 25 miles per hour. Suddenly there was a loud explosion, and lots of sparks coming from the wires overhead. We did not see the damage, owing to the tunnel, but the train definitely stopped. All the next day there were no trains on that line except what we think were repair gangs going backwards and forwards.[2]

The following four days were spent moving cross-country in an easterly direction towards the Prato–Bologna mainline. Greville-Bell related that it was trying not to have any news of the main Army. The men were also getting very weak through hunger, eking out their depleted rations with potatoes and grapes, but they did not wish to ruin their chances of operating by going to houses for food until all the explosives had been used up.

On day eleven, the party reached the railway south of Vernio (about 19 miles north-west of Florence) and carried out a reconnaissance of the line. Next day, they placed a charge on the right-hand line, this time using a pull switch, and sought to hit a south-bound train, having been told before departure that railway traffic kept to the right. However, when a train came along, it went down the left-hand line. The saboteurs blew the charge without being able to see the result immediately, so the train passed unscathed, but the men were slightly comforted by the thought that at least one of the lines had been put out of action temporarily.

Next day, after gorging on a few tomatoes and about 10 lb of grapes each, the trio set a charge on the line about 1 mile south of the point of the previous night, reverting to the use of a fog signal igniter. A train of twelve mixed-goods carriages blew the charge and came off the line, noisily tearing up a section of track. There were also some enemy casualties, as screams and groans were heard. The next day, there was a heavy concentration of railway traffic in the area waiting to get through on the single remaining track.

The party started for the south after what Greville-Bell described as a period of 'semi-starvation'. Their rations were finished and they felt very weak, so they gingerly went down to a house and bought some bread and apples. The residents were very frightened when their callers pretended that they were Germans.

The men walked to the east of Florence through a German convoy in the village of Vaglia, which was unguarded. When buying some food, they heard that a reward of 1,800 Lire was being offered for the recapture of escaped prisoners of war, with a bounty of 10,000 Lire for parachutists. On day eighteen, the party reached Fiesole and they were well looked after by Marchesa Roberti, whose sister happened to be a friend of Greville-Bell. From the Marchesa's elegant villa, they watched the Americans bomb the tenement area of Florence from a great height, with casualties estimated as at least 4,000, which, they thought, would inevitably fan anti-American feeling.

After leaving Fiesole, the trio marched in wind and rain for three days and felt exhausted, cold, and wet. They stole a boat after cutting its chain with an 'A' Force special lock knife, crossed the River Arno, and found refuge with another noble, Count Paglietti, who was half-English and had just been released from imprisonment for his anti-Fascist sympathies. He put the parachutists in touch with a band of partisans operating north of Incisa. They included Yugoslav army officers and were well armed. Greville-Bell decided to spend a little time trying to organise them and was soon able to send out twelve parties to cut telephone wires.

Four weeks after dropping at Castiglione, the lieutenant and Sgt Daniels wandered into Florence in civilian clothes to check on the Italian rumour of German preparations for demolitions in the city. They found that the bridges over the River Arno had been mined, apart from the Ponte Vecchio. Access to two areas was also being denied to civilians, including one around the central railway station. The pair found time to call in for a beer at the Loggia bar in Piazza Michelangelo. Greville-Bell recalled: 'It was full of German officers and "other ranks", mostly drunk, who were paying for about one drink out of five'. He added: 'The beer in this bar is very bad'.

The next day, the lieutenant took Daniels and two of the Yugoslav partisans to reconnoitre a suitable point for attack on the Florence–Arezzo railway line south of Florence. The following night, they blew up a heavy south-bound train. The trio were unable to check the results, but civilians reported that the train had been wrecked.

After a week with the partisans, Greville-Bell judged that his efforts to organise them were a failure; he wrote later that they 'were not all that good, but the Chianti was excellent'. It was time to leave. The lieutenant took along one of the two rebels who had been on the railway raid, a Yugoslav Naval Reserve Officer called Radomir Kalomira, who acted as their guide. A fluent Italian speaker, a good shot with all weapons, intelligent, fearless, and keen to join the British Army, he proved invaluable in obtaining food for the party, which had been a problem since the civilians were afraid to help armed men. They decided to walk by day whenever possible.

Eight days later, the four men were overtaken by two Germans in a truck while marching along an open road near the famous wine centre of Montepulciano, 77 miles south-east of Florence. A sergeant got out of the vehicle and opened fire with an automatic. The men countered with their carbines and the two Germans surrendered. They were identified as Luftwaffe personnel on their way to the aerodrome at Lake Trasimeno. Greville-Bell recalled: 'We ditched the truck which had six bullet holes through the engine and told the Germans to clear off, which they did quickly. I was reluctant to shoot them as we were near the house of an English Marquis who had helped a great many prisoners of war and I was afraid of reprisals'.

On day fifty-two, the quartet passed through the Lazio village of Leonessa, on the border with the region of Abruzzo. After two days, they came upon an isolated village, which here will remain nameless. The men were persuaded to stay in a shed on the edge of the settlement by the mayor, who promised that he could obtain 40 kilograms of gelignite for them. However, they were betrayed by an Italian informer, and at dawn on the second day, the village was surrounded by two trucks of German infantry.

The SAS party only just managed to escape into the mountains in civilian clothes. The Germans did not find the kit that they had been forced to leave, but local Italians did and stole the lot, including weapons and uniforms. By threats, the raiders managed to retrieve 2,000 lire, one set of overalls, and three carbines (one with the sling missing), but they were forced to stay another week in an attempt to exchange their civilian clothing for battledress with Allied escapers, of whom about forty lived locally. The effort eventually succeeded and they were able to leave.

On day sixty-one, the quartet crossed Monte Cagno in a blizzard at about 1,000 metres. They were lost in snow for several hours and on the verge of collapse, until they managed to find food and shelter in the village of Roverè in the nick of time. Both Greville-Bell and Daniels developed slight snow-blindness; the lieutenant also had a touch of frostbite where there was a hole in his boot.

Three days later, the men crossed the Rome–Pescara road near Castel di Ieri, walked through German anti-aircraft positions and by-passed a column parked on a road. After travelling through Anversa, they came upon the village of Frattura, well-known as a haven for escapers wishing to cross the lines, and took refuge in a cave. Sgt Daniels had developed a bout of dysentery and an Italian had to take him into the village for treatment. The weather was very bad, with heavy snow and high winds, and the locals all said that it was impossible to cross the final barriers of Monte Greco and the River Sangro. The parachutists thought this was probably an exaggeration, but also noted that many parties had returned. On day seventy-one, Sgt Daniels came back to the cave, as the Germans were searching Frattura for escapers. He decided that he felt well enough to start next day.

The quartet set off for Monte Greco at dawn and walked in snow a metre and a half high at a height of 1,500 metres. They halted for the night in a shepherd's hut. There were already about thirty Italians there and they claimed that it was impossible to cross the lines as the weather was too bad, there were too many Germans, and the River Sangro was impassable. Nevertheless, the SAS men and the Yugoslav partisan started off at 2.45 p.m. next day and reached the forward German positions at 4.30 p.m.; they waited for darkness and then picked their way across three or four enemy strong points and crossed the river just east of Alfedena. Neither German nor Allied infantry were encountered south of the Sangro and the quartet reached the British 168th Field Regiment at 2 a.m. on 18 November 1943. It was the seventy-third day since the parachute drop at Castiglione in Tuscany and the men had walked at least 250 miles through enemy-occupied territory.

The lieutenant was granted an immediate DSO on his return. The citation read:

> This officer was one of a party of two officers and five men dropped by parachute north of Florence on 8 September 1943, with the object of disorganising enemy railways and communications. Despite two broken ribs and other injuries sustained when landing in rocky country, Lieutenant Bell took command of the party as the other officer was missing after the drop. Although in great pain he lead the party for another twenty-four hours after which, finding himself forced to keep taking morphine on account of his injuries, he handed over command of the party to the senior NCO although continuing to keep up with the party as well as he could. Two days later he felt well enough to re-assume command, and continued to lead his men under conditions of great hardship owing to lack of food and bad weather. With his party he derailed one train in a tunnel on the Pistoia-Bologna line, and later another on the Prato-Bologna line. Working around to the south of Florence they derailed a third train. Three weeks after dropping, Lieutenant Bell, on the way back through central Italy towards the Allied lines, organised a band of Italian partisans in telephone wire-cutting and train-wrecking operations. On the fortieth day his party had a brisk exchange of fire with a German mobile patrol, capturing two prisoners, shattering the rest of the patrol and destroying a truck. Seventy-three days after dropping, Lieutenant Bell brought his party intact through the enemy lines, after a march of 250 miles. This officer showed outstanding powers of leadership and unfailing judgement in most difficult circumstances. He was an inspiration to the small force under his command.[3]

In a glowing testimonial to Anthony Greville-Bell, the commanding officer of 2nd SAS, Lt-Col. Bill Stirling, wrote:

> Tony took part in operations in Africa, various enemy-occupied islands and Sicily, but distinguished himself most notably on a classic SAS operation against the railways in northern Italy, which was a true strategic operation in that it probably did, as was intended, alter or at least affect the course of the war.... Tony commanded the party on the central sector. He was badly injured in the drop, but continued to lead his party and destroyed three trains, completely putting the railway out of action for nineteen days. After pausing for a few weeks in the Tuscan mountains to raise and train an army of Italian partisans, he continued south, and had the satisfaction of seeing, while trying to cross the road

> south of Florence, an apparently endless column of tanks heading for the battle, mostly on their tracks. It must have been depressing for their commander to know that that with an effective track mileage of only 250 miles, they had a journey of more than 300 miles in front of them.
>
> Suffering badly from near starvation and very severe weather conditions in the Apennine mountains, Tony finally led his party through the enemy lines and re-joined his unit, a journey of some 300 miles.
>
> Tony Greville-Bell was the best type of officer. He was serious about his job, enjoyed life and wanted everyone else to enjoy it as much as he did, and above all, he took care of his soldiers for whom he had the greatest regard.[4]

Sgt George Daniels was granted an immediate MM on his return from Operation Speedwell. The citation read:

> This NCO was dropped north of Florence on 8 September 1943 and returned to our lines seventy-three days later. The commander of his stick, Lieutenant Bell, 2nd SAS Regiment, broke two ribs on landing and being in considerable pain for three days, handed over command of his party to Sergeant Daniels while he was taking morphine to ease his pain. Sergeant Daniels succeeded in keeping Lieutenant Bell with the party and was conspicuous throughout the operation during which three trains were sabotaged and much other damage caused to enemy lines of communication. By his leadership he made the operation a great success when failure seemed likely.[5]

The post-combat report on Operation Speedwell included a short precis of Sgt Robinson's account of the activities of his group:

> Sergeant Robinson, Sergeant Stokes and Parachutist Curtis split from Lieutenant Bell's party on 9 September 1943 and set out for their objective on the Bologna–Prato railway line.
>
> They reached a point overlooking the line on 13 September. On the 14th they laid their charges fog-signal fashion between a station and the mouth of a tunnel, hoping in this way to cut both tracks and block the tunnel. They observed the charge explode but were unable to assess damage caused.
>
> On 21 September they joined up with a band of Italians but split from them on 24 September, as they considered them useless.
>
> On 7 October Sergeant Stokes was left in a farmhouse suffering from a rupture and Sergeant Robinson and Parachutist Curtis moved on alone. They finally got through to our lines and contacted the Canadians on 30 October 1943.[6]

Sgt Robinson and Parachutist Curtis had changed into civilian clothing and started the first part of their return journey by rail. They finally reached Allied forces at Frosolone. Both went on to serve with 2nd SAS in France. However, Leonard Curtis lost his life in a plane crash on 23 July 1944 at the age of twenty-two. The remaining member of the detachment, Sgt Horace Stokes, was from Birmingham. He joined the Territorial Army in August 1939 and was mobilised immediately on the outbreak of war in September. He joined 12 Commando and the Small-Scale Raiding Force and had also taken part in Operation Basalt, the assault on Sark. After recovering at Fabriano in the Marche region, Sgt Stokes made his way to the Italian capital on a bicycle. He was taken under the wing of the underground British organisation in Rome for Assisting Allied POWs, but was eventually recaptured and deported to Germany. He was held in two camps, including Stalag VIIA at Moosburg. In peacetime, Stokes was a greengrocer and a publican. He seldom discussed his wartime experiences.

In his personal post-combat report, Tony Greville-Bell criticised several aspects of the mission and made suggestions for future operations. The main points read:

1. Food: I consider the food we took to be most inappropriate and was a very bad choice on our part, consisting as it did of cheese, sardines, biscuits, sugar and 'compo' tea [in a tin, with powdered milk and sugar already added].
2. Weapons: The carbine is an excellent operational weapon unless the operation is definitely anti-personnel, when a heavier automatic weapon is really necessary. Automatic pistols are not good on a long operation if bad weather is expected. The 'A' Force knife is extremely useful and we found occasion to use wire cutters and saws.
3. Boots: American boots are entirely unsuitable for an operation liable to last over four weeks. They were also useless and even dangerous on wet rocks or mud. However, in good conditions they are ideal for short periods, being both comfortable and silent.
4. Maps: When we reached the Tiber, we were off our 1/250,000 map, and had to use our cloth maps, which are almost useless. For all operations I think it is better to have too much coverage than too little, since maps do not weigh much.
5. Wireless: We would have been glad to have a walkie-talkie set, since it is impossible to get the truth out of an Italian, and they were too frightened of the Germans to listen to Radio London. It was rather depressing and very lowering to the morale of the troops not to know where our army was.

6. Clothing-American overalls are unsuitable for anything but a hot climate. I suggest the SOE camouflaged overalls and jumping jackets. Italian rucksacks are very good and comfortable to carry. Sleeping bags are unbelievably efficient but need a waterproof cover for snow. A great many pairs of socks and spare boot laces should be carried. Some form of hood or balaclava is better than the beret for cold weather.

General: Three we found to be a very handy and easily controlled party for this type of operation. Boldness pays at night. Nervousness is apparent to a sentry immediately.[7]

Anthony Greville-Bell was promoted to lead an SAS Squadron in France and finally left the army in 1956 with the rank of Maj. in the SAS Territorials. He went on to become a well-known Hollywood script writer (*Perfect Friday*, *Theatre of Blood*, and *The God King*), a successful sculptor, and a keen amateur musician.

9

Operation Speedwell Two

Group Two of the Speedwell Operation to disrupt enemy rail communications across the northern Apennine passes in order to reduce the flow of German reinforcements to the south landed in the area north of Florence. The mission was commanded by Capt. Patrick Dudgeon, MC, Royal Corps of Signals, veteran of Operation Marigold and several Commando raids. Second in command was Lt Thomas Maclagan Wedderburn, Royal Artillery, from Edinburgh, aged twenty-seven. He was nicknamed Tojo (after the Japanese war leader) owing to his short stature and thick glasses, but was powerfully built and a proficient mountain climber. He was elected president of the Cambridge University Mountaineering Club for 1935–1936 and even managed to make some climbs during the war when serving with the Army in Tunisia.

The rest of the party were Warrant-Sergeant William 'Geordie' Foster, Royal Artillery, from Workington, aged twenty-eight; Cpl James Shortall, Royal Fusiliers (City of London Regiment), from London, but born in Ireland, aged twenty-four; L/Cpl Harold 'Tanky' Challenor, Royal Army Service Corps, from Bradley in Staffordshire, another veteran of Operation Marigold, aged twenty-one; and Private Bernard Brunt, Royal Artillery, from Rotherham, also aged twenty-one.

Challenor recalled that the sun was dipping low over the horizon as they took off from Kairouan in Tunisia on 7 September. There was a lot of aimless chatter in the cramped plane, and at 11.30 p.m., they were almost there. The aircraft attracted some flak over the coast, but this ceased as they flew inland. He was sixth in the dropping order, the last man out, and saw that the rest of the stick were strung out in a perfect formation. From the direction of the city of La Spezia, they heard the wail of an air-raid siren. It was a cloudless and moonlit night and down below the Apennines looked like gentle hills. The planned drop zone was Borgo Val di Taro in Emilia, but the actual landing took place near the village of Barbarasco in the sparsely populated commune of Tresana, 10 miles south of Pontremoli, and inside the present Province of Massa-Carrara in the region of Tuscany.

It was a high drop at 7,000 feet and Challenor's first parachute night-time jump; he plunged into a small tree and spent a frustrating time tearing his parachute from the branches and burying it. He had landed in a small wood on the mountainside and began to look for Lt Wedderburn, using a low whistling sound to attract his attention, as they had agreed previously. Within an hour, all six men had linked up; they posted a sentry and settled down for the night. In the morning, they located the containers, checked their bearings, and arranged a rendezvous 'for seven nights ahead, at a point on a stream between Pontremoli and Villafranca', which was not far north of the drop zone.

In the evening, the party divided. Capt. Dudgeon and Parachutist Brunt, and Sgt Foster and Cpl Shorthall, were to make separate attacks on sections of the main railway line running along the coast between Genoa and La Spezia, known as the Riviera di Levante (the coast of the rising sun). Challenor recalled: 'Our partings were low key, in typical unemotional SAS style, just a cheery wave and a call of "Good luck". The other four marched off in a single file along a wooded mountain track. That was the last I saw of them'.

Lt Wedderburn and L/Cpl Challenor checked their bearings once more and set off for a section of track north of Pontremoli on the branch line between La Spezia and Parma. Challenor carried a Schmeisser machine pistol, a .32 Colt pistol and a Fairbairn-Sykes fighting knife strapped to his leg; a smoker, he also had a minute compass secreted in the stem of his pipe and a silk map of Italy in the tobacco pouch. The lieutenant always called him 'Tanky' and he replied with a 'Sir', but in practice, they became as close as brothers. After spending six nights following mountain trails, they found a long, unguarded tunnel, and at around midnight on 14 September, they placed charges at each end on the up and down lines. Sticks of plastic 808 were taped to the track and connected by cortex fuse to a fog signal detonator inserted in a gun cotton primer.

The pair were making their way back to the entrance when they suddenly heard a train approaching fast, making the line hum; it was on the down-line, where they had placed the first set of charges. Running and falling, they just cleared the mouth of the tunnel when the train thundered in. Challenor related: 'With a rumbling "boom" the explosion echoed down the tunnel. There followed a crashing, banging, screeching sound of metal piling up. As we left the scene we both heard it—a train on the up-line. We listened in awe. "Boom!" Again, more crashing sounds and then an eerie silence'. They had claimed two trains in one go and undoubtedly blocked the railway line as ordered.

The duo marched farther down the valley and arrived at the rendezvous point, which was by a small church near a stream below Villafranca; the road was being used by German lorries, so they lay up in the mountains during the day and emerged at night. Challenor recalled: 'We were surprised to find that Capt. Dudgeon was not there. He had issued strict orders that no one was to wait more than three nights, and time was not on our side'. Unshaven, hungry, and exhausted, they finally decided to sleep in a ditch among trees not far up the mountain. Challenor awoke to find the sun in his eyes and a heavy boot prodding him in the ribs. He went to grab his Schmeisser machine pistol, expecting to feel the butt of a German rifle at any second, and wanting to make a fight of it; instead there was the smiling face of an elderly Italian farmer. He immediately recognised that they were British soldiers and took them to his farmhouse, where his wife prepared a meal of spaghetti, warm bread, and wine. He was Pietro Massimo Petriccioli whose holding at Barbarasco, in the commune of Tresana, on the right-hand slope of the Magra Valley, overlooked the road and railway between La Spezia and Parma.

The farmer was able to converse with Wedderburn in French, probably because of local links with France through migration to seek employment. That night, the parachutists slept in a warm barn, a great improvement on nights on the mountain in sleeping bags. They remained for another day, but as there was still no sign of the others, Wedderburn decided that they would have to leave after using the remaining explosives.

Petriccioli told them that some trains were still running on the line below the area where they had blocked the tunnel. The parachutists offered him payment for their food and shelter, but he refused, only accepting a gold sovereign as a memento. They left a chit to the military authorities and moved on, but ironically, they were replaced 'almost immediately' by Capt. Dudgeon and Parachutist Brunt. The newcomers actually heard the sound of the explosion that their colleagues caused on the railway bridge in front of the house, and, according to the farmer, they left about six days later, on 24 September.

Challenor recalled the final attack on the railway system:

> It was on 18 September, eleven days after we landed, that we placed our second charges. When we had completed the task we crossed the rails and headed for high ground in readiness for the long haul back to safety, but we had only reached the foothills when we heard the whistle of a train. We paused and listened, waiting for the inevitable.
>
> As an ear-drum-shattering explosion echoed round the hills, we burst out laughing, shook hands, and headed south, making for what we believed to be the Allied lines.[1]

The parachutists decided to walk by day, confident that by keeping to high ground they would avoid towns and villages occupied by the Germans; they followed the Apennines in a south-easterly direction, the route taken by thousands of escaped POWs. The pair walked in the sun and in the rain, sometimes eating chestnuts from the trees and washing them down with water from the numerous streams. They learned essential Italian words and phrases and readily obtained food and shelter for the night from poor farmers; the only hostility came from a priest who could not get rid of them quickly enough. Challenor went by his family name of Peter, translated into Italian as 'Pietro'.

The duo lost track of time, but every day brought new adventures and new risks. On one occasion, they crossed paths with two German soldiers, but they were raw, base troops and too scared to challenge two heavily-armed, bearded and swarthy men; another day, Challenor succumbed to the charms of a beautiful, lonely widow while Wedderburn slumbered in the hay; elsewhere, they paid a poor farmer, who had spent time in New York before the war, to obtain a wheel barrow-load of bottles of wine for them and they soon felt better than they had for months; one morning they were hidden underneath a pile of washing by women doing their laundry in a stream when German troops emerged from a car to flirt with them; and in a village that was completely clear of enemy troops, the locals made a great fuss of them and provided a barber to trim off their beards, so as to make them look more like clean-shaven German soldiers.

The two parachutists had travelled a considerable way, but as days turned into weeks and weeks into months, they began to have doubts about completing the journey. One day, Challenor collapsed against a wall with the early symptoms of another attack of malaria while travelling through a village occupied by the Germans, but he was smuggled by the locals into a large house, where he was treated by a doctor for jaundice as well.

After three weeks' recuperation, the pair moved on, but now the first snow was falling on the mountain peaks and the wind cut through them like a knife. They were both in poor shape, so at the beginning of November, they decided to rest up in the village of Coppito, 3 miles from L'Aquila in the Abruzzo region. They had travelled over 200 miles and were only 80 miles away from Cassino, where the front line was static. The pair were directed to the Eliseo family, who were already assisting escaped British POWs on their farm overlooking the village. The husband had left to settle in Australia, but his wife, Domenica, and their two children, Domenico (Mimmo), aged twenty-one, and Anita, aged twenty, had been unable to follow him owing to the outbreak of war. The redoubtable 'Mamma', aged about fifty, small, plump, and clothed from head to toe in black, would play an important part in their lives over the next few months.

The parachutists lived in a small hut in the fields, visiting the farmhouse for meals and helping with the daily round of farming chores whenever they could. They wanted to appear less conspicuous and so Domenico arranged for the local tailor to pay them a visit and to measure them up for civilian clothing. Both of them had plenty of operational money to pay him and the dark pinstripe suits he produced were smart and made them look like villagers.

On the snowy Christmas Eve of 1943, the locals began their celebrations, calling on neighbours with their best wine, and moving from house to house. Challenor joined in, and by midnight, he was completely drunk; he felt himself being pushed into the church for mass and blearily tried to make sense of the book he had been given. As he glanced across the aisle he saw row upon row of men in field grey uniforms, troops of the German Army, stiffly mouthing the unfamiliar hymns. Once everyone left the church, it was apparent that the Germans had also been drinking heavily, as they began to pelt one another with snowballs; some of the villagers joined in and Challenor felt for a heavy stone that he could encase in snow to target the enemy, but then he was violently sick and was forced to stagger away while the soldiers continued their fight.

On Christmas Day, Wedderburn and Challenor noticed increased German troop movements in the mountains and heard that several POWs had been recaptured. They decided that it was better to split up. Wedderburn went to stay with a lady called Filomena on the outskirts of the village, while Challenor moved to a grotto filled with straw on the hillside near to the farm. Around 3 a.m. on 27 December, he was awoken by bursts of gunfire and the beat of engines; not daring to leave his refuge, he learned later what had happened from Anita. Filomena's house had been raided by Fascist militia, the lieutenant and two POWs had been captured in a hut in the fields, and she had been executed for harbouring them.

Wedderburn escaped from a prison train taking him to a POW camp in Germany, but he was recaptured and beaten up. He was to make two more ultimately unsuccessful attempts at escape and was held at Oflag 8-F at Mährisch Trübau in Czechoslovakia (now Moravská Třebová in the Czech Republic) and at Oflag 79 in Braunschweig (Brunswick in English). Challenor recalled: 'Worried as I was about Wedderburn's fate, I knew there was nothing I could do to help him'. He decided to leave before a thorough search of the area was made.

On the drab morning of 20 January, Challenor said goodbye to Domenica and Domenico; Anita accompanied him as far as L'Aquila and made her tearful farewells. By nightfall, Challenor had travelled through the town of Popoli and along the Pescara road, jumping into an icy ditch by the roadside whenever a German vehicle passed. With his head down and feeling exhausted, he did not realise that he was approaching a village until he was stopped in his tracks by a sentry's challenge. The blinding light of a torch shone into his face prevented him from pulling his gun out of his pocket, a rifle was pushed into his chest, and a demand made to see his papers. Challenor pretended to be an Italian, but the guard was suspicious and marched him to a nearby hut, where he was interrogated by a sergeant, who eventually sent for an Italian translator. Realising that the game was up, Challenor immediately confessed that he was British and half a dozen soldiers raised the barrels of their rifles. He was searched and his pistol and silk map were found, but not the compass concealed in the stem of the pipe.

Challenor reluctantly gave his name, rank, and number, and the next morning, he was taken under armed guard to army headquarters and interrogated by an elderly officer. He said: 'You are armed, equipped with a map and dressed in civilian clothes. This is a serious matter. I am required to hand you over to other people'. These turned out to be two brutal SS officers who drove him to jail in Popoli. 'You are not a soldier,' said one of them. 'You are a spy and will be shot if you do not help us.'

Challenor recalled that he wondered how he could prove that he was a soldier, not a spy, without endangering any of his comrades. He told them that he was a member of the SAS and that he had been on a train-blowing job in the north of Italy; his uniform had been stolen while he was very ill with malaria. However, they beat him 'until they were very tired' and put him in a little cell with dirty straw and nothing else. He related: 'This went on for nearly a week when, for no understandable reason, they told me they were sending me to Aquila prisoner of war camp and that I would probably be shot as a spy'.

As soon as he was in the camp, Challenor looked for a plan of escape, 'impelled by the desperation of a possible death sentence'. His attention soon focused on a large hatch on the side of the prisoners' cookhouse through which they received their food. He also noticed that a number of Italian women who acted as domestic helpers entered and left the camp without hindrance. With the help of other prisoners, Challenor obtained items of clothing that would make him look like a washerwoman. On 2 February, three of his companions pushed him through the hatch and he walked out of the front office of the camp without being challenged. Challenor ran across the fields, hitched a lift with a man on a cart, and returned to the Eliseo family in the village of Coppito. They fed him, provided a change of clothing, and begged him to stay on the farm as he was obviously ill, but he recalled that he felt that they had taken too many risks already and that he should go back to the grotto: 'I made my way up the mountainside and flopped down on the bed of straw. It was like returning home after a long absence'.

However, Challenor woke in the night feeling seriously ill, suffering not only from malaria but also from pneumonia brought on by exposure and his prison experiences. 'Mamma' Eliseo obtained a hypodermic syringe and a supply of quinine from L'Aquila and, with the help of Anita, injected him with regular doses in his bottom; they also fed him with spoonfuls of warm milk with bread in it, but as his condition worsened, they decided that a move to a more comfortable hiding place was required.

The engineer of L'Aquila and his wife provided a room in their house outside the village, taking it in turn with the Eliseo family to nurse the patient. However, his escape was common knowledge in the neighbourhood, and once he felt stronger, he decided that his position was precarious and that he should leave before the Germans found him; he climbed to a hut high in the mountains where a group of escaped POWs was said to be in hiding, but found that they had already left. Reluctantly, Challenor returned to the engineer's house, managing to knock on the door before collapsing. In the morning, he was taken back to the grotto where Domenica continued with the full doses of quinine. One night, she lit a candle and said a prayer over him. In the morning, the fever had abated. After the war, 'Mamma' Eliseo succeeded in taking her children to Australia to join her husband, and they became a prosperous farming family.

It was only on 1 April 1944 that Challenor felt strong enough to head for the British lines again. He travelled across the Gran Sasso mountain range, often walking knee-deep in snow and always wet. One day, he was surprised and comforted to discover that he had a companion walking beside him. He too was dressed in a civilian suit, wore a trilby hat, and said that he was British prisoner on the run. As they headed higher into the mountains, the stranger kept repeating: 'Keep going. Not long now. We'll rest soon'. They managed to reach a farm in the village of San Rocco, were given a good meal, and slept between the oxen in the byre. In the morning, the man was gone.

Challenor never found out if his companion existed in the flesh or was a product of his semi-delirious state, being afraid to ask his hosts in case he had arrived alone. He reached the high ground overlooking the Pescara River and found that the only crossing was over a low dam guarded by a solitary sentry. He walked towards him and said '*Buongiorno*', but the German completely ignored him and he passed unchallenged. Challenor met a guide and four South African evaders, but they all said that it was too dangerous to cross the lines. Several notices in Italian warned that civilians found in a military zone would be shot without warning.

Challenor decided to press on alone. He had lost his compass, but in the darkness could see the muzzle flashes of British guns and knew that he only had to walk in that direction. On the night of 5 April, Challenor reached the outskirts of Guardiagrele, which had changed hands several times, but two suspicious Germans suddenly emerged from the shadows and he quickly identified himself as a British soldier to avoid the risk of being mistaken for an Italian civilian and shot.

The troops took Challenor to Company HQ, which was dug in on the side of a steep hill and subject to an intense artillery barrage from British guns. The men appeared shell-shocked and were drinking heavily. The captain in charge accepted Challenor's story that he was an escaped POW and that an Italian had stolen his uniform while he was ill with malaria. He was moved to a hut that was less exposed to the shellfire and invited to join the three guards in drinking from a large barrel of wine in the corner of the room, an offer that was cheerfully accepted.

On the morning of 7 April, Challenor noticed that the soldiers were half asleep after the excesses of the night before and he decided to escape. He left his shoes in the hut to lull his captors into a sense of false security and fled across rocky soil in his bare feet to a deep gully; no one followed, and he sprinted 2 miles across no-man's-land.

Challenor was suddenly pulled up by a shout of 'Halt!'

'Take it easy, chum,' he replied. 'I'm English.'

A giant Indian soldier appeared from behind a wall and searched him for weapons; he was convinced by Challenor's story that he was a member of the SAS returning from an operation and took him to a forward post. In a short time, Challenor was sitting on an ammunition box with his back against a tree, soaking up the sunshine, with a mug of tea in one hand and a cigarette in the other, and all he could say over and over again was 'I've done it, you bastards'.

Looking back at his experiences, Challenor related: 'In seven months I was never betrayed and I will never forget the generous help that I was given and the risks the Italian people took for me', adding that it would have been impossible to survive a winter in the Italian mountains without food, shelter, and, in his case, injections of morphine.

In August 1944, Challenor was behind the lines in France as part of Operation Wallace and, as he wrote, 'in the happy position of being able to repay the German SS brutality'. He went on to serve in Germany, Norway, and, finally, Palestine, after being promoted to sergeant. When the SAS regiments were disbanded in 1945, Challenor transferred to the 17th Parachute Battalion and became company quartermaster sergeant; he was demobilised on 17 February 1947 with his character assessed as 'exemplary'.

His award of the MM was gazetted on 7 November 1944. The citation read:

> This NCO was dropped by parachute near Borgo Val di Taro, north of Spezia, on 7 September 1943. The total detachment consisted of two officers and four 'other ranks'. After landing, the detachment split, Lance-Corporal Challenor accompanying one officer. This small detachment succeeded in derailing two trains on the Spezia–Parma line on the night of 14 September at a point north of Pontremoli. Again, on the night of 18 September a third train was derailed south of Villafranca. Having no further explosives, the detachment started to return to our lines. During this time, the enemy was continually searching for escaped prisoners of war and on 27 December the officer was captured. Lance-Corporal Challenor continued southwards alone. He was captured north of Chieti, but succeeded in escaping later from Aquila prisoner of war camp. He continued south and on 5 April 1944 was again captured while attempting to pass through enemy lines; on 7 April he again escaped and reached our lines. Throughout the seven months spent behind enemy lines this NCO displayed the highest courage and determination.[2]

In the Foreword to Challenor's memoir, *Tanky Challenor, SAS and the Met*, Maj. Roy Farran, DSO and Bar, MC and two Bars, French *Croix de Guerre*, and American Legion of Merit, related:

> Harold 'Tanky' Challenor is a friend of mine. Years ago when the world was in turmoil, I just knew him as a Corporal under my command in the Special Air Service.... He was always a resolute soldier, ready to brighten up our darkest moment with his quick smile and ready wit of a Londoner.... In a type of warfare where there was little distinction between officers and men, we all loved Tanky. We knew we could rely on him in a pinch and that he would never let down the team. He came to us from the Commandos and was totally in his element in the SAS where the lives of men in a small group depended so much on the actions of each other.

Commenting on the events that led to the 1964 'Brick Case', Farran said that Challenor's comrades understood and did not forsake him: 'They knew that every man has his breaking point and that when it is reached his actions may not be rational. Tanky Challenor is now fully recovered. He served his country well as both soldier and policeman. And I am glad to be called his friend. With a few more Challenors, the war would have been over sooner'.

Lt Thomas Maclagan Wedderburn was liberated with the other prisoners at Oflag 79 Braunschweig on 12 April 1945 by the US Ninth Army. The following year, he was elected to the Alpine Club, founded in 1857 as the first club for mountaineers.

It was a considerable time before Challenor learned from Sgt Robinson what had happened to the men of Speedwell One. In his memoir, he wrote: 'Tragically, Captain Pinckney was never seen again after they parachuted into Italy. An extensive search was made of the dropping area but there was no trace of him'. As we have seen, five men from the group eventually reached Allied lines, with the other, Sgt Stokes, being captured in Rome and deported to a POW camp in Germany. The fate of Challenor's four companions from Speedwell Two remained a mystery.

10

The Missing Men

In early 1990, Harold 'Tanky' Challenor was in contact with a Sgt John Baxendale—through the pages of the SAS journal *Mars and Minerva*—over the fate of the four missing members of the regiment from Group Two of the Speedwell mission. The sergeant had been attached to 78 Section, War Crimes, Special Investigation Branch, and in the summer of 1945, he investigated their disappearance in Italy.

It was Sgt Baxendale who first reported that Capt. Patrick Dudgeon and Parachutist Bernard Oliver Brunt had arrived at the Petriccioli family home in Barbarasco close on the heels of Challenor and Wedderburn. The farmer had told him that the new arrivals stayed about six days, and during this time, they constantly sought intelligence on enemy strength and dispositions; at about 8.30 p.m. on 24 September 1943, the pair left, with the captain saying that it was their intention to seize a German car on the main road north and that they would use lethal force if necessary, though they would retain their uniforms to ensure their safety in case of capture.

At around 10.30 p.m. on 30 September, Dudgeon and Brunt flagged down an open German car with their torches near the village of Santissima Annunziata, on the road just south of Pontremoli. The occupants were a sergeant-major and his driver, a corporal, both from the 65th Infantry Division. The captain used his fluency in German to order them to stop and to get out, but an altercation developed, which led to the Germans being shot and pulled out into the road. The sergeant-major, apparently a family man with five children, was killed instantly, and the corporal was seriously wounded. In the process, the windscreen of the car was shattered and the seats were splattered with blood.

The SAS men turned the car around and drove towards the Cisa Pass (1,040 metres) on the border between Tuscany and Emilia, a distance of about 14 miles over a rough, winding road. When they arrived in the hamlet at the top of the pass, they were challenged at a German checkpoint. Capt.

Dudgeon ordered the troops to lower the barrier and to let them through, but was told that they had to show their papers; the captain said that his had been lost, but the sentry did not believe him, and ordered them to get out of the vehicle; when they did, they were arrested and detained in the guardroom of a small barracks. The parachutists' hands were tied and they were interrogated by an English-speaking officer, 2Lt Victor Schmit, a Luxembourg national who had volunteered to serve in the German Army in 1941 and held two Iron Crosses for service in Russia and in Italy at Anzio.

Three days after the victory in Europe on 8 May 1945, Schmit wrote to the captain's father, Lt-Col. Christopher Dudgeon, MC, in Hampshire, with an account of these events:

> Dear Sir,
>
> By this letter I fulfil my word pledged to the bravest of English officers I met in all my life. This officer is your son, Captain Dudgeon, who fell for his country in Italy on 3 October 1943. Before he died I had to promise him to give you information about the circumstances and the spot where he was buried.
>
> I was at that time a platoon commander in the 65th Infantry Division of the Germans. My unit lay in the Passo della Cisa, about 30 miles west of Parma on the road Parma–La Spezia.
>
> About one o'clock a.m. I was wakened by my men who told me they had captured two English soldiers driving in the direction of Parma; their clothes were smeared with blood; in their bags they had about 40 pounds of explosives. I went down and found in the Guardroom two English soldiers, one of whom was a Captain. When I asked who they were, they gave me their military cards. I reported to the Company Commander and later to the Division. The Divisional Officer on duty told me that half an hour ago a German Sergeant and a private driving towards La Spezia had been shot and the car stolen.
>
> This having happened several hundred miles behind the lines, and the two soldiers carrying explosives, they had to be treated as irregulars and would probably be shot.
>
> The Battalion commander who had arrived in the meantime tried to get out of your son anything about his purposes, where he was coming from, etc., etc., I being the interpreter. When the German insisted, your son asked me to translate: 'If you were my prisoner should you betray your country by talking about your mission?'
>
> Upon this, my Captain told him that probably he had to be shot by an existing order of the Führer. Captain Dudgeon took the news, answering something like this: 'Alright, I'll die for my country'.

When my Captain had withdrawn I sat beside your son on the straw and we were speaking together all night long. He told me he knew little of Germany [and] that he had been to Switzerland, etc. on his holidays.

In the morning the Divisional Commander, General von Ziehlberg, informed the Battalion that he would come and see the English Captain before he was to be shot. I told him (your son) that the German officers were scandalised that an enemy who had behaved in so brilliant a manner had to be shot but were powerless against an order of the Führer. To me the behaviour of the young officer, twenty-three years old, had made such an impression that I couldn't help telling him when we were alone: 'Your country may be proud of you. If you were not my enemy I should ask you to be my friend.' Captain Dudgeon gave me his hand, saying: 'I thank you for telling me that'.

The interview with the General was quite without result. At the end of it (all German officers were present) the General told me to translate to your son the following sentence—'Tell him that I have every respect for his bearing. He will be shot in an hour, together with his comrade'.

Your son saluted militarily and left the General. He asked me to stay with him until it would be over. He gave me your address, asking me to inform you. He asked for a Protestant priest. Before he died, he asked to die with his hands free and his eyes open. He knelt down for a short while, praying with his hands in front of his face.

Then he got up and died like a hero.

I wasn't allowed to give you notice of your son's death by way of the Red Cross, as the enemy was to have no information whatever regarding the efficiency of the parachutists. So I had to wait and keep the address hidden up to now. The grave of Captain Dudgeon is 200 metres south-west of the chapel on the Passo della Cisa, going in the direction of La Spezia, 100 metres behind the last of the buildings.

I am, Yours Sincerely, Victor Schmit[1]

Schmit eventually managed to escape from prison and fled to Argentina, where he settled and raised a family. His grandson, Rodrigo Quiroga Schmit, related that he had told him that there was no hope for Dudgeon and Brunt from the moment they were captured: 'Several attacks against railways had been carried out in the area during those days and Hitler, who was furious, had personally ordered that any soldiers captured in those circumstances had to be considered as irregular troops'. This equated them with partisans, who were to be shot on sight. The Commander of the 65th Infantry Division, *Generalmajor* (equivalent to brigadier or brigadier-general in the British Army) Gustav Dietrich Adolf Heisterman von Ziehlberg, had also already said on the telephone that he could not refuse to fulfil Hitler's personal orders. Though some senior divisional officers were said to have opposed the executions, they were overruled, and they were carried out.

The *generalmajor* went on to lead his division in fierce fighting against the Allies on the River Sangro in south-eastern Italy. On 28 April 1944, he was promoted to major-general (*generalleutnant*) and appointed commander of the 28th Jäger Division; he was also awarded the Knight's Cross of the Iron Cross on 27 July. However, shortly afterwards, the general was accused of negligent disobedience for his failure to arrest his staff officer, Maj. Joachim Kuhn, who was accused of being involved in the failed July plot against Hitler and then defected to the Soviets. Von Ziehlberg was sentenced to nine months' imprisonment, but was subsequently pardoned owing to his past service, and allowed to return to his unit. Suspicions remained, however, and the general was rearrested, again brought to trial, and sentenced to death on 21 November. Ironically, on 2 February 1945, he was himself executed by firing squad.

The fate of Challenor's last two comrades from Speedwell Two also came to the urgent attention of the British Army's Special Investigation Branch and Sgt Baxendale in the summer of 1945, when their disappearance was still unexplained. Sgt William Foster and Cpl James Shortall had been tasked with sabotaging the main coastal railway line from Genoa to La Spezia, which runs along the Riviera del Levante. On 20 September, they were on the outskirts of Liguria's second city of La Spezia, home to Italy's largest naval base and an important railway junction. The pair, in uniform and carrying explosives, money, and pistols, were walking along the main road north-west of the city towards the village of La Foce. They were also only a few miles east of the railway track running through the picturesque fishing villages of the Cinque Terre. From the train, there are a few tantalizing glimpses of sheer cliffs and turquoise sea, as it enters one tunnel after another, which were undoubtedly their targets.

At the time, eight German divisions were deployed in the north of the country under Army Group B, commanded by Field Marshal Erwin Rommel. Of these, the 24th Armoured Division and the Hitler SS Armoured Division were based in the Parma–Bologna areas, and four infantry divisions, the 65th, 76th, 94th, and 305th, were stationed in the Sestri Levante, Val Taro, Pontremoli, and Apuania areas.

The raiders walked straight into a temporary camp set up by troops of the German 65th Infantry Division on the side of the road and they were quickly apprehended and taken to the local Italian police station, which was near the unit's headquarters at Ponzano Magra. The pair were held separately and taken for interrogation in an empty villa at hourly intervals from midnight to early morning, but refused to give any information apart from their name, rank and number.

Discussions took place at the German headquarters as to how the two prisoners should be treated, and the divisional commander, Gen. von Ziehlberg, decided that they should be executed. He issued the necessary command and referred to the Führer 'Commando Order' of 18 October 1942. It was basically designed to curtail the activities of hostile forces engaged in special missions. Hitler was said to have been particularly incensed by the alleged mistreatment of German prisoners during the Dieppe raid of 19 August 1942 and during Operation Basalt, the raid on Sark of 3–4 October 1942, in which, by coincidence, four of the men of the Speedwell mission had taken part: Captains Pinckney and Dudgeon and Sergeants Robinson and Stokes.

From October 1942, personnel captured during commando-type missions would not be treated as POWs, but as terrorists or bandits, liable to be shot on sight. Chief of the Operations Staff of the German Armed Forces High Command Gen. Alfred Jodl said that the document was issued 'in connection with the destruction of enemy terror and sabotage squads' and that in no circumstances was it to fall into enemy hands.

The order read:

1. For a long time now our opponents have been employing in their conduct of the war, methods which contravene the International Convention of Geneva. The members of the so-called Commandos behave in a particularly brutal and underhand manner; and it has been established that those units recruit criminals not only from their own country but even former convicts set free in enemy territories. From captured orders it emerges that they are instructed not only to tie up prisoners, but also to kill out-of-hand unarmed captives who they think might prove an encumbrance to them, or hinder them in successfully carrying out their aims. Orders have indeed been found in which the killing of prisoners has positively been demanded of them.
2. In this connection it has already been notified in an Appendix to Army Orders of 7.10.1942 that in future, Germany will adopt the same methods against these sabotage units of the British and their Allies; i.e. that, whenever they appear, they shall be ruthlessly destroyed by the German troops.
3. I order, therefore: From now on all men operating against German troops in so-called Commando raids in Europe or in Africa, are to be annihilated to the last man. This is to be carried out whether they are soldiers in uniform, or saboteurs, with or without arms; and whether fighting or seeking to escape; and it is equally immaterial whether

they come into action from ships and aircraft, or whether they land by parachute. Even if these individuals on discovery make obvious their intention of giving themselves up as prisoners, no pardon is on any account to be given. On this matter a report is to be made on each case to Headquarters for the information of Higher Command.

4. Should individual members of these Commandos, such as agents, saboteurs etc., fall into the hands of the Armed Forces through any means—as, for example, through the Police in one of the Occupied Territories—they are to be instantly handed over to the S.D. [The abbreviation for the *Sicherheitsdienst*, the security service of the SS]. To hold them in military custody—for example in POW camps, etc.—even if only as a temporary measure, is strictly forbidden.
5. This order does not apply to the treatment of those enemy soldiers who are taken prisoner or give themselves up in open battle, in the course of normal operations, large scale attacks; or in major assault landings or airborne operations. Neither does it apply to those who fall into our hands after a sea fight, nor to those enemy soldiers who, after air battle, seek to save their lives by parachute.
6. I will hold all Commanders and Officers responsible under Military Law for any omission to carry out this order, whether by failure in their duty to instruct their units accordingly, or if they themselves act contrary to it.

A. Hitler[2]

At 12.45 p.m. on 21 September 1943, vehicles and motorcycles carrying German soldiers arrived at the police station in Ponzano Magra and took William Foster and James Shortall away. They were led to a wood alongside a stream near the Vaccari ceramics factory and shot by a firing squad composed of ten German soldiers from the 65th Infantry Division.

In August 1948, the killings at Ponzano Magra and the Cisa Pass were brought before a British Military Court sitting at Hamburg in the British Zone of Occupied Germany. The Judge Advocate, Frederick Honig, Barrister-at-Law, a former German refugee, summarised the facts as follows:

> The accused in this case are charged with committing a war crime in that they, in the vicinity of Ponzano di Magra, Italy, on or about 22 September 1943, in violation of the laws and usages of war, were concerned in the killing of Sergeant Foster and Lance-Sergeant Shortall, both of the 2nd Special Air Service Regiment, prisoners of war. That is the first charge, which concerns all the accused before you in this court.

> Further there is a second charge which concerns only the accused Feurstein and Menges and which charges these two accused with committing a war crime in that they, in the vicinity of the Passo della Cisa, Italy, on or about 2 October 1943, in violation of the laws and usages of war, were concerned in the killing of Captain P. Dudgeon and an unidentified non-commissioned officer, both of the 2nd Special Air Service Regiment, prisoners of war.[3]

The men had been shot in accordance with Hitler's infamous Commando Order of 18 October 1942 on the orders of Maj.-Gen. von Ziehlberg, Commander of the 65th Infantry Division, into whose hands the men had fallen.

The defendants on trial at the British Military Court were Gen. Valentin Feurstein, a sixty-three-year-old Austrian, who had been Commander of the 51st Mountain Corps, which was part of Rommel's Army Group B; Capt. Dietrich Wilhelm von Menges, who was Feurstein's Intelligence Officer; Lt-Col. Klaus von dem Knesebeck, who had been Chief of Staff to Gen. von Ziehlberg, commander of the 65th Infantry Division (one of the units in the 51st Mountain Corps); Capt. Hans Sommer, who was the HQ divisional camp commandant and commander of the HQ defence platoon; and Lt Zastrow, who had led the military police platoon belonging to the division. Both Sommer and Zastrow were alleged to have taken part in the Ponzano Magra executions. A sixth officer, Lt-Col. Moll, who was the Intelligence Officer of Army Group B, was also charged, but not arraigned as it proved impossible to bring him before the court.

The prosecution at the trial argued that the killing of unarmed POWs constituted a war crime, and alleged that although none of the defendants had fired the fatal shots, they had set the machinery in motion by which the four men were shot. In his summing up, the Judge Advocate would define this type of indirect degree of participation as being 'the cog in the wheel of events leading up to the result which in fact occurred'.

Feurstein argued that he had no advance knowledge of either shooting and that any information received from the division would have only gone as far as his Chief of Staff, Col. von Altenstadt, since deceased. Von dem Knesebeck admitted to having made arrangements for the executions at Ponzano Magra but argued that he had done so in accordance with the orders from von Ziehlberg, and that, in addition, he believed the exercise of the Commando Order to be a lawful reprisal. Von Menges also made this point and in addition argued that although he had known about both shootings, as Corps' Intelligence Officer, he had no powers of command. Sommer argued that he had not been present at the Ponzano Magra executions, though witnesses said that he took a leading part. Zastrow also claimed not to have been present at the execution, and although Von dem Knesebeck had originally said that he had appointed him to lead the firing squad (as commander of the military police platoon), he retracted this statement under questioning at the trial.

In his summing up, Frederick Honig, the Judge Advocate, submitted that Hitler's Commando Order was contrary to international law and that the defence of 'superior orders' was not available to the accused. In other words, they were unable to rely on a plea not to be held guilty for actions which were ordered by a superior officer. The defence of 'superior orders' had been used extensively during the earlier Nuremberg war crime trials, but its application had been redefined by reference to Article 8 under the London Charter of the International Military Tribunal of 1945, which set down the laws and procedures under which the trials were to be conducted. It read: 'The fact that the Defendant acted pursuant to order of his Government or of a superior shall not free him from responsibility, but may be considered in mitigation of punishment if the Tribunal determines that justice so requires'. In other words, the defence of superior orders was not considered enough to escape punishment, but might affect its nature and duration.

The Judge Advocate also referred to the Geneva Convention Relative to the Treatment of Prisoners of War, agreed in 1929 by the delegates of thirty-eight nations. The signatories included the United Kingdom of Great Britain and Northern Ireland, Germany, and Italy, and the provisions were binding between individual states. The agreement came into effect in 1931 and so was the relevant international humanitarian law throughout the Second World War (and had currency until 1949, when it was superseded by a new convention). War was seen as an open conflict between two or more nations. A soldier serving in the army of a country that was recognised as being at war with his captor's nation, and who was taken prisoner in the course of a military operation, was entitled to POW status, provided that he was a member of a properly constituted military organisation and wore a uniform.

Article 2 of the convention emphasised: 'Prisoners of war are in the power of the hostile Government, but not of the individuals or formation which captured them. They shall at all times be humanely treated and protected, particularly against acts of violence, from insults and from public curiosity. Measures of reprisal against them are forbidden'. In the eight articles headed 'Judicial Proceedings', Article 61 read: 'No prisoner of war shall be sentenced without being given the opportunity to defend himself. No prisoner shall be compelled to admit that he is guilty of the offence of which he is accused'. Article 64 said: 'Every prisoner of war shall have the right of appeal against any sentence against him in the same manner as persons belonging to the armed forces of the detaining power'. Article 66 read: 'If sentence of death is passed on a prisoner of war ... The sentence shall not be carried out before the expiration of a period of at least three months from the date of the receipt of this communication by the Protecting Power [which at the time was Switzerland]'. None of these legal requirements had been met in the cases of the Ponzano Magra and the Cisa Pass killings.

The British Military Court made its ruling on 24 August 1948. Feurstein, von Menges, and Zastrow were all found not guilty. Von dem Knesebeck and Sommer were convicted on the first charge, of 'being concerned in the killing of Sgt Foster and L/Sgt Shorthall' at Ponzano Magra, and were each sentenced to six months' imprisonment. The convictions and sentences were confirmed by superior military authority. No one was ever convicted on the second charge of 'being concerned in the killing of Captain P. Dudgeon and an unidentified non-commissioned officer' at the Cisa Pass. What became known to the legal profession as 'Feurstein and others (the Ponzano case)' has frequently been cited in the context of criminal joint enterprise.

A memorial to William Foster and James Shortall was erected at Ponzano Magra in 2003, and its inauguration was attended by serving members of the SAS. A street in the village was also named 'Largo XXI *Settembre* 1943' in their honour in 2005. A memorial to Patrick Dudgeon and Bernard Brunt was inaugurated at Cisa in 2004, in the presence of Keith Killby, one of the Italian SAS originals and founder of the Monte San Martino Trust. A service to remember these brave men is held every year, with the participation of British and Italian service representatives, veterans, and local civic leaders.

11

Jeep and Sabotage Operations

In early September 1943, Roy Farran's 'D' Squadron of 2nd SAS embarked on an American cruiser at Bizerta to travel to the port of Taranto in support of the 1st Airborne Division's Operation Slapstick. On the evening of the 8th, the Italian surrender was announced over the loudspeakers and the ship was soon swept with speculation that the Allies would be in Rome in a week.

About 3 p.m. the next day, the men sighted the shores of Italy around Taranto Bay. The ship was the first one into the naval base and berthed with the help of heavily armed Italian sailors, who days earlier had been their enemies. The Italian Naval Squadron succeeded in escaping from the Germans to Malta, escorted by the British battleship HMS *King George V*. The first wave of the SAS moved into the city of Taranto and soon reports came back that it was proving to be a peaceful occupation.

Farran's jeeps were unloaded from the cruiser in darkness. The US Army Willys MB Truck provided a perfect platform for weapons; the ¼-ton 4×4 vehicle was a general-purpose carrier, especially adaptable for reconnaissance or command, with a crew of two, and up to three passengers. A conventional three-speed transmission equipped with a transfer case provided additional speed for traversing difficult terrain. The jeeps were equipped with the gas-operated, .303-calibre Vickers Class 'K' machine gun, which was being replaced in the RAF. The weapon was designed to deliver a high rate of fire (between 900 and 1,200 rounds a minute) in the brief window presented to air gunners, and proved highly effective during hit and run raids by the SAS.

Farran's orders from Brig. John Hackett (later of Arnhem fame), Commander of the 4th Parachute Brigade, were to push inland immediately as far as possible up the main road to the west of the port. It was certain that there were enemy units in the area, but their strength and dispositions were uncertain.

The jeeps drove through the darkness on alternate sides of a silent tree-lined avenue, with the squadron's second in command in the lead vehicle. Lt James 'Jim' Hamilton Mackie was a tall, sandy-haired Scot from Edinburgh, whose medical studies had been disrupted by the outbreak of war. He stopped suddenly and beckoned Farran forward from the second jeep. A group of armed men were standing around a bridge. As the rest of the convoy ground to a halt, an Italian guard shouted a challenge. Farran called back '*Inglesi*' and began to walk towards the men; he had just reached the bridge when one of them rushed towards him with a brandished rifle and fired a round through his legs at under five yards range; Farran's gunner, Sgt-Maj. Charles Mitchell, fired a whole magazine of Bren bullets into the Italian and he fell dead in the gutter. Farran recalled: 'And then there were profound apologies on both sides when we had established our identity'. The Germans were first encountered on the outskirts of the village of Massafra, when in the early hours of the morning a hail of bullets hit the convoy from an olive grove, but tracer from the Vickers guns on the jeeps soon silenced the attackers.

New orders from Brig. Hackett told Farran to push out to the north-west along the coast to see if he could locate the limits of the German position; if possible he was to infiltrate to their rear areas. The raiders attacked an enemy convoy at a crossroads near the village of Ginosa, 'unleashing a colossal barrage of fire' at close range, which resulted in the capture of forty-two troops and four trucks, the destruction of eight other vehicles, and about six enemy fatalities.

For several days, Farran continued the reconnaissance, hoping to find a gap in the German line. On 16 September, contact was made with forward elements of the advancing Eighth Army north of the village of Pisticci. Canadian soldiers in a Humber armoured car advanced on the SAS Headquarters and 'after a few minutes of mutual suspicion', they were shaking hands and slapping each other on the back. At the time, the progress of Farran's patrols was being obstructed by a blown bridge near a railway station and he was delighted to receive help from the Canadians in erecting a makeshift bridge over the ravine out of concrete railings and telegraph poles.

However, Farran did not want to stay with the main force. He sent Lt Mackie to take a patrol on foot through a railway tunnel in the mountain, leaving two men to guard the entrance at the far end. He was 'to appreciate the German strength, kill as many as he could with a few surprise bursts and then withdraw back the way he had come'. The patrol found itself in the middle of an enemy battalion and fought its way back to the tunnel, only to find the mouth occupied by a German section. The two guards that Mackie had left had fled back to safety. After what Farran described as 'a rather lucky little action', the party managed to return from the other side of the mountain. The two men who had abandoned their positions were immediately returned to their parent units (RTUd), the SAS's ultimate sanction.

After further duelling with enemy forces in the Grassano area and the loss of two jeeps, it became clear to Farran that there was no further hope of infiltrating through this sector of the front. He related that they had achieved a certain success in shallow penetration, but the results were not sufficient to justify them remaining in the area any longer; they were now 80 miles beyond the nearest airborne troops and supplies were running low, so he decided to return to Taranto for further orders.

Soon afterwards, the squadron was ordered to Bari to link up with the 4th Armoured Brigade and found a billet in a large school overlooking the sea. Their first task was a long-range patrol to report on the progress of the French Canadians, who were pushing inland with armoured cars and trucks. After being greeted as liberators in several villages on the way, the patrol found the Canadians in the hill village of Rovereto, about 30 miles from the port.

The two groups fraternised in a coffee bar, but Farran neglected to post lookouts in the excitement. He recalled: 'Only the prompt action of Sgt-Maj. Mitchell saved us from disaster when about fifty Germans entered the village from the other side'. The first notion of danger was a sudden burst of Bren from the rear of the column. Mitchell seized the gun and charged the enemy platoon after rallying the crews of the last jeeps, who had dismounted to talk to civilians. Firing from the hip, he drove the enemy troops out of the village and down the hill on the other side. They were pursued until they were pinned down in a river bed by his fire from above; four wounded Germans were also captured in the streets of the town. For the gallantry he showed in these engagements, Sgt-Maj. Mitchell was awarded the MM.

After the skirmish, the squadron turned north again towards Melfi and clashed with the enemy on high ground overlooking a steep-sided gorge. The SAS deployed at least seven machine guns, but withdrew when the Germans opened up a new flank and began to fire a mortar from the direction of the town.

The squadron was placed in reserve near Canosa while the 4th Armoured Brigade crossed Puglia's largest river, the Ofanto, but they were suddenly called upon to conduct a detachment of their French SAS colleagues across the river to Cerignola, the next town in the line of advance. The commander of the brigade, Brig. John Currie, a friend of Farran from the desert, then gave him the task of patrolling on the left flank while the main force advanced on Foggia. In a place called Stornarella, the SAS men were once again treated as liberators, but suddenly it became apparent that half of the village was still occupied by the Germans. The squadron was forced to withdraw after street fighting all morning and faced a further ambush when returning to the brigade.

The SAS moved with them to Foggia and Farran was given the task of reconnoitring the town of Lucera. He led the squadron through vine-covered fields for about 5 miles and at nightfall decided to take a foot patrol into the town after discovering three enemy 88-mm guns firing from the surrounding woods. As the men were climbing the last ploughed field before reaching houses there was a tremendous explosion and they threw themselves to the ground, fearing that their presence had been discovered. Clods of earth and brick came whistling down and Farran was hit in the side of the face by a large piece of masonry; blood poured over his shirt, and he thought his jaw was broken. His men helped him into the shelter of some vines as he gave orders to Lt Jim Mackie to find a safe house to act as a base and a place where he could recover.

Farran finally staggered to his feet and led the rest of the patrol to the outskirts of the town. Mackie eventually returned and took them to the house of an elderly priest, who was terrified that the Germans would discover their presence. His sister bathed and bandaged Farran's wounds, while he sent out three patrols with orders to snipe at the enemy but not to get involved in a firefight. They covered most of town and discovered that the explosion had been caused by the Germans demolishing a road in preparation for withdrawal; they left by one in the morning after mining the area, but the locations were subsequently carefully plotted by the SAS.

Farran recalled: 'It was certain by morning that there were no further Germans about so we sallied forth in our great strength of twelve to take over Lucera. The Italians turned out in their thousands to welcome the conquering army'. After two days, Farran received permission to move farther north along the San Severo to Castellana road, but when his jeeps were targeted by German 88-mm artillery, firing armour-piercing shells, he decided to withdraw. He related: 'It was plain that the front was becoming too stable for our game of shallow infiltration and I decided to make my way back to the main force'.

At the end of October, Roy Farran was tasked with his last venture in Italy in 1943, which he described as 'a true SAS operation behind the enemy lines'. The squadron had moved to a rambling country house at Gioia del Colle, with the benefits of an Italian cook, a large garden, and a horse in the stable. While receiving reinforcements, the squadron was briefed on the new mission by a staff officer from the Eighth Army. Codenamed Candytuft, it involved targeting railway lines and communication targets in the coastal area between Ancona and Pescara, and was scheduled to run from 27 October to 2 November. The objectives were set out in the post-combat report:

> The plan was to land by sea on the coast between Ancona and Pescara, and attempt to derail a train near a curve on the coast railway. Naval craft were to look for signals on the first four nights in November, and take off the party after the operation had been completed.
>
> Four parties of four men were to be landed on the southern bank of the River Tronto, 25 miles north of Pescara. They were to be landed at 22.00 hours on the night of 27–28 October and to make their way inland for between 4 and 5 miles and lie up until the night of 28–29 October. On the night of 28–29 October all parties would rendezvous at the track junction at 21.00 hrs. The centre party would then attempt to derail a train by 02.00 hours. If by this time there had been no success, the performance was to be repeated on the night of 29–30 October, and again on the night of 30–31 October if necessary.
>
> As soon as a train had been derailed, a party would blow large gaps in the line on either side of the train, and one party would mine the main coast road. Telephone communications would also be cut.
>
> If no success had been achieved by the night of 31 October–1st November all parties would demolish the railway and mine the road regardless of trains. After the demolition had been completed all parties would make their way southwards to hide out in the River Salinello valley. They would then make their way, by night, to the embarkation point. Signalling to the Navy would be by torch flashes from 23.59 hours to 02.30 hours.[1]

A distraction exercise would also be carried out off Pescara, when a mock landing party would appear off the shore several days after the railway line was blown in order to direct the attention of the enemy away from the raiders on their dangerous return journey. Three of the four parties of four men were from 'D' Squadron: the first was led by Capt. Farran, the second by Sgt Hawes, and the third by Sgt Seddon. The fourth party, from 'B' Squadron, was led by Lt Grant St John Hibbert, who had already taken part in a mission in the region as commanding officer of the seaborne beach party in the San Benedetto–Pescara area during Operation Jonquil to rescue escaped Allied POWs.

As the Italian motor torpedo boat neared the shore, the British captain of the vessel suddenly ordered the engines to be switched off. With the aid of binoculars, he had discovered that what appeared from a distance to be a large rock in the mouth of the River Tronto was in fact a German submarine charging its batteries, only 500 yards from the landing point.

Farran recalled: 'My nerves were so tense that I could barely speak. It was incredibly bad luck to run into perhaps the only submarine on the coast. But the sailor seemed quite happy to go ahead with the plan'. One engine was started up gently and the motor torpedo boat floated ever closer to the shore. Two rubber dinghies and a Goatley collapsible boat were launched and the men made a hurried departure in the darkness, keeping one eye on the submarine and the other on the sandy beach ahead. Everyone landed safely without provoking a reaction from the enemy vessel, but the rain was beating in their faces and their rubber-soled boots slipped in the mud. The four parties made their way inland, with orders to rendezvous at the target site at 9 p.m. on 28 October. They were to stay ashore for approximately a week, cause as much damage as possible, and then rendezvous with another vessel south of Giulianova and the River Tordino, farther down the coast.

Farran's detachment blundered into a small village by mistake, dogs barked, and a light came on in one house, but no one emerged to challenge them. They then went to ground in a bamboo grove near the river and stayed there for the rest of the night and for most of the next day. In the evening, one of the men sent on a scouting mission returned with the news that they were only 500 yards away from a railway bridge guarded by two German sentries. Farran related: 'At last I had got my bearings'.

Once it was dark, the men made a detour to avoid the guards and followed small tracks and narrow lanes until they reached the railway line. Keeping to the shadows, they scrambled up the embankment, down the other side, and on to the main road. Suddenly, an old man carrying an umbrella appeared. Farran recalled: 'Pretending that we were Germans, I asked in broken Italian the way to the crossroads. He conducted us down to them and then said goodbye to us in English'. Two of the other three detachments also reached the rendezvous, but there was no sign of the one under Sgt Hawes. On the suggestion of Lt Hibbert, it was decided to postpone the attack till the next night, on the grounds that they were too wet and miserable to do the job efficiently and also in no fit state to undertake the long escape march. In the meantime, they would hide on remote farms and confine the occupants to their houses.

Farran took his own party about a mile to the west in heavy rain and found a cosy billet with a poor farmer, his wife, and their teenage son. The sound of overhead aircraft broke the men out of their slumber at 11 a.m., and through the farmhouse windows, they watched a flight of Curtiss P-40 Warhawk fighters and ground-attack aircraft bombing the submarine in the mouth of the river. The planes scored a direct hit and a large lump of metal flew into the air.

At 10 p.m., the raiders left to meet their comrades. The original plan was that one party under Sgt Seddon would lay mines on the road and blow up telegraph poles, while the other three groups were targeting the railway line. However, on the night, there was still no sign of Sgt Hawes' men.

The rain drove hard into the faces of the men as they trudged across the fields and scrambled up a grassy bank leading to the railway. They dumped their rucksacks and formed a defence party while Cpl Linton carefully laid the charges. At 11.30 p.m., the men squeezed their half-hour time pencils and rolled down the embankment. They struggled up muddy paths into the hills and suddenly heard the comforting sound of explosions and saw flashes through the rain. The men split into their groups of four and began the long trek back to the rescue craft, moving inland across rough country to avoid the coastal plain.

After four hours, Farran's detachment had only covered 10 miles instead of the planned 20 miles, and so he decided to move down to the main road, even though the risk of capture was greater there. They came upon a hamlet, with a railway station and a bridge over a river, which meant that they had travelled over a third of the distance, but Farran suddenly noticed a German truck parked in the railway yard. It was too late to turn back, so they padded on silently with their eyes firmly straight ahead and were soon back in open country. Sgt Seddon and his men were less fortunate when they followed later. They were challenged and fired on, and the Sgt and Parachutist Richards were captured. They were subsequently posted as 'missing, believed to be prisoners of war'; the two other men in the group escaped.

Farran's party spent the night outside a village, which an old man on the road told them had Fascist sympathies. They slept among the cattle in a byre underneath the house on a prosperous farm, and in the morning were treated as honoured guests by the family. The next night, the four parachutists settled down among the oxen in the stable of a farm where three families of evacuees bombed out of Bologna were staying, and even here found no animosity.

In the morning, the group by-passed another village, which a farmer said contained Fascists, and trekked as fast as they could across ploughed fields in the direction of the coast as darkness fell, knowing that the motor torpedo boat sent to pick them up was due in at around midnight. Farran became separated from the others in the final dash to the beach, as they scattered to avoid a German armoured vehicle on the road. He arrived at the rendezvous an hour late, to find Lt Hibbert signalling with his torch, but without receiving any response. The men withdrew in their four groups and arranged to meet again next day.

Farran plodded across wet, ploughed fields and found shelter on a small farm 2 miles from the beach. He slept until midday and was delighted to hear from his hosts that surrounding farmers were also sheltering parties of Britons. They included Sgt Hawes' detachment, which had not arrived at the original rendezvous. He reported that they destroyed three trucks and had also blown the railway line as soon as they heard the sound of the main party's explosions.

When all the men had gathered on the beach in the evening, Sgt Hawes was put in charge of a party to watch the road and to lay mines before leaving for the boat. The men started signalling with a torch behind a blanket at 11 p.m., and almost an hour later, they noticed the long, black shape of a vessel creeping into the shore. There was the fear that it could be one of the German E-boats that were based at Giulianova, a few miles to the north, so the men hid in the dunes, until they saw a rubber dinghy bouncing over the surf. Maj. Sandy Scratchley jumped on to the beach, and the men were taken to the motor torpedo boat for the voyage back to Termoli in four trips of the rescue craft.

The main raiding party had blown the railway line in sixteen places, demolished seven telegraph poles, and brought down an electric pylon. In addition, Sgt Hawes' group had destroyed three trucks and also blown the line as soon as they heard the first explosions.

Back at their billet in Gioia del Colle, Farran was modest about their achievements, reflecting that holes in a railway line are easily repaired. But, he recalled, Eighth Army HQ seemed satisfied and had intercepted radio messages that showed that a certain amount of panic had been caused: 'General Montgomery was so pleased that he sent us down his usual "good boy" gift of newspapers and cigarettes. Little gestures like that make the men think that their endeavours are really worthwhile'.

Maj. Scratchley returned to the same area on 18 December 1943 in an operation codenamed Sleepy Lad. His party split into separate groups and attacked enemy road and rail communications, but their pickup by sea proved impossible, and they returned to Allied lines by stealing a boat.

The 2nd SAS Regiment went back to North Africa in January 1944 and returned to the UK in March to prepare for the D-Day operation. They would be back in Italy in December, as we shall see.

12

Rescuing POWs

On the late afternoon of 2 October 1943, seven men from the 2nd SAS Regiment and an interpreter from the American Office of Strategic Services (OSS) parachuted from an Armstrong Whitworth Albermarle transport aircraft in the Abruzzo, only to find that it was in the wrong place and at the wrong time. As it was still daylight, the men were clearly visible from the ground, and as they descended, they discovered that they were over Chieti, a major urban centre instead of the planned remote drop zone in the countryside.

CO Lt Alastair McGregor could see German troops running to their vehicles, and moments later, they reappeared on the road below. For a few seconds, he thought that his party would land in the middle of them, but the wind suddenly changed direction and blew them away from the centre of the town and over a large field. Once on the ground, the parachutists were welcomed by a crowd of excited Italians, who had gathered to view the unfolding spectacle. McGregor said later: 'They were shaking my hand before I even touched the ground'. By now, the Germans were approaching, and so he decided to dump the containers in a ditch.

The interpreter found a uniformed Italian Customs Officer (*Guardia di Finanza*), who volunteered to help. There was no time to doubt his good intentions, and he quickly led the party down to the River Pescara; the men hid there, while the Italian returned to the drop zone and persuaded some local farmers to conceal the containers. On his return, he took the party 7 miles across country to a farm; after lying low there for two days, during a frantic enemy search of the area, the parachutists began their secret mission.

In October 1943, this and other groups from the 2nd SAS Regiment were part of a large-scale effort to find former POWs at loose in the Italian countryside after the armistice of September 1943 and to guide them to beachheads on the Adriatic Coast for pickups by Allied craft. The task was coordinated by 'A' Force, the special operations agency under G-2 Operations at AFHQ in Algiers, which was 'responsible for deception and cover plans and for the organisation of escape chains'. The rescue work was delegated to the escape and evasion agencies, the British MI9 (known in Italy as 'N' Section of 'A' Force, until 20 August 1944, when it became IS9) and the American MIS-X. Both worked together in the field.

The inspiration for the mission in Italy came from the highest level of British Government. Prime Minister Winston Churchill had great regard for the fate of POWs, which was born out of his own escape in South Africa during the Boer War. As early as 26 July 1943 in a message to President Roosevelt entitled 'Thoughts on the Fall of Mussolini', he wrote (in point six out of twelve):

> Another objective of the highest importance, about which there will be a passionate feeling in this country, is the immediate liberation of all British prisoners of war in Italian hands, and the prevention, which in the first instance can only be by the Italians, of their being transported northwards to Germany. I regard it as a matter of honour and humanity to get our own flesh and blood back as soon as possible and spare them the measureless horrors of incarceration in Germany during the final stages of the war.

Three days later, the two leaders agreed eleven articles that would be the basis for an Italian surrender; the third one read: 'All prisoners or internees of the United Nations [are] to be immediately turned over to the Allied Commander-in-Chief, and none of these may from the beginning of these negotiations be evacuated to Germany'. When the Italians signed the instrument of armistice and surrendered at Cassibile in Sicily on 3 September, the provisions on Allied prisoners in Italian hands again appeared as article three, with similar wording to that of 29 July.

The official history of IS9 related that just two officers from 'N' Section were landed on the beach at Syracuse during the invasion of Sicily in July 1943. They had their kit, but no transport, and no idea as to their purpose in life apart from the instruction that they were to find out how rescue work might best be accomplished with an army in the field. During a miserable fifteen-day hitch-hike around the island, the pair soon learned the vital lesson that no rescue work of any kind would be possible unless an 'N' Section team was self-contained and mobile. The history noted that the war establishment in 1943 'was woefully weak both in personnel, transport and means of communication, and an idea of this weakness will be gathered when we state that our total transport consisted of one eight-cwt utility truck and one motor cycle. No means of communication by way of radio existed, of course'.

Lt-Col. David Stirling, creator of the SAS Regiment, and later a POW in Italy and Germany.

Lt-Col. Miles Dempsey (left), Commander of XIII Corps, in Sicily in July 1943. He related that he was originally only lent the Special Raiding Squadron (SRS) for the attack on the guns of Cape Murro di Porco, after which it was to have returned to the Middle East, but then went on to carry out three more successful operations in Italy.

Field Marshal Sir Harold Alexander, Supreme Commander of the Mediterranean Forces, standing in front of a map of Italy at his HQ in the Royal Palace of Caserta.

German Field Marshal Albert Kesselring (centre), Commander of Army Group 'C', during an inspection tour in the Italian Apennines in 1944.

Lt-Col. Robert 'Paddy' Mayne in the desert near Kabrit, future commander of the SRS in Italy and the 1st SAS Regiment.

Members of 2nd SAS Regiment on parade for an inspection by Gen. Montgomery, following their successful participation in the capture of the port of Termoli. *Front left*: Maj. Alexander Scratchley, commander of the detachment. *Front right*: Capt. Roy Farran.

HMS *Safari* (P211), the famous submarine that carried the SAS raiders to and from Sardinia during Operation Marigold in May 1943.

Troops of the British 5th Infantry Division passing bomb-damaged buildings in Syracuse on the opening day of the invasion of Sicily, 10 July 1943, hours after the SRS had destroyed enemy coastal batteries in their landing zone.

HMS *Mauritius*, which assisted the SRS's landing at Augusta, Sicily, on 12 July 1943 in a shore bombardment role. The light cruiser is shown here ready for action off the Anzio beachhead in March 1944. The SAS supported the landings in January with operations to impede German reinforcements.

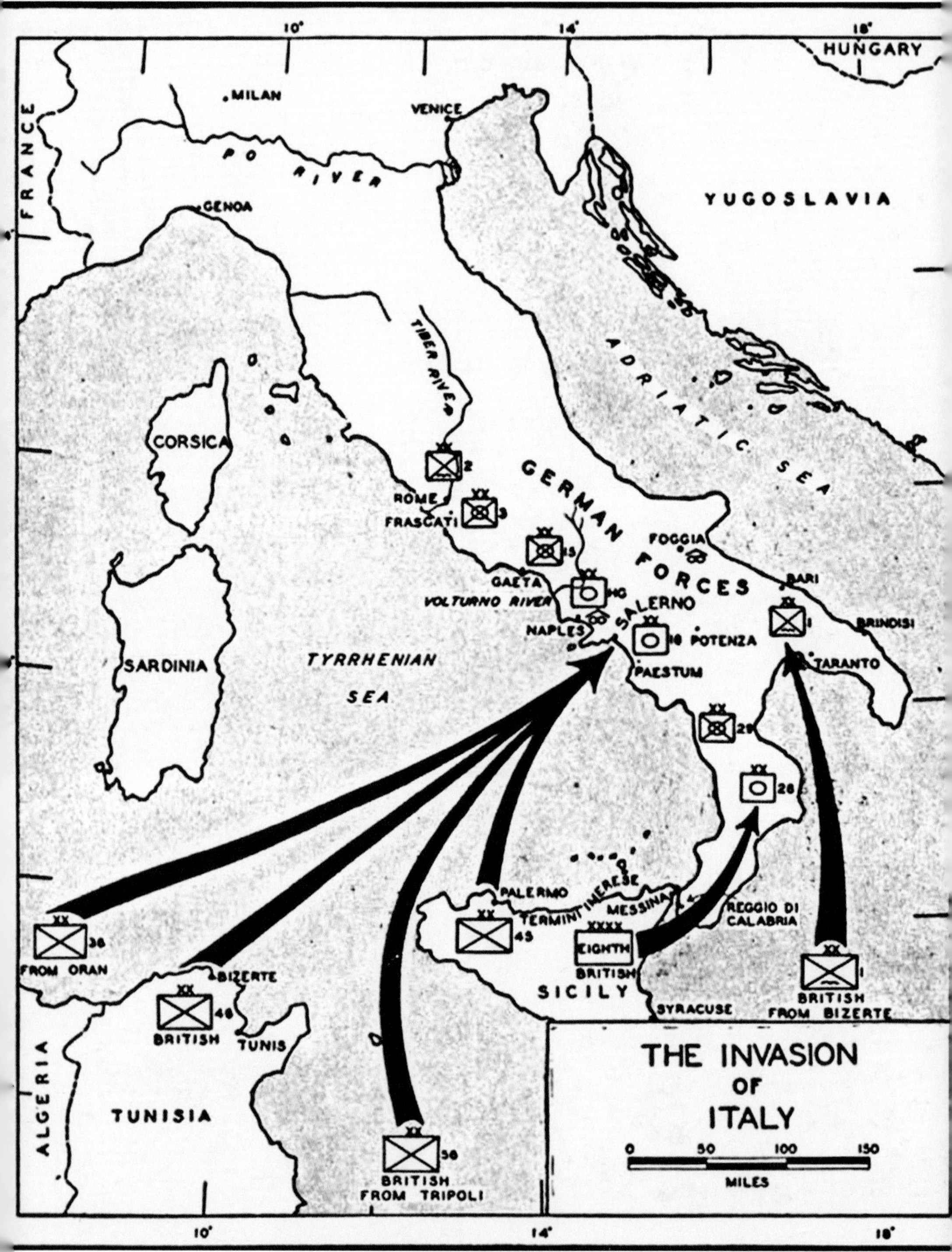

Map of the invasion of mainland Italy in September 1943.

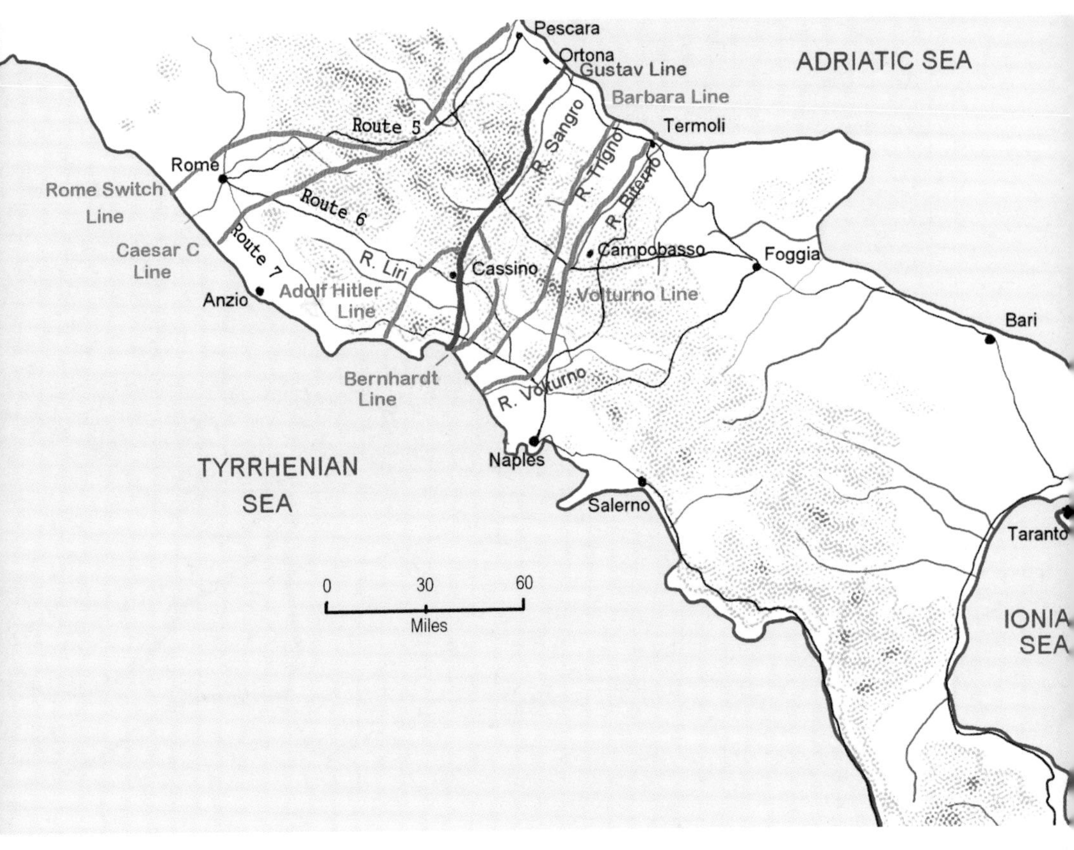

German defensive lines south of Rome, 1943–1944.

Next page: German defensive positions in northern Italy, June to December 1944.

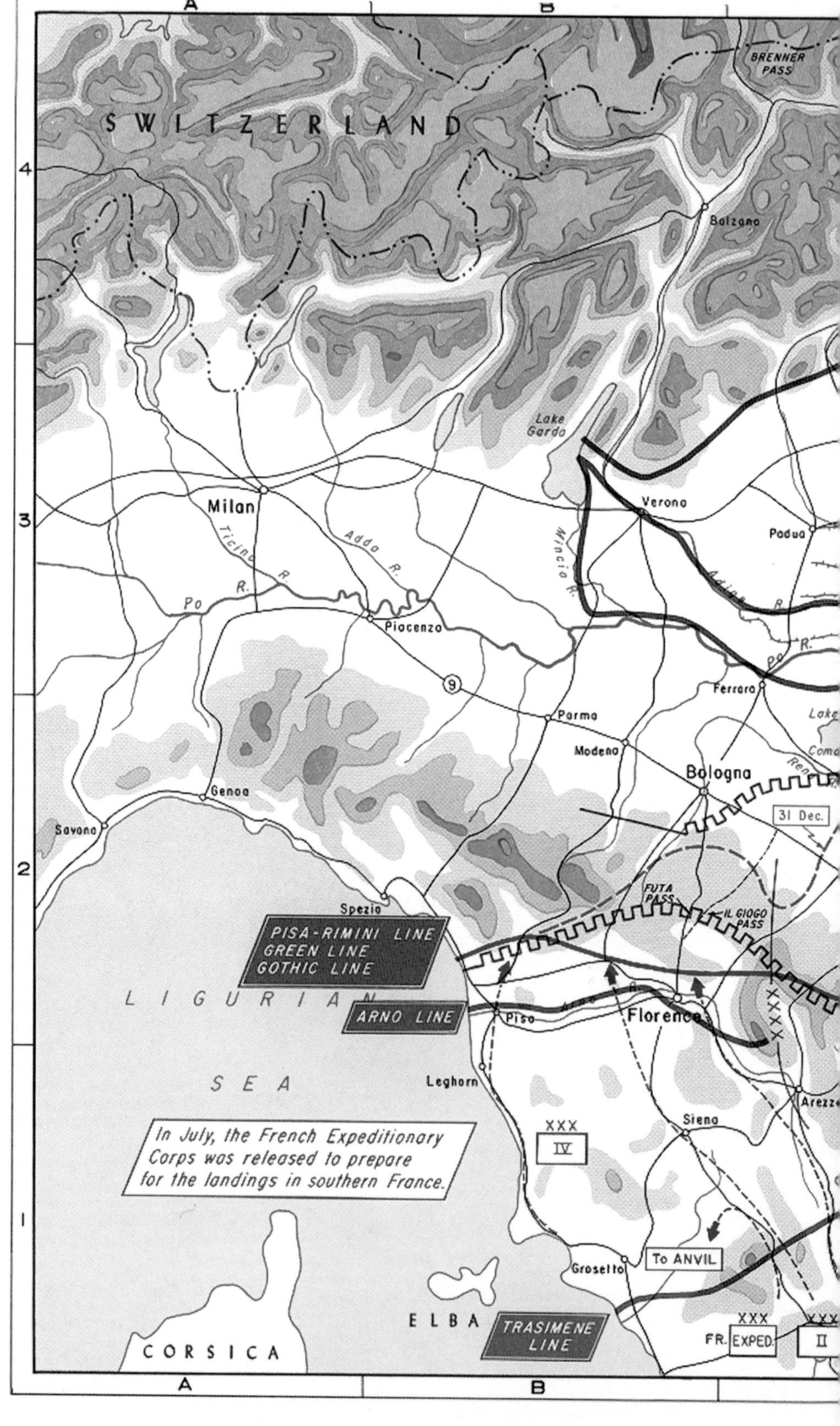
SWITZERLAND
BRENNER PASS
Bolzano
Lake Garda
Milan
Verona
Padua
Ticino R.
Adda R.
Mincio R.
Po R.
Adige R.
Piacenza
9
Ferrara
Parma
Modena
Bologna
31 Dec.
Genoa
Savona
FUTA PASS
IL GIOGO PASS
Spezia
PISA-RIMINI LINE
GREEN LINE
GOTHIC LINE
LIGURIAN
SEA
ARNO LINE
Arno R.
Pisa
Florence
Leghorn
Arezzo
Siena
XXX
IV
In July, the French Expeditionary Corps was released to prepare for the landings in southern France.
To ANVIL
Grosseto
ELBA
TRASIMENE LINE
CORSICA
FR. EXPED.
II

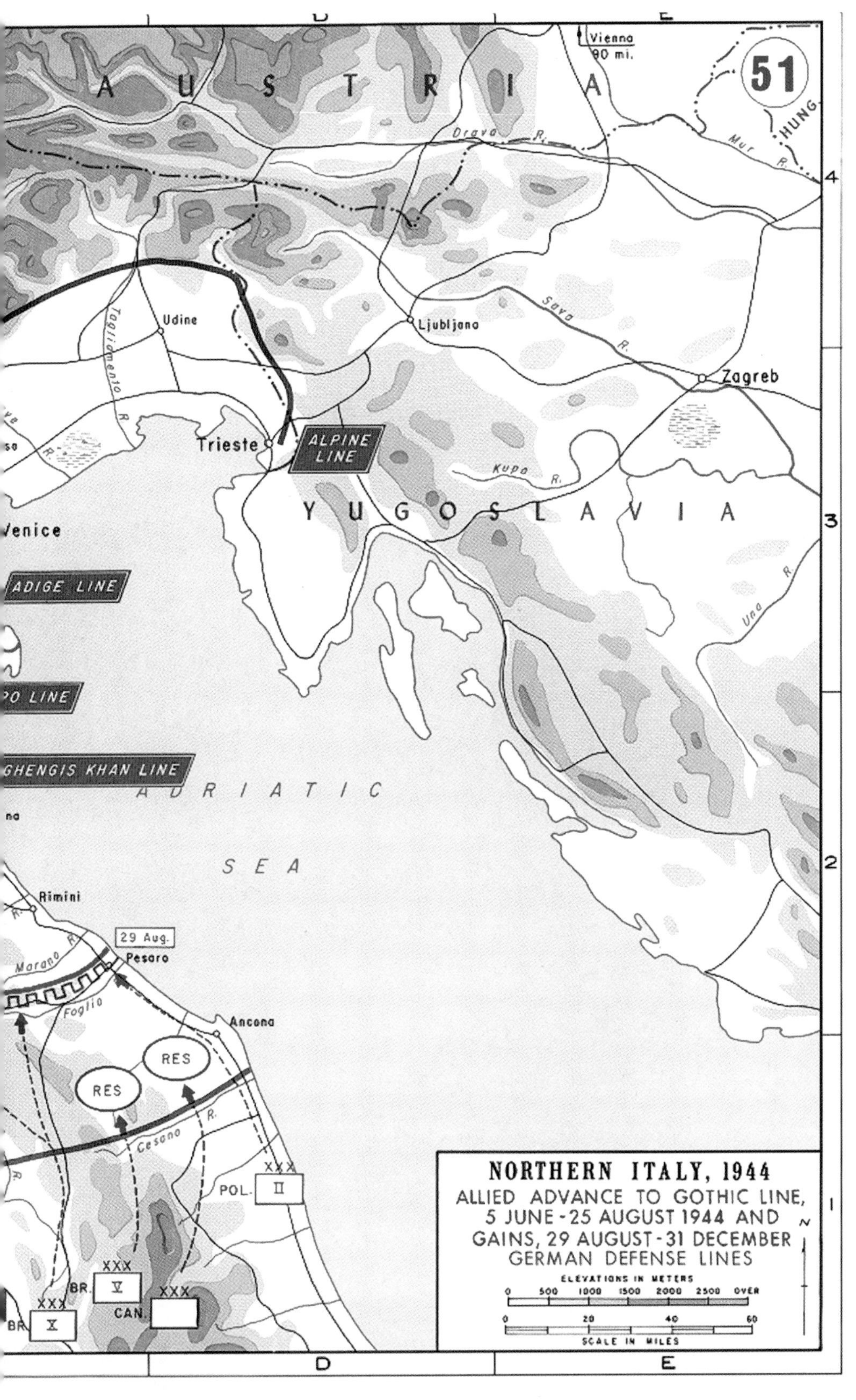
51
AUSTRIA
Vienna
90 mi.
HUNG
Drava R.
Mur R.
Sava R.
Udine
Ljubljana
Tagliamento R.
Zagreb
Trieste
ALPINE LINE
Kupa R.
YUGOSLAVIA
Venice
ADIGE LINE
Una R.
PO LINE
GHENGIS KHAN LINE
ADRIATIC
SEA
Rimini
29 Aug.
Pesaro
Marano R.
Foglia
Ancona
RES
RES
Cesano R.
POL.
II
XXX
BR.
V
CAN.
X
NORTHERN ITALY, 1944
ALLIED ADVANCE TO GOTHIC LINE, 5 JUNE - 25 AUGUST 1944 AND GAINS, 29 AUGUST - 31 DECEMBER
GERMAN DEFENSE LINES
ELEVATIONS IN METERS
0 500 1000 1500 2000 2500 OVER
0 20 40 60
SCALE IN MILES
D
E
1
2
3
4

Monte Altissimo (1,589 metres) in Tuscany, climbed on 14 February 1945 by the SAS Troop in Operation Galia when exfiltrating to Allied lines.

Above: Two USAAF Douglas C-47 Skytrains, the preferred transport of the SAS and other parachutists in Italy.

Below: Interior view of the Douglas C-47 Skytrain.

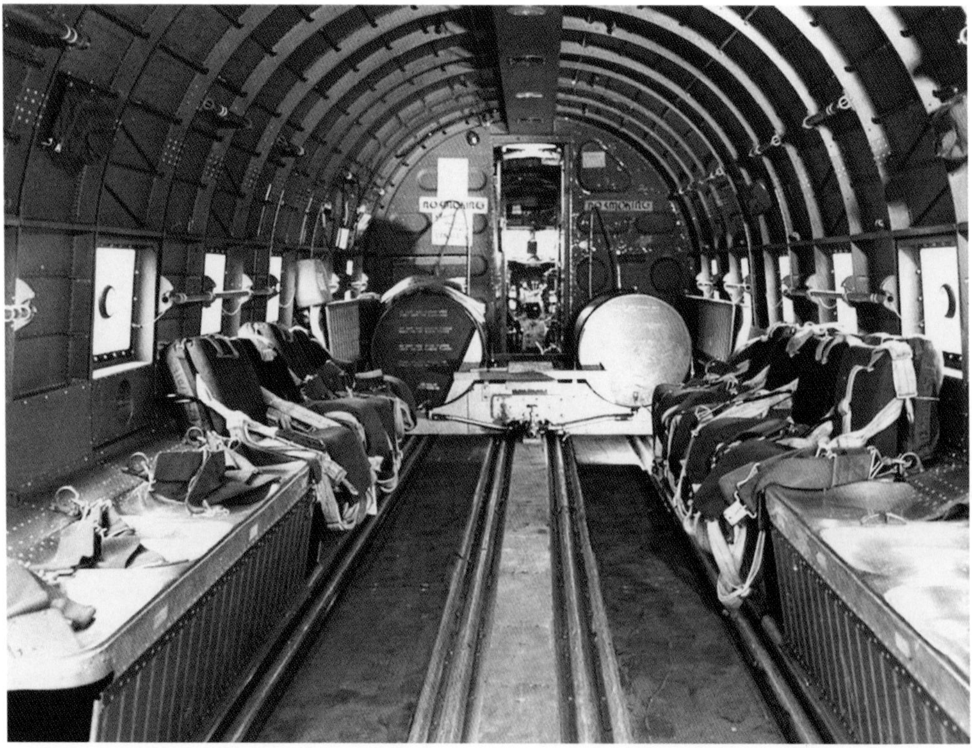

On 25 September 1943, Prime Minister Winston Churchill, from the Cabinet War Rooms in Whitehall, London, authorised the urgent mission to rescue escaped Allied POWs in southern Italy. An operational headquarters codenamed SIMCOL was set up in Bari, with a forward base established at Termoli in October. Former Special Operations Executive operative Lt-Col. Anthony 'Tony' Simonds of MI9 landed at Taranto with the 1st Airborne Division and set about assembling parties to send up to 50 miles ahead of the 5th and 8th Armies to locate the servicemen and to guide them back within the lines. Capt. Christopher Soames, Coldstream Guards, who in 1947 married Churchill's daughter, Mary, led one of the field escape sections with orders 'to utilise all known available means to produce a network of helpers behind the enemy lines and make local plans for the early rescue of ground troops and air crews at large within enemy territory'.

On 26 September, the day after the Prime Minister's order, Maj. Symes of 2nd SAS reported to Col. Simonds after two troops of the regiment had been placed under his command for deeper penetration operations. A detailed plan for the rescue of the POWs was prepared, with a seaborne element (Operation Jonquil) and an airborne element (Operation Begonia). The coast between Ancona and the front line (a distance of over 400 miles) was designated as the operational area for the mission and it was divided into four sections. Two parties were to be introduced into each area, one seaborne as a beach party, and the other airborne, tasked with locating and guiding the escaped POWs to the beachhead for evacuation by sea.

The areas and the parties allocated were as follows (from north to south along the Adriatic Coast):

Area A: Ancona to Civitanova: Squadron Sergeant-Major (SSM) Marshall and six men (seaborne beach party), and Eighth Army 1st Airborne Division (airborne search party).

Area B: Civitanova to San Benedetto del Tronto: Capt. Power and six men (seaborne), and Airborne Division (airborne).

Area C: San Benedetto del Tronto to Pescara: Lt Hibbert and six men (seaborne), and Airborne Division (airborne).

Area D: Pescara to the south: Capt. Baillie and six men (seaborne), and two airborne parties: Lt McGregor and six men (SAS), plus Lt Borrow and twelve men from the US Office of Strategic Services (OSS).

There was also an extra protection party in the most southerly area D, as it was closest to the Gustav Line, the German winter defensive position. The group consisted of Capt. Lee and seventeen other men from the Free

French Squadron of the SAS. Many members of the regiment used an alias and the captain was one of them. Though he now went by the name of Lee, he was born Raymond Couraud on 12 January 1920 at Surgères, Charente-Maritime, in south-western France. A former French Foreign Legionnaire, he helped run an escape line for refugees from German occupation, all members of the intellectual and artistic community, until in April 1941, he crossed the Pyrenees and offered his services at the British Consulate in Barcelona. In October, Couraud joined Free French forces in London, and two months later, he was recruited by SOE and commissioned as 2Lt Jack William Raymond Lee. Owing to his unorthodox methods, he left the agency under something of a cloud in January 1943, but then joined 62 Commando and finally the SAS Regiment. When the French Squadron was formed in March 1943, 'Capt. Lee' was appointed its commander, owing to the bravery and leadership he had demonstrated in a wide variety of raids; two months later, he took out British citizenship.

On 5 October 1943, Capt. Charles Henry Duffett, Naval Liaison Officer with the Eighth Army, received orders from 15th Army Group to proceed with all speed to Termoli to take command of the landing craft there and to establish what cooperation was required for the evacuation of escaped prisoners of war. He arrived at 11 p.m., when Germans were on the edge of the town, men of the 38th Brigade were disembarking from Landing Craft (Infantry) (LCIs), and the harbour was being periodically shelled and attacked by dive bombers. There was no naval officer in charge of the port. The only officer present was Lt Hilton, RNVR (Royal Naval Volunteer Reserve), who was acting as Liaison Officer to the Special Service Brigade. He was doing what he could, but a more senior officer was required, as the Army looked to the Navy for a decision on many questions that were arising.

Capt. Duffett met Col. Tony Simonds and he was briefed on what had already been done; together they worked out plans for the evacuation of escapers by sea. The captain selected three LCIs for this purpose, sending the remaining four south to Barletta. On 6 October, the town and the harbour in Termoli were again shelled and dive-bombed, but without damage to any naval craft, and operations by the three LCIs were able to begin that evening using the beaches extending as far north as Grottammare in the region of Le Marche.

In his final report to 15th Army Group on his activities, dated 17 October 1943, Capt. Duffett related that exact information regarding POWs was most difficult to obtain and even then it was usually out of date and mostly hearsay. However, it did appear that some 2,000–4,000 men might be lying up in the country between Ancona and the front line. A large number of them were being looked after by Italians who, having been threatened by the Germans with death if they were found sheltering POWs, were not unnaturally extremely reluctant to disclose information to any persons who might well be enemy agents; Allied POWs appeared equally wary.

In enemy territory itself, the parachute landings had all been made in from Albermarle aircraft on 2 October. The three Airborne Division parties experienced similar problems to those of Lt McGregor's SAS group. The parties for areas A and B were both dropped in the same place and the one for Area C was dropped half an hour too early in broad daylight.

Lt Alastair McGregor, commanding the SAS airborne search party in Area D (Pescara to the south), was born on 5 September 1918 at Hendon, north-western London, and educated at Epsom College in Surrey, where he excelled in sports. After graduating from the Royal Military College, Sandhurst, McGregor was commissioned in the Royal Scots (The Royal Regiment) in 1938 and took part in the evacuation from Dunkirk in 1940. He served with the 1st Airborne Division in North Africa, and after being posted back to the United Kingdom following an altercation at battalion headquarters, simply got off a train at a desert station and sought out 2nd SAS.

Following the problematic parachute drop over Chieti on 2 October 1943 and lying low for the two days, McGregor's group split up to contact escaped POWs over a wide area. About 300 men were directed to the beachhead between 4 October and 12 October. Capt. Duffett temporarily halted LCI operations at this time, owing to a bright phase of the moon, and as no more of the craft were expected at the rendezvous, Lt McGregor decided to send the escapers along a land route that he had already reconnoitred. About 250 prisoners went through Popoli and Scanno and many succeeded in reaching Allied forces near Alfedena. On 10 October, the three LCIs brought back to anchor about 3 miles south of Termoli were dive-bombed at around 11.30 a.m. There were several near misses, but any damage to the craft appeared superficial.

Around 20 October, a detachment of SS troops moved into the Chieti area and began to track down escaped POWs. The lieutenant decided to organise the ambushing of road convoys in order to divert the attention of the enemy from the escapers to his own party. He commandeered a small 8-cwt truck and his men attacked two convoys, killing six Germans and wounding seven more.

At the beginning of November, bad weather was setting in and the prisoners were shivering in their summer clothing. Lt McGregor requisitioned a new Fiat six-cylinder car, which was being hidden until the end of the war for King Emmanuel of Italy, and called on well-known Fascists in the area with two men armed with Tommy guns on the running board; they solicited donations of clothes and money for distribution to the fugitive servicemen, which would tide them over during the winter and facilitate their journey through the lines. At this time, at least three Italians who were informing on escapers in exchange for money were shot.

Early in January 1944, the SAS party was preparing to return to Allied lines when it was attacked by a large group of German troops, and split up according to a pre-arranged plan. Lt McGregor and Parachutist McQueen reached liberated territory after an arduous 40-mile journey on a stolen rowing boat. The fate of the remaining men was not known, though the post-combat report said that there was no reason to suppose that any of them had been taken prisoner or shot, as no such reports were received by Lt McGregor for a period of ten days in a country 'where such news travels like wild fire'. Alastair McGregor was awarded the DSO for his gallantry in action in Italy, and the MC later in France.

The seaborne parties, which established the defended positions to allow the evacuation of ex-POWs brought to the beaches by the airborne search parties, are the topic of the next chapter.

13

Amphibious Operations

As part of the combined operation of Begonia-Jonquil to rescue ex-POWs at large in the Italian countryside after the September 1943 armistice, the seaborne parties were landed shortly after the airborne parties, and experienced similar problems.

The seaborne groups in Area 'D' (Pescara to the south) were landed by schooner 7 miles south of the planned landing point at the mouth of the River Foro on 4 October. However, the German counterattack on the port of Termoli disrupted subsequent operations. The harbour was no longer safe and the use of schooners off the coast by day was considered impracticable. They were therefore replaced by the Landing Craft (Infantry) of Capt. Duffett. As the speed of these vessels was not sufficient to reach the beach serving Area 'A' (Ancona to Civitanova) and return in darkness, the beach was abandoned and both the parties for Areas 'A' and 'B' were landed on the night of 5–6 October in Area 'B' (Civitanova to San Benedetto del Tronto), though this was at Grottammare, 4 miles from the proposed landing point at the mouth of the River Menocchia. A successful landing by the party for Area 'C' (San Benedetto del Tronto to Pescara) took place the following night, just north of the River Tronto, which was 8 miles away from the intended site at the mouth of the River Salinello.

The leaders of the SAS parties landed together in Area 'B' were SSM Marshall and Capt. Power. On the night of 9–10 October, contact was made with a boat at the mouth of the River Menocchia, but no POWs had yet been sent down by the inland group. The vessel withdrew and the group split into four detachments to search the countryside themselves, as the airborne party did not appear to have been able to operate. A rendezvous was fixed for 22 October and a rear party was left under SSM Marshall. It was arranged that the naval craft were to return on the night of 24–25 October, which was during a dark phase of the moon.

However, on 21 October, a large party of Germans stormed the rear party's headquarters. Parachutists Cook and Fitzgerald were captured and taken away, despite SSM Marshall killing two of the attackers. He hid in a bush for several hours, and the enemy patrol left after throwing grenades and taking pot shots at anything that moved. Fortunately for Cook and Fitzgerald, the Germans handed them over to the Italian *Carabinieri* (who were not subject to Hitler's Commando order) and the pair managed to escape with a group of former Allied POWs during an air raid at Monturano on 18 November.

On 24 October, the SAS search parties arrived back with 300–400 ex-POWs. Capt. Power established contact with a motor torpedo boat just after midnight as planned, but as the escapers began emerging from the bushes to cross the road overlooking the beach, they heard random gunshots and most of them stampeded back into the hills, despite the fact that they would probably have been able to reach the craft unobserved. Twenty-three men were able to embark for Termoli, including the main SAS party.

More than fifty years later, I was in contact with one of the former POWs who had been rescued on this occasion. Lt Geoffrey Scott Stavert, 'E' Troop Commander, 155th Battery, 172nd Field Regiment, Royal Artillery (and a future lieutenant-commander in the Royal Navy), had been captured by the Germans at Sidi Nsir in Tunisia on 26 February 1943. He remembered thinking: 'Oh well, perhaps I'll go to a prison camp and become somebody by making a famous escape'.

The lieutenant was one of the officers and men who marched out of Camp 49 Fontanellato at noon on 9 September 1943. He told me that he and a fellow gunner officer (Lt Harold Magee, who did not survive the war) at transit Camp 66 Capua, near Naples often used to discuss escape plans when they were both POWs, little thinking that they would have the chance to put them into practice:

> Neither of us fancied the necessities of a border crossing in Switzerland, and still less the hazards of getting through the fighting zones to reach 8th Army in the south. The idea of making for the Adriatic coast (easy walking in the plain) and then circumventing the lines by sea, in contrast, seemed to have a lot of potential advantages, and certainly the least risk if we were careful of any encounter with the enemy. Of course, neither of us had any experience of handling a small boat or of the elements of navigation, but these were practicalities that we felt could be dealt with when the time came. It is just as well that we never had to put this part of our scheme in operation!
>
> I was taken to PG 49 via PG 66 Capua in May 1943, part of a batch of officers captured after the tank battle in Tunisia (1st Army types,

not 8th Army). I remember the closing days of PG 49 exactly as you have described them. After the camp broke up, I was in a party of four who were given old clothes and taken to a farm a little to the north of Fontanellato. It was run by a family called Carrara. They were all, of course, friendliness and help personified. After lingering there for a week we started walking east, in the opposite direction to your family's farm. In ten days we got to the coast near Rimini, where our idea was to steal a small boat and sail it south. Nothing doing, however, so we carried on walking south over the foothills and had got nearly to Pescara when we made contact with a small force of parachutists from 2nd SAS who were hoping to gather escapers like ourselves.

We had started walking on Saturday, 18 September, and first met the SAS on Tuesday, 12 October at a small house in the country, a mile or two inland from Monterubbiano. The SAS were a party of three under a Captain Power and part of a total group of nine, they said. They had been dropped with hopes of rounding up as many as a hundred or so ex-prisoners of war and evacuating them by sea. The Captain named a quiet beach just below the mouth of the little River Menocchia, and told us to get there by midnight on the Sunday week, 24 October. This was only a day's walk away, and the following evening we encountered his reception party, another trio in the charge of Squadron Sergeant-Major Marshall, a big cheerful Scot, billeted in a friendly cottage about a mile from the beach. Up above, to our left, on its hill, was the town of Ripatransone, reputed locally to be the home of several Fascist sympathisers. The third trio of SAS men were said to be farther inland, towards the mountains.

We were left with over a week to wait, which we managed to pass without any major incident, and we duly got ourselves down to the beach with over an hour to spare. Unfortunately, there was a big scare at the last minute, and when the Infantry Landing Craft at last turned up, several hours late, only about a dozen ex-prisoners of war including ourselves were there to be picked up. One curiosity was that Captain Power, who met us, did not take part in the beach rescue; his opposite number then turned out on the night to be a Captain Timothy. What happened to the two of them, I never did find out.

The landfall at Termoli took place only thirty-seven days after Geoffrey Stavert, and his three companions from Camp 49 had left the Fontanellato area. He related: 'We must, indeed, have been one of the earliest parties to get through, and I was actually "Home by Christmas"'.

Three men were left behind to help any remaining fugitives at the mouth of the River Menocchia in October 1943: Captains Power and Tong and

Parachutist Maybury. They were evacuated by schooner, together with fourteen more escapers in separate journeys on 12 November and 20 November, making the total number of former POWs evacuated by the parties in Areas 'A' and 'B' thirty-seven.

The SAS party for Area 'C' (San Benedetto del Tronto to Pescara), led by Lt Grant St John Hibbert, was landed on the night of 6–7 October, just north of the River Tronto, instead of at the at mouth of the River Salinello as planned. They made their way inland and then southwards to the sea at the intended landing place, a journey of 8 miles. The lieutenant made contact with the Airborne Division search party and seventy-five escaped POWs. On the night of 9–10 October, the beach party gave the required signals by torch flashes, but it was unable to establish contact with any craft, and most of the prisoners of war dispersed. On the night of 11–12 October, the SAS and the Airborne Division parties were evacuated to Termoli by schooner, together with the remaining escapers. Lt Hibbert would return to the same area just over a fortnight later as second in command of the sabotage mission led by Capt. Roy Farran (Operation Candytuft).

The SAS party for Area 'D' (Pescara to the south), the first to land on the night of 3–4 October, moved north to the intended landing point at the mouth of the River Foro under the command of Capt. Baillie, while Capt. Lee (the alias of Raymond Couraud, as mentioned) and his protection party went inland. On the night of 5–6 October, Capt. Baillie signalled on the shore and heard a boat's engines, but the light of his torch was not seen by the craft. The captain repeated the process three days later, but again with no result. By 10 October, 200 escaped POWs had been collected and the protection party had returned to the rendezvous. Three hours before the scheduled time for a boat to arrive, a bright light was observed coming from a vessel that looked like a motor torpedo boat; it was answered by a light from the shore, and Capt. Lee became suspicious. He went to investigate and discovered three Germans hiding behind a motor boat and shot them. The boat shone its searchlight on the beach for some seconds and then made off northwards at high speed. The escapers were told to disperse, as nothing more could be done for them.

The SAS parties under Captains Baillee and Lee moved separately inland to the Cugnoli area. One of the men, Parachutist Fawthorpe, accidentally shot himself in the foot while cleaning his weapon; he was left behind in a farmhouse and, after recovering, escaped to Allied forces on 24 December 1943. The rest of the group moved to Civitella and contact was made with the SAS airborne search party under Lt McGregor on 15 October. Capt. Baillie and Lt Louis Gabriel Saltet de Sablet d'Estières led a raid on the local *Carabinieri* headquarters, and the policemen were disarmed and told to go home. Their commandant, who had been away on the night, returned and led a frantic search by enemy troops, forcing the two seaborne groups to move into the commune of Silvi, about 9 miles north of Pescara.

Capt. Lee left by schooner together with some members of 1st SAS Regiment who were escaped POWs, arriving in Termoli on 24 October. The captain promised to return within a few days to collect the rest of the party. Three days later, two members of the SAS arrived at the beach in Silvi with instructions to contact a Maj. Gordon, who was in hiding in the mountains and was in contact with many other escapers. Lt E. C. Lyte, parent unit, the 4th Royal Horse Artillery, a future recipient of the MC, was accompanied by Sgt Scott, one of the 1st SAS ex-POWs who had been evacuated by Capt. Lee. Lt Lyte contacted the major and gave him money and supplies, returning safely to the coast on 1 November. On the same day, Lt Saltet de Sablet d'Estières set out with the rest of the French party to return to Termoli.

On the night of 2–3 November, Lt Lyte was on signal duty and he was forced to watch helplessly as Italian motor torpedo boat 74, bringing Capt. Lee back, was hit by heavy machine gun and artillery fire from the coast when it was less than 2 miles offshore. The craft flipped on its side, went on fire, and finally exploded. Three survivors from the crew swam ashore: Capt. Lee and Lt Calf and Midshipman Draper from the Royal Navy. However, as they ran from the beach into the trees, Lee was hit in the arm by enemy fire. The trio joined Capt. Baillie's party. On 7 November, a fishing schooner sailed into Termoli harbour, carrying the captain's party of seven, the two naval officers, and two former POWs. 'N' Section noted: 'From their report, it appeared that the boat was attacked by a shore battery while lying to and sunk'. Little definite news was available of Capt. Lewis, an American officer working for the section, who was also on board the boat, and it was a relief when he walked through the lines on 17 December. Capt. Lee had been left behind with two orderlies, as he could only move very slowly. They were picked up on the night of 9–10 November, together with Maj. Gordon, an Italian officer, and four more escapers.

A further SAS party, with a total strength of eight men, led by Maj. Symes, the most senior SAS officer involved in the operation, arrived at the same landing point 7 miles south of the mouth of the River Foro in Area 'D' (Pescara to the south) on the night of 15–16 October. The region was now full of German troops and movement and concealment were proving increasingly difficult. Two patrols were sent inland to the Chieti and Casoli areas to contact escaped prisoners of war and other SAS troops. By the night of 21 October, thirty escapers had been sent to the beachhead, and the major moved with them to a more secure hiding place in the surrounding countryside to await developments.

On the night of 22–23 October, Symes managed to establish contact with a motor torpedo boat after an hour's signalling, but when it was close inshore he saw a German soldier coming towards him, followed by two others at a distance of twenty yards. One of the men doubled back to raise the alarm at their platoon post, while his companions cocked their weapons and stood on the railway line looking rather silly. The major gave a warning flash seaward with his torch and jumped into the bushes. The SAS men then began to crawl away up the mountainside, while the escapers crashed through the undergrowth like a herd of elephants. By this time, the Germans were tearing down the railway line and the boat was pushing off. When the fugitives reached the top of the slope, they had to stop and hide for a few minutes to let a long column of horse-drawn infantry pass along the main road, but then, fortunately, Symes recalled: 'Our pursuers were so delighted with the contents of my pack and my night glasses, which had been left on the railway line, that they lost valuable minutes and we were able to cross before they arrived and before some lorry-borne troops made their appearance on the scene'. The major ordered the prisoners of war to split up and to rendezvous at the mouth of the River Foro three days later, knowing that they would be able to return to their Italian hosts in the meantime.

Symes signalled again on the night of 25–26 October—this time there were fifty escapers on the beach—but once more there was no result. On the next night, the number of POWs had grown to 120, but just as the major was starting to marshal them for the beach, he received warning that a party of Germans were lying in wait for them. A reconnaissance confirmed this report, and the escapers were told to return to the houses where they were receiving food and shelter. By 4 November, and after repeated and fruitless efforts to get a boat, Maj. Symes decided to walk back through the lines and advised all the POWs to do the same. However, an Italian came forward on the same day and offered him a small boat, which would hold ten men, for the cost of 10,000 lire. The major and thirteen men embarked in the craft within 50 yards of a German sentry and returned to Termoli on 6 November.

Capt. Charles Duffett, Royal Navy, was relieved as the Flag Officer, Taranto Area, on 15 October 1943 by Commander Nicholls. The captain's report to 15th Army Group, which he wrote two days later, did not hide the problems experienced in coordinating land and sea activities:

> Operations with three LCI's were commenced on the night of 6–7 October using the beaches extending as far north as Grottammare. These were continued on subsequent nights until 9–10 October when I decided that as it was imperative to avoid detection thereby compromising all future schemes, operations should not be carried out during the period of

> bright moonlight except to follow up reliable information. One further expedition however was carried out on the night of 12–13 October. All these operations produced no result beyond the evacuation of some twenty prisoners by fishing boat.
>
> Although prearranged signals to indicate the correct rendezvous had been instituted, the exact location of the beaches proved a matter of extreme difficulty in the dark and actually contact with shore parties was achieved at only one beach, two and a half miles north of Grottammare, where, however, no prisoners of war had been brought down.
>
> On the night of 9–10 October an operation in the vicinity of Pescara which might have proved fruitful was prejudiced by the presence of what the beach party thought was a German patrol boat, earlier in the evening. After inquiries I believe this to have been one of our own motor torpedo boats on patrol.
>
> Communications throughout were extremely slow and all signals were passed by Army channels through 15th Army Group. Air cover, which was requested from dawn to about noon on each day of operating, was always supplied.[1]

On 1 November 1943, 'N' Section's own Boating Section took over from SIMCOL, at a time when several missions the headquarters mounted were still bringing results. The official history of IS9 recorded:

> Every day fishing craft of all sizes, sailing boats, and small dinghies would heave to in the minute harbour of Termoli, bringing down parties of refugees, prisoners of war and Simcol mission personnel. A total of eighteen prisoners of war arrived at Termoli between 1 November and 11 November and all were evacuated by the efforts of Simcol personnel. From official interrogations and normal conversations with the returning personnel it was possible to gain a very good idea of the effects which members of Simcol missions had created in the Abruzzi and Marche. They had made their presence felt among both escapers and evaders and the peasant families and a very definite connection had been established between both sides of the line. It now remained for us to arrange the necessary means of evacuation for the many parties of escapers and evaders with whom we were in contact. Unfortunately this contact was not good and we had to rely on word of mouth instead of direct wireless telegraph (W/T) communication. Had we had reliable wireless communication, it is reasonable to support that the successful sea evacuation of large numbers of escapers and evaders would have been achieved. At this stage, however, we had to rely on the slow and doubtful system of pre-arranged beach rendezvous.

Once rescue operations were approved, there were two choices as regards craft: the section's private fleet of motor fishing vessels, or Italian light coastal craft, under the command of the Royal Navy. However, all too often, IS9'S requests to conduct an evacuation would coincide with Navy operations by motor torpedo boats or destroyers and they would not be allowed to take place. The history of the agency noted: 'We had no means of letting the escapers and evaders know. Such was the problem presented by a complete lack of wireless telegraphy communication in enemy-occupied territory'.

An even more infuriating situation would often arise owing to cancellation of a mission on the sailing date due to heavy seas that would prevent a coastal approach. In contrast, enemy interference was evaluated as a minor problem owing to operations only taking place at the appropriate phases of the moon. The history related: 'The coastline was very lightly defended and excellent for our work, yet the great disadvantage was a road and railway which ran parallel along its whole length and within 50 yards of the beach. To have attempted operations during the moon period would have asked for disaster'.

Largely due to the influence of these factors, many of the veterans of the 2nd SAS Regiment viewed the operation to rescue escapers and evaders as a failure. In addition, it was even suggested that their deployment was not even appropriate. Roy Farran, though not personally taking part in the mission, went so far to describe it in his memoirs as having only an indirect connection with the war:

> Many British prisoners had escaped at the time of the surrender and now at large behind the enemy lines. In response to pressure brought to bear by politicians at home, a force was organised to do what it could to facilitate their rescue. We were their tools. A number of small parties equipped with wireless sets were dropped in the foothills all along the Adriatic coast from Ancona to Pescara. Their job was to direct ex-prisoners to beach parties who had been landed from motor torpedo boats on the coast. Between the beach parties and the parachutists in the hills, foot parties of SAS would act as guides. Periodically landing craft or motor torpedo boats would come into the beach parties in answer to a torch signal to pick up the refugees.
>
> The operation went on for two months but was never a resounding success. There were many reasons. Sometimes large parties of ex-prisoners got down to the beaches alright, but they were usually scattered by the Germans before they could be picked up. The Navy found it difficult to make exact landfalls on a featureless beach, and above all most of the men were so demoralised that they were not

> prepared to exert themselves. Contrary to public opinion at home, many of them preferred to stay in comparative safety in an Italian farm than to risk their necks in a hazardous escape.[2]

Despite the reference to the provision of 'wireless sets' in this piece, the post-combat Jonquil report noted: 'Signalling arrangements were not satisfactory. Walkie-talkies between shore and ship would have prevented the ignorance of the parties of the amended orders issued'. The revised instructions mainly referred to the decision to suspend pick-ups by landing craft during the bright phase of the moon.

Rescue operations continued on the Adriatic coast right up to the breaching of the Gustav Line in May 1944, and in the rest of Italy until the end of the war in May 1945, but, perhaps fortunately, the SAS usually had other tasks to complete.

14

Support for the Anzio Landings

During December 1943, the 2nd SAS Regiment was required to prepare plans to disrupt enemy rail communications in central Italy in conjunction with the proposed landing at Anzio. Two plans were produced, one dealing with the railways in the Orte to Terni area, through which all traffic from the north and south of Rome had to pass, and the other with the line leading from Ancona to Rimini. The plans were submitted to 15th Army Group on 10 December, and permission to proceed was granted a week later. Weather conditions were bad both for flying and for seaborne work, and there was a thick layer of snow on the higher ground. The operation was given the codename of Maple, with its separate missions identified as Thistledown and Driftwood.

After two false starts due to bad weather, three Dakotas took off from the airbase at Gioia del Colle in Puglia on 7 January 1944. Two of the planes carried four parties for Maple-Thistledown to a drop zone at Colle Futa, near the village of Termine in the commune of Cagnano Amiterno, north-west of Aquila in the Abruzzo region. The third plane carried the two parties of Maple-Driftwood to a drop zone in the commune of Jesi, north-east of Ancona, in the Marche region. All the charges were to be set on the night of 13–14 January to gain the maximum effect, and the parties were briefed to exfiltrate on completion of their tasks.

Just before midnight on 7 January, the seventeen men of Operation Maple-Thistledown parachuted in bright moonlight from Dakotas 439 and 681 at a height of about 800 feet to the drop zone at Colle Futa. They landed successfully in 4 feet of snow and had no difficulty in collecting the paniers of supplies, but contact was lost between parties one and two, who dropped from one plane, and parties three and four, who dropped from the other.

Party one consisted of Lt Worcester, Sgt Smoker, Cpl Phillips, L/Cpl Lawrence, and Parachutist Hehir. Their rail sabotage task was the Orte to

Terni line. Party two consisted of SSM Lloyd, Cpl Davis, and Parachutists Pepper and Todd. Their rail sabotage task was the Orvieto to Orte line. Party three consisted of Lt Parker, L/Cpl Bennett, and Parachutists Claridge and Monk. Their rail sabotage task was the Terni to Foligno line. Party four consisted of Sgt Hill, Lance-Corporals Hughes and Roberts, and Parachutist Medlin. Their rail sabotage task was the Terni to Perugia line.

Parties one and two moved off together in a north-westerly direction over difficult country, but at first progress was slow owing to the snow. After three days, they reached the main road 2 miles south of Posta, a village in the province of Rieti, just inside Lazio. All the men felt exhausted, as their packs weighed about 45 lb and the windproof suits that they wore over their battledress overburdened them with clothing. As a result, they eagerly accepted the offer of food and shelter for the night from an Italian civilian.

Lt Worcester's party moved off on 11 January to cross the Terni–Rieti Valley, and they reached the village of Cantalice four days later; they stayed two days before travelling through Cottanello and finally establishing a headquarters near the small village of Le Capannacce. On 22 January, Lt Worcester detailed two parties to attack the railways. He reconnoitred the railway bridge at Orte, together with Parachutist Hehir and a South African ex-POW, but found that it was too heavily guarded to attack. In addition, they discovered that the line to Terni was already damaged by Allied bombing. However, at the end of January, Sgt Smoker, L/Cpl Lawrence, and an Italian officer succeeded in derailing a goods train on the branch line between Terni and Rieti. A close watch was kept on the local railways, and as no further traffic was observed over a period of one week, the lieutenant decided to make up his remaining plastic explosive into 61-lb bombs for use against road transport.

An attempted raid against the German airfield and petrol dump at Rieti in the second week of February was unsuccessful, as the SAS party was challenged; the raiders evaded the ensuing search and returned to their base. Instead, a large number of attacks were made on the Terni to Rome road. Lt Worcester related that one staff car was stopped by four rounds from a .45 revolver: 'My party was hidden in the ditch beside the road and fired from point blank range'. On another occasion, they were about to cross the road when a staff car came up suddenly: 'Parachutist Hehir drew his two revolvers and walked up the road, firing at the car which was approaching at about 30 miles per hour; the car stopped and both its occupants were killed'. Over a period of ten days, twenty-five vehicles were destroyed, usually by throwing bombs in the back as they passed at reduced speed owing to snow on the ground; the bombs were detonated by short lengths of safety fuse, which was fired as the traffic approached.

On 20 February, Lt Worcester sent Sgt Smoker, L/Cpl Lawrence, and Parachutist Hehir to reconnoitre a route to Civitavecchia, north-west of Rome, for a possible exfiltration of the party by boat, but they had to turn back 20 or 30 miles from the coast because of lack of cover in an area which was a training area for enemy troops. On the way, they saw the German 1st Parachute Division moving down to Cassino, but were unable to pass on the information as they had no radio. By the end of the month, the lieutenant decided to return by land as the weather was improving and their chances of crossing the lines in the Castel di Sangro area seemed good. The party was divided into three groups: Lt Worcester, Parachutist Hehir, and L/Cpl Cobley, an ex-POW from the Sherwood Foresters, in the first; Sgt Smoker, Cpl Phillips, Jackson, who was an ex-POW from the Durham Light Infantry, and Edwards, an American pilot, in the second; and L/Cpl Lawrence and two South African escapers in the third.

Lt Worcester's party was very short of food, but in spite of this, the men did some hard marching, covering an average of about 25 miles a day, and even 38 miles on one occasion. It proved difficult to move along the edge of the mountains as anti-aircraft emplacements were sited on the hill slopes defending the Avezzano basin, which was a concentration area for troops. Trying to get through the valley the trio had a brief skirmish with a German patrol, turned back to Castelvecchio, and decided to stay the night.

At the end of the war, Lt Worcester related what happened next:

> On 4 March, I was rudely awakened at 02.30 hours to find myself covered with a Schmeisser. I was taken next door and asked for my papers, then stripped of everything worth taking. We were generally treated fairly well during this examination. Hehir, Cobley and I were left in a room with five Germans to guard us. At about 06.00 hours I noticed that the enemy, who were middle-aged, were becoming drowsy so I asked for some water. A bottle of wine and a glass were produced and I threw these at the first two Germans. We then made an attempt to escape. I was hit in the leg by Schmeisser fire early in the scrap and I saw Cobley go down in the corner with two Germans on top of him. Hehir was hit twice, first in the arm and then in the leg, but kept fighting and eventually a German stood over him as he lay on the floor and emptied the whole magazine from his Schmeisser at him. Fortunately' only four bullets hit him in the stomach. My leg was useless and I though Hehir was dying. We were laid on the bed and I managed to give Hehir a shot of morphine which made him lose consciousness. We were not moved until approximately 16.30 hours and we were then carried about 3 miles on ladders. At Santa Maria, all the inhabitants, totalling about four

> hundred, turned out to see us carried through. From there we were taken by ambulance to Carsoli, where we stayed for sixteen days. Thence by varying stages we were moved northwards towards Germany.[1]

Lt Worcester and Parachutist Hehir subsequently recovered from their wounds when held as POWs.

L/Cpl Lawrence set out with the two ex-POWs making up his party at the same time as Lt Worcester and his men, but heavy snow forced them to spend a fortnight at Marano. At the end of March, they were near Morro and their presence 'heartened the local partisans to carry out a series of attacks on local transport'. This caused the Germans to search the area, and the men then moved south, but they were eventually captured at Artena on 1 June after being given away by a farmer, who, as we shall see, had already betrayed the members of Sgt Hill's No. 4 party three months earlier.

Sgt Smoker, Cpl Phillips, Jackson (the British ex-POW), and Edwards (the American pilot) only set out on 29 March as they had been unable to leave earlier owing to the corporal being unwell. On 4 April, together with some ex-POWs, the sergeant ran into a group of Germans on the railway and he was taken prisoner. The corporal and his two companions made for the Maiella mountain range, but when they joined a large group of escapers, they were surprised by German mountain troops and captured at Montefalcone on 13 April.

After separating from Lt Worcester and his men at the house near Posta on 10 January, SSM Lloyd led his No. 2 Party to a point overlooking Terni and discovered that they were being followed by men with dogs. When they came too close, a single shot caused them to scatter and make off. The parachutists then marched along mountain tracks north of Leonessa and crossed a tributary of the River Tiber after a brush with a German patrol, reaching the target railway line on 16 January. Charges were placed at the approach to a tunnel, with a two-day delay in case the pressure switches failed to operate. On the return journey, SSM Lloyd placed a further charge on the Terni to Spoleto line; the men met Lt Parker's No. 3 party in Favischio and here they heard from a Greek, who appeared to be well informed, that all railway traffic had ceased in the target area.

The following day, the parties separated, and SSM Lloyd's group set out towards Tufo. On the way there, they held up some *Carabinieri*, smashed their rifles, and took their boots for the use of three escaped POWs who had joined them. SSM Lloyd met a South African captain from the Medical Corps, who was in touch with a Sicilian said to be operating a radio transmitter, and gave him details of a petrol and ammunition dump near Sassa for transmission. Owing to the large number of German troops concentrated in the area, SSM Lloyd decided to split the party for the next stage and to rendezvous at Marcellina on 1 February. He arrived there on time, but as none of the others had appeared after a wait of one day, he left for Rome, 25 miles away, reaching the city the same evening. He made contact with local partisans and took part in various attacks before deciding to cross the lines in the Aprilia area. On 24 April, SSM Lloyd was in sight of British positions, but during the night, he was captured by a German patrol in no-man's-land.

The two other parties under SSM Lloyd's command—one consisting of Cpl Davis and an American ex-POW, and the other of Parachutists Pepper and Todd and a South African ex-POW—set out at an interval of twenty-four hours. Both groups then returned independently to Nespolo after failing to rendezvous with the sergeant-major at Marcellina. The men were suffering from influenza and took shelter in an empty house, but they were surrounded and captured by the enemy at 5 a.m. on 1 March.

Party No. 3, under Lt Parker, and Party No. 4, under Sgt Hill, made their way northwards together after being dropped some distance from the other two parties on the Colle Futa drop zone. They obtained guides for each party at a farmhouse at Salto del Cieco and then separated on 11 January. Lt Parker led his men to the target area on the railway between Terni and Spoleto on the night of 13–14 January and laid an 8-lb charge with a twenty-four-hour delay time pencil in case the pressure switch did not operate. They returned by the same route to the farmhouse, where they were reunited with Party No. 4. The lieutenant briefed and equipped partisans to carry out a similar raid on the railway when it started working again. Both parties moved to Favischio on 18 January, but separated next day. Lt Parker continued southwards with his party and three ex-POWs who had joined them, arriving in Vallepietra on 28 January. They were immobilised here for over a month in a house on Monte Autore (1,854 metres), as Parachutists Bennett and Monk had fallen ill, and bad weather had returned, with heavy snow and drifting. During this time, they cared for seventeen ex-POWs.

On 7 March, when the weather had improved sufficiently to set off again, the lieutenant decided to cross the lines. The party was divided in two, with Lt Parker taking Flying Officer Jowett, an ex-POW from the RAAF, with him, while L/Cpl Bennett took Parachutists Claridge and Monk. Both groups arrived at Collelongo without incident. In the meantime, the lieutenant rescued a South African pilot, Flying Officer Pitout, who had baled out of a Spitfire. On 20 March, as a detachment of fifty Fascists was seen to be approaching the hut in which the men were living, they moved off to the south in two parties: Lt Parker with Parachutist Monk and Flying Officer Jowett started out first, leaving L/Cpl Bennett, Parachutist

Claridge and Flying Officer Pitout to follow twenty-four hours later. On 21 March, while making for Castel di Sangro, the lieutenant's party was challenged and captured by Germans on the road from Gioia dei Marsi to Alfedena. L/Cpl Bennett and his men were at large until 6 May, when they were captured in the Maiella mountain range. Flying Officer Pitout was subsequently reported to be a POW, but there was no further news of the L/Cpl or of Parachutist Claridge.

After separating from Lt Parker and his No. 3 party near the drop zone, Sgt Hill set out with his No. 4 party for their railway target on 12 January. They rested for the night at a farmhouse. During the evening of the 13th, they were guided to the railway by the farmer's son and laid two scissor charges in a tunnel on the line from Terni to Perugia. L/Cpl Roberts remained on guard outside and sowed anti-personnel ground-burst small arms mines (Switch No. 8, anti-personnel) in the area. The parachutists then returned to the farmhouse. The next day, 14 January, Sgt Hill's party laid a further charge on the railway line from Terni to Spoleto, using a twenty-four-hour time pencil, as Lt Parker had blown this line the night before and no trains were running. The anti-personnel mines were again laid in the area. The raiders then travelled southwards by way of Belvedere and stayed at a monastery.

On 18 January, Nos 3 and 4 parties met up again at Favischio, and the following day, Sgt Hill set off with his men for the original drop zone at Colle Futa and remained there until 21 January. From then until 2 February, they followed a route through Castello di Corno, where they heard for the first time of the Anzio landings, which led them to give up their plan of crossing the lines on the central front and to make for the beachhead. On the way, they met three ex-POW, two South Africans and an American, and took them with them. On 3 February, the party of seven left Vignola with the intention of crossing the lines near Velletri. After a march of 15 miles through a thunderstorm, they sheltered in a barn outside Artena. The following morning, they were surrounded and captured by Germans, whom Sgt Hill saw paying the reward to the farmer who had betrayed them.

Over the course of the war, no further news was received from the airborne parties, although escaped POW brought in scraps of information. It was only on the return of the men at the end of the war that it was possible to complete the full story. The official report on Operation Maple concluded:

> Charges were laid on the following lines: Orte-Orvieto; Terni-Spoleto, at three separate points; Terni-Perugia; and Terni-Rieti. Party one of Maple-Thistledown found that their objective had already been put out

> of action by Allied bombing raids, but later attacked the Terni-Rieti line; party two successfully accomplished their task on 16 January, while parties three and four reached their objectives on the night of 13–14 January and laid their charges as scheduled. According to a German intelligence officer, accidents were caused on the lines concerned, which information is substantiated by local reports. In addition, Lieutenant Worcester's party operated against the roads and destroyed twenty-five vehicles in a period of ten days.
>
> Prisoners of war: seventeen (two of this number were never reported by the enemy, but there is clear evidence that they were taken prisoner of war).
>
> A number of factors increased the difficulties which had to be overcome on the return journey. The weather in the early spring of 1944 was stormy and cold. The snow on the ground still made the going arduous and tracks were visible. A large number of ex-prisoners of war were known to be attempting to cross through the line, which led to extra enemy vigilance and raids in the villages where they were sheltering. The Anzio bridgehead had not expanded as quickly as had been expected when this operation was planned; it was then considered possible that men would be overrun rather than that they should have to undertake the long return march through a static enemy line in bad weather conditions.
>
> Partly because of these factors and partly because not sufficient care was taken to guard against Italian informers, all members of parties one to four were taken prisoner on dates between 4 February and 1 June 1944. It is natural that after two months in enemy territory precautions should be relaxed, and the small size of the parties prohibited continual guards when the men were exhausted by hard marching. It is considered more probable too that the Maple parties would have succeeded in returning had they not split up into small groups of SAS men each with some ex-prisoners of war. The exfiltration of ex-prisoners of war was not the object of the operation and, as has been shown in Operation Jonquil, the ex-prisoners in the main added considerably to the difficulties of movement and evasion of capture. Also, as they were unarmed, they were powerless to resist even the smallest enemy force.[2]

A paper entitled 'SAS Report, Operations Maple and Baobab' (dated 9 April 1945) from Maj.-Gen. Richard Gale, Commander of the 1st British Airborne Corps, to the Under Secretary of State at the War Office, noted:

> It should be remembered that these operations were carried out when 2nd SAS Regiment had only just started to operate in an airborne role.

> They had none of the signals communications which SAS troops had on [Operation] Overlord and no close tie-up with the Air Force, as with 38 Group. Although, therefore, the ground parties were able to achieve considerable success, the lack of signal communication made their final evacuation impossible.

The eight men assigned to the sub-mission Maple-Driftwood were parachuted by Dakota 391 to a drop zone 8 miles west-north-west of the commune of Jesi in the Marche region on 7 January 1944. The CO was Capt. John St George Gunston, born on 17 February 1919, son of Sir Derrick Wellesley Gunston, first Baronet, and Evelyn Bligh St George; he was educated at Harrow School and Trinity College, Cambridge University, and commissioned in the Irish Guards. The other members of the captain's party (designated as number five of Operation Maple) were Cpl Albert Pugh and Parachutists William Dodds and Herbert Loosemore. Their rail sabotage task was the Urbino to Fabriano branch line.

The second party of four men (designated number six of Operation Maple) was led by Sgt Robert Benson, from Stockport in Cheshire. The other members of his group were: Sgt William Glen and Parachutists John Evans and Alan Lockeridge. Their rail sabotage task was the Ancona to Rimini mainline. It was planned to reinforce this party by a seaborne mission equipped with sufficient explosive to demolish a bridge between Fano and Pesaro on the target railway, but this proved impossible owing to adverse weather conditions. The operation was mounted independently at the end of January as Operation Baobab.

On completing their task, the Driftwood personnel were to be evacuated by sea from a point on the beach 5 miles south-west of Fermo, near Torre di Palme, on the night of 25–26 January, but neither of the parties arrived at the rendezvous. Another member of the 2nd SAS Regiment, Parachutist Cook, who was seeking to cross the lines, met Capt. Gunston near Fermo a few days later and was told that he still had a further task to complete and would then evacuate his party by sea. Another contact, Capt. Matthews, from the South African Corps of Signals, recalled that, on 4 February, he met an Italian girl who helped POWs at the hospital in Fermo. She told him that a parachutist and some others were leaving that night by sea. Her cousin then guided the South African to the rendezvous, where he met the captain. Matthews related: 'He said that he was leaving by sea for the Allied lines with eight parachutists, Captain Clubb, New Zealand Expeditionary Force, and one other man. On 7 March, Captain Gunston's party left from a point a little south of Porto San Giorgio in a twenty-two-foot boat. I never heard of their safe arrival and no message was subsequently received from them'.

The men were initially posted as 'missing' and at least some of their relatives received telegrams stating that they were 'prisoners of war'. However, in June 1945, they were declared 'missing, presumed to be dead'. The official report suggested that Capt. Gunston's party may have been attacked by Allied aircraft (who were instructed to fire on craft off the enemy coast) or have been capsized some distance from the shore. Less plausibly, the report stated that there was also the possibility that they were forced to land again in enemy-occupied territory, noting that a German Intelligence Officer had read out the names of Capt. Gunston, Sgt Benson, and Parachutist Loosemore as SAS captured in Italy when interrogating three SAS prisoners in 1944. The mystery of their disappearance remains.

The eight men are commemorated on the Cassino War Memorial (all with the date of death given as 7 March 1944): Capt. John St George Gunston, aged twenty-five, Irish Guards; Bombardier Albert Henry Pugh, aged twenty-five, Royal Artillery; Sapper William Dodds, aged twenty-five, Royal Engineers; Private Herbert Loosemore, aged twenty-one, Durham Light Infantry; Sgt Robert Thomas Benson, aged thirty, Cheshire Regiment; Sgt William Osborne Glen, aged twenty-nine, Royal Artillery; Sapper Alan Lockeridge, aged twenty-four, Royal Engineers; and Private John Evans, aged twenty-six, Cheshire Regiment.

At the end of January, the seaborne operation codenamed Baobab was mounted on the main coastal railway between Ancona and Rimini. The objective was the demolition of a bridge over a small stream on a section of track roughly equidistant between Pesaro and Fano (a distance of 8 miles). At 2 p.m. on 29 January 1944, an advance party consisting of Lt Laws and Signalman Dowell was embarked in motor schooner MFV 2041 at Molfetta, north of Bari. At 12.30 a.m. the following day, they were landed north of Pesaro, instead of to the south, as intended, owing to heavy fog.

The pair hid their folbot and then climbed the cliff face and took shelter in an inland cave. At 8 a.m., Lt Laws signalled by wireless that he had landed. He then carried out a daylight reconnaissance of the countryside south of Pesaro and observed a detachment of nine Germans marching towards Fano. At 2 p.m., the lieutenant sent a further message stating that the area was patrolled and that it would be dangerous for the main landing to take place before 11 p.m. In the meantime, he located a house near the bridge that was being used as a barracks by a detachment of *Carabinieri*. He approached the building and discovered that there were about nineteen men inside, some wearing uniform, but the majority in shirt sleeves; he jammed the outward-opening door of the house with a large stone without being noticed and withdrew. At 11.15 p.m., Lt Laws went to the shore and began to signal the boats in.

The main party for the Baobab mission had embarked in the destroyer HMS *Troubridge* at Molfetta at 3 p.m. on 29 January. The vessel proceeded to Manfredonia and that night a rehearsal for the raid was held in the port, which included drills on manning the boats and returning to the ship. At noon on 30 January, the *Troubridge* left Manfredonia, escorted by another destroyer, HMS *Tenacious*; both ships arrived off the rendezvous point at about 10 p.m. Shortly after the time set by the lieutenant of 11 p.m., they began to signal to shore. Fifteen minutes later, they thought they saw a faint reply, and took a bearing, but the simultaneous presence of lights from cars using the coastal road prevented a definite identification. Capt. Power decided to send Capt. Cameron inshore anyway and the boats were manned, as provided for in the operation order if no signal were received.

The dories left the vessel at 11.50 p.m., and the men made contact with Lt Laws on the beach at 12.15 a.m. on 31 January. He took the demolition party to the bridge and the defence party to the positions that he had selected. The charges were laid by explosives expert Lt Miller in a single strip across the bridge under both the up and down tracks after the ballast had been removed. The process took about half an hour, and by this time, the Italian *Carabinieri* had emerged from the barracks and arrived to challenge the men on the bridge. When asked brusquely what they were doing, Cpl McGuire replied in Italian that they were a working party detailed to carry out repairs to the line, and he managed to pacify the policemen for a few minutes. The main party returned to the boats and Lt Miller was about to set the charges, which had a ten-minute delay, when the Italians opened fire. He completed the operation, jumped over the bridge, and joined his companions on the beach.

The little flotilla then put out to sea, pursued for the first 400 yards by Italian gunfire from the bridge and its surrounds. The beam of a torch could be seen in that area, pointing downwards as if a search was taking place. At 1.12 a.m., twelve minutes after the lieutenant had fled the bridge, a violent explosion blew it to smithereens. The official report recounted: 'It resembled the petals of an orange coloured flower opening, while fragments of incandescent material were thrown through the air. It is reasonable to assume that a considerable proportion of the *Carabinieri* were among this debris, as they were last seen on the bridge. Blue flashes came from the overhead electric power lines, which must have also been damaged'. At 1.33 a.m., the returning dories were hoisted aboard the destroyer, and the SAS party was landed in Molfetta on the same afternoon, no casualties having been sustained.

An immediate damage report confirmed that the bridge had been destroyed, both railway tracks had been cut, and up to nineteen *Carabinieri*, Fascist Militia, or Customs Guards had been killed or injured by the explosion. Photographic reconnaissance revealed that the railway line was closed to traffic for six days as repairs were carried out.

A review of the mission concluded: 'Baobab is interesting as the last of a series of seaborne tasks carried out by the 2nd SAS Regiment in Italy and Sicily. It illustrates that for geographically convenient targets the use of sea transport enables a greater quantity of explosive to be carried and provides a reliable means of withdrawal for the attacking force'.

The contrast with the airborne missions could hardly be greater.

15

Operation Pomegranate

Only five days after Operation Maple was launched, another mission with similar military aims was under way. At 8 p.m. on 12 January 1944, a six-man squad of parachutists from the 2nd SAS Regiment took off in a Douglas C-47 Dakota from the American base at Gioia del Colle in Puglia on Operation Pomegranate. Their task was to raid the airfield at Sant'Egidio, 5 miles from the city of Perugia, in the Umbria region of central Italy, to destroy German reconnaissance aircraft which would pose a threat to the imminent Allied landing at Anzio (Operation Shingle).

Leading the raiders was twenty-nine-year-old Maj. Edward Anthony 'Tony' Fitzherbert Widdrington, of the 5th Royal Inniskilling Dragoon Guards, who came from a service family in Felton in Northumberland. He joined the Army in 1934, took part in the Syrian and Tunisian campaigns, and was awarded the MC and was also mentioned in dispatches four times.

Second in command was twenty-three-year-old Lt James Quentin Hughes, a free-thinking maverick, who was always known in the Army as 'Jimmy'. He was born in Liverpool, the only child of a vicar of the church in Wales, and claimed descent from Oliver Cromwell and the Welsh evangelist Thomas Charles of Bala. After attending Rydal School in Colwyn Bay, Hughes began studies at the Liverpool University School of Architecture, but they were disrupted by the outbreak of war. He volunteered for the Royal Artillery and saw service in Malta during the siege, before joining the newly created 2nd SAS Regiment at Philippeville in Algeria.

The other members of the squad were L/Cpl J. Malloy and Parachutists T. Cox, S. McCormick, and A. Todd. The party parachuted safely at 10.30 p.m. near the village of Col Piccione, east of Lake Trasimeno, around 150 miles behind enemy lines. The plane turned for home, but was never heard from again. To distract attention from the drop, a force of Wellington bombers had raided Perugia at the same time and crews reported conditions of icing and 9/10 cloud. It was presumed that the Dakota had crashed in the mountains due to the weather conditions. Italian researchers have established that the plane was lost on Monte Tezio (961 metres above sea level and east of the drop zone), which also claimed a German plane during the war.

In his report on the mission, Quentin Hughes related that the landing was soft and sticky, but too near the road, where they were seen by some inquisitive Italians. Three of the party joined him quite quickly, but Maj. Widdrington and Parachutist McCormick had caught their parachutes in trees and it was half an hour before they could be found. Once the men had regrouped, they buried their parachutes, located the supply containers, and marched through the night to a wooded ravine. They were discovered there by some Italian foresters who had followed their tracks; they reported that the Germans had found the parachutes and were searching farmhouses in the valley. The party began the approach march on Sant'Egidio at dusk. The route lay north and east of Perugia before moving south and closing on the target. It involved two days of hard climbing with heavy rucksacks over Monte Tezio. Descending to the Tiber, the men found it in flood and unfordable. Fortunately, they came upon an overhead cableway, with a cradle that could be pulled to and fro across the river. The whole group crossed successfully in four journeys, but L/Cpl Malloy suddenly announced that he had left his carbine on the far bank of the river. He was winched back to retrieve it, but this time the noise alerted a German sentry and he challenged them. Maj. Widdrington did not want to start a firefight and ordered his men to disperse through surrounding houses and into the fields.

The two officers were reunited, but they were never able to make contact with the others in the party and set off alone. They arrived at a wood about 3 miles north of the airfield at dusk on 17 January. The pair hid their rucksacks and carbines and easily penetrated the perimeter fence. Once inside, they each primed twelve Lewes bombs, finally pulling the pins from the lead-delay timers. This job was normally done after the bombs were placed on the target, but they reasoned that the type of timer they had been given would provide one hour's delay at 65 degrees Fahrenheit, or two or more hours at the lower temperatures that night. After months of experimentation in the Western Desert, Jock Lewes had developed this lightweight bomb, which could destroy an aircraft by igniting the fuel. Thereafter known as the 'Lewes Bomb', or the 'sticky bomb', it was made by mixing a pound of plastic explosive with thermite and diesel oil.

The airfield lights came on and four Junkers Ju 88 bombers flew in. A fifth crashed on landing and burst into flames, and in the commotion, it was 10.30 p.m. before the bombs could begin to be placed on the seven remaining aircraft. Hughes recalled that by 2 a.m., they had reached the southern side of the airfield and could not find any more aircraft to attack. They sat down and began to disarm the remaining bombs:

> I had finished my work and was about four yards away from Major Widdrington when a bomb in his hands blew up, about one hour and twenty minutes after it had been set. We were using 'L' delays and not time pencils. I was blinded and nearly completely deaf and my trousers were blown off. I managed to feel Major Widdrington's body and discovered that he had lost both hands and was badly wounded in the right leg and in the chest. I found my morphine syringe, but dropped the piercing pin and as I was blind I could not find it. I made a fire of what papers and maps I could find and fired my automatic in the air to attract attention. Some German sentries arrived and later an ambulance. Major Widdrington appeared to be dead. I was taken to a dressing station.[1]

Hughes added: 'I would not care to use "L" delays again'. The next day, 19 January, he was taken to Perugia Military Hospital in the San Giuliano Convent and initially placed in a ward with other wounded British personnel. However, within half an hour of an interrogation by a German Intelligence Officer, he was moved to a private room and told that contact with other Allied troops was forbidden and that he was a 'prisoner' and not a 'prisoner of war'.

In the following days, Hughes developed a high fever and was interrogated on several occasions. The Intelligence Officer told him that the secret police wanted to have him handed over, so that he could be shot in pursuance of Hitler's Commando Order. At this time, Hughes found a protector in the adjoining ward of the hospital, a major who was friendly and pleasant and told Hughes that he was the G-2 (head of the Intelligence Section) of Luftwaffe Italy. He and the doctor who was treating the lieutenant contacted the Gestapo and managed to arrange a temporary reprieve. The doctor told him that his fate would be sealed if he were to be handed over to the secret police.

However, on 4 March, the German major reported that the demands for Hughes to be executed had started once again. He had partially recovered, by this time, though he remained blind in one eye and deaf in one ear. The German drove to Field Marshal Kesselring's headquarters and arranged with the G-1 (head of the personnel section) to have the interrogation report altered to show that Hughes was a POW and not a saboteur. It was also decided that he would travel on a hospital train to Padua and then on to a Luftwaffe-run camp in Germany, where he would be safe from any further trouble, rather than being sent to a POW collection centre, where it was likely that he would have to face further interrogation.

On 10 March, Hughes went by train to a military hospital in Florence and was put in a ward with other wounded POWs. Together with Technical-Sergeant Bradburn, USAAF, and Sgt-Maj. Taylor, Royal Corps of Signals, he planned to escape down a drainpipe, but in the evening, they were loaded on to the hospital train bound for Padua. Despite warnings of on-board machine gunners, sentries at every station, and guards on tunnels and bridges at night, the trio decided to try to climb through the train window and to jump down on to the track. The first attempt was a failure, as Taylor had his shoulder and one arm encased in plaster and could not get through the window. However, around 2 a.m. on 11 March, when the train was pulling slowly out of Modena station, his two companions pushed him feet first through the window on to the running board and watched him jump down. Bradburn followed, and finally Hughes, who dropped through the opposite window on to the track:

> I lay flat, my heart pumping wildly as the endless train passed us. What an age it seemed, but at last it was gone and no shots were fired. No one had missed us. We collected ourselves and, making a large circuit of the town, crossed the railway at the far side. With the dawn we felt exhausted, and timidly approaching the nearest farm, asked for assistance. They were kind, hiding us in a cold stable during daylight. By afternoon they took us and fed us and exchanged some of our clothes for scarecrow apparel.
>
> From there we wandered south by day, avoiding towns and villages, but I fear deceiving no one of our true identity in this ragged turnout, always making for the range of mountains which seemed so far away.
>
> A succession of high ridges and deep valleys confronted us as we moved slowly southwards, getting weaker all the time. Weeks in hospital had not assisted our stamina. The American had a score of wounds, many still open, and Taylor was little better.
>
> At last on 22 March we contacted a partisan patrol, and after a good meal, were guided to their Brigade Headquarters at a little church in the tiny village of Strabatenza.[2]

Here they met another group of Allied escapers, which included Brig. Bertram Frank Armstrong, DSO, Commander of the 5th South African Infantry Brigade, and Brig. Stirling of the 13th/18th Royal Hussars. They had been among those held at the senior officers' camp PG 12 Vincigliata, near Florence, and had escaped after the September 1943 Armistice, together with Generals Richard O' Connor and Philip Neame, the most senior officers captured in North Africa. The generals had already been evacuated from the Adriatic coast by 'A' Force, the Allied Force HQ deception and escape service, after several earlier attempts had failed.

Hughes joined the brigadiers in a new venture, which was organised by the same agent, Ruggero Cagnazzo, a dynamic, young Italian Jew, said to be an engineer from Pesaro, who went by the alias of 'Keg'. The lieutenant had to leave Technical-Sergeant Bradburn and Sgt-Maj. Taylor behind in a partisan hospital, as they felt too weak to travel. The Germans later attacked the headquarters, and the pair were recaptured.

The party made good progress, as they now had plenty of money to pay local guides and to buy food. Using forged identity cards, and sometimes riding in pony carts, they went through the partisan walled stronghold of Cingoli, travelled down to Appignano del Tronto, passed unchallenged through a police check point at Monte San Giusto, and reached the valley of the Tenna, at last in sight of the sea.

The escapers reached the rendezvous at a farmhouse on 14 April, hoping to be picked up by boat the next night from a beach near Porto San Giorgio. However, the craft approached the shore at the wrong point, was fired upon by coastal batteries, and fled. Ruggero Cagnazzo had swum ashore, but his radio operator was lost. As a result, the beach party had to communicate with the Allies through couriers on bicycles sent to a radio operator belonging to SOE (known in Italy as Special Force), who was embedded with the partisans at Cingoli, 35 miles inland across enemy territory. Finally, the escapers were able to set off south once more, passing between Fermo and the sea and reaching Torre di Palme on the coast at 11 p.m. on 9 May 1944. In a detailed account, written in the third person and now held in the IWM's Department of Documents, Hughes recalled:

> Little groups drifted into the rendezvous out of the dark night. The agent had gone ahead and made the arrangements, and now they knew that they had agreed to purchase an old fishing boat which lay high on the beach on the other side of the main road. The deal was fixed so that if the two Italian fishermen would take them all south of the Allied lines a reward would be paid for each person safely landed, and the fishermen would be assured the safety of the seas in which to fish unhampered by enemy or Allied air strikes. This was certainly something which was denied them behind the German lines.
>
> Twenty-two people were to make the voyage, plus one white rabbit to bring them luck, and now the tasks were allocated. The long and heavy mast took six hands, who lifted it carefully and, waiting for a pause in the heavy German traffic on Route 16, raised it and trooped silently across the road. They were followed by another party of four who carried the sail and a large white sheet inscribed in bold black paint with the letters

> 'POW'. This was a safety precaution against Allied air attacks, for it was rumoured that the last boat which made the trip had been shot at with a total loss of life. Others carried a demi-john of water and the caged rabbit, plus the various bits and pieces which would make up the cargo for the voyage.[3]

The escapers turned south along the beach, crunching noisily over the pebbles for a hundred yards until they came upon the boat, a clinker-built craft of considerable size, which had not been launched for two years. The mast was erected and the stays secured and each man took up his position around the craft, swinging it easily in a big arc and quickly manhandling it down into the sea:

> It was a chilly night and late and, as the bows of the old boat pushed into the breakers, each man stopped walking out, fearful of getting his clothes drenched by the sea. The inevitable happened. The second breaker hit the bow at an angle and swung the whole boat round, so that it lay parallel to the beach. The next one swamped its gunwales and poured into the craft. In a sort of panic most of the personnel realised that if they were to get the boat into the water, they must soak themselves and, plunging up to their waists, they tugged and pulled until the bows came round and the boat headed into the waves. The shore shelved sharply and the water soon was deep. All climbed aboard. The oars were on the rowlocks and they were pulling clear of the shore line, which slowly lost all shape and dipped into the darkness.
>
> Soon they were well out, a couple of hundred yards, and the boat was drifting and being propelled in a southerly direction. Only then did the predicament dawn on those on board. The water level inside was as high as that of the sea outside. The ship was awash but still floating. She rolled sloppily in the heavy swell, making little headway. Each man took his trilby hat and began to bale furiously. The odds and ends of luggage and the big demi-john of water were all jettisoned overboard, but no one had the heart to sacrifice the rabbit which lay cold and half drowned in the bows of the boat. They argued hotly about the best course of action. If the boat was going to sink it would be better to cling to the coast, but in doing so they ran the risk of being seen by German patrols. Sitting up to their waists in water, baling continuously with flimsy water-logged felt hats, they made the bold choice and headed farther out to sea. The time was two o'clock in the morning and they hoisted the jib. Now the gentle breeze was filling it, blowing them gently east by south on the compass. It began to look as if their luck was in and the constant baling was beginning to show results. The clinker planks of the boat were swelling

in the sea water, the gaps were sealing and soon the water was no more than a slopping puddle around their feet. No one slept. They were too cold, wet and miserable for that as they baled and waited for the dawn.

After they had been going for what seemed hours, there was a sudden sharp crack in the boat and the single mast split and fell, bringing with it the jib. Its old timber had been unable to take the strain and now they cut it loose and cast it, with the sail, into the sea. Slowly the darkness gave way to a light in the east which spread evenly across the sky. It would be a day of even, solid cloud and then they saw the mountains on their right—the great high massif of the Abruzzi e Molise and, rising imperiously in its midst, the bulk of Monte Corno and Gran Sasso d'Italia. They were abreast of the highest peaks, but surely this was not possible. As the light improved 'Keg' took out the panoramic sketch which showed the coastline and mountain ranges. They looked at it in amazement for the rough silhouette agreed with the skyline to the west. They really were abreast of the high mountains and they must have made incredible speed during the night, catching both the wind and the tide in their favour. 'Keg' explained that about once a year, the sea, forced by the wind, built up towards Venice with a north-westerly current and then backed, running down the Adriatic with the following wind from the north.

The sea was now calm with just a gentle breeze, and then, with daylight, came the first aircraft flying high above them. It was a Spitfire. As they heard it approach they held out the big white sheet, hoping that the pilot, before taking any precipitous action, would be able to read the bold letters 'POW'. They waved it to attract his attention, but he was high and flew on unconcerned, with other tasks to fulfil.

By mid-day they could see the flashes in the hills as the guns exchanged their lethal charges. Soon there was a fast motor boat heading out towards them, but, as it grew larger, it suddenly turned and slowly made its way back towards the coast. Then they could see a railway engine chugging up the coastal line, its white puffs of smoke outlined against the dark hillside. That must be the Allied lines. No German trains were running along the coast. By three in the afternoon they were moving in among the little fishing fleet and could see the tiny port ahead of them—no anchorage, but a welcome stretch of friendly beach—and within the hour, the keel struck land at San Vito Chietino, just south of Ortona a Mare.

If they had expected a red carpet reception they were mistaken, but a little reception party did stand waiting to arrest them and interrogate them—two British Military Policemen and an Italian *Carabiniere*. Clean, smart, with polished boots and blancoed webbing, they stood

> imperturbably as the sodden, weary party stepped gingerly, one by one, from the old boat which had brought them home. The Sergeant led them up the beach to a little house and each was given a cup of hot, sweet, tea.[4]

Quentin Hughes would become one of the first soldiers to inform the British military authorities of Hitler's Commando Order, but at first his superiors were sceptical, dismissing it as a mere interrogation technique.

The other four members of the detachment, who had become separated from the officers at the Tiber crossing, also made their way to the airfield, but arrived after the attack had been carried out. They made a successful withdrawal and eventually crossed the lines to liberated territory. Maj. Widdrington was buried by the Germans on 20 January 1944 with full military honours and now rests in the Assisi War Cemetery.

Hughes was awarded the MC for his part in the raid on Sant'Egidio airfield. The citation said that he and Maj. Widdrington had destroyed four Junkers Ju 88 bombers, two Fieseler Fi 156 Storch liaison aircraft, and one Junkers Ju 52 transport. Both officers were praised for their courage, determination, and devotion to duty. On 9 November 1944, Hughes was granted a Bar to his MC for his escape, 'in recognition of gallant and distinguished services in the field'. Typically, he joked that the second award was given because the authorities had forgotten that he had received the first.

Quentin Hughes rejoined the 2nd SAS Regiment at Prestwick, Ayrshire, and subsequently moved to Colchester in Essex as chief instructor and training officer. He was appointed commander of the HQ Squadron in July 1945, but a jeep accident forced his early retirement and he left the Army with the rank of major. Hughes completed his studies at Liverpool University, gained his architecture degree and became a noted conservationist, academic, and expert on military architecture, particularly fortresses.

16

The Return of 2nd SAS

In December 1944, Maj. Roy Farran returned to Italy in command of No. 3 Squadron, 2nd SAS Regiment. The unit had been raised in the UK following the completion of operations in France. They arrived in southern Italy by air on 15 December, with the heavy equipment following by sea. Some of the men had seen action in France, but most were volunteers from the airborne divisions, and in many cases, they had not faced the enemy before. Farran related: 'They were an excellent lot, varying in age between twenty and thirty-five, many of them being regular soldiers. If anything, their discipline was better than that of the two other squadrons, and during the whole of the operations we did not discover a single passenger'.

In this last stage of the war in Italy, the SAS had the benefit of close liaison with the subversion and sabotage agency, the SOE, which in Italy was known as Special Force. Farran recalled: 'It was a privilege for me to work so closely with our friends in SOE. Without them, our scope would have been limited and the results far less satisfactory'. In the autumn of 1944, Special Force had set up a forward tactical headquarters, known as TAC HQ, which was housed in a villa on the Via delle Forbici, on the high road between Florence and Fiesole. In command was a charismatic, young major, Charles Macintosh, born of New Zealand parents in Uruguay, and working for Royal Dutch Shell in Venezuela on the outbreak of war.

TAC HQ was controlled and administered by Special Force, but operationally it was directed by Fifth Army HQ. Special Force's TAC HQ assumed command of six British and Italian missions within the tactical area, one in Bologna, and five in the Apennines; three more, in Modena, Reggio, and Modena, were controlled by the national base in Monopoli. The missions were tasked with strengthening their own organisations and those of the partisan units to which they were attached, stocking up on supplies, and extending their intelligence reporting. Sabotage operations were to continue, but they were to be of such a nature as to avoid the

Germans reacting in strength. The Fifth Army front would largely remain unchanged from the end of October 1944 to April 1945.

Farran arrived at Special Force's TAC HQ in Florence just before Christmas 1944. The officers were delighted at the prospect of having SAS parachutists working with their Apennine missions, though Charles Macintosh feared that once the major was in enemy territory he would largely act as he pleased; SAS training and Farran's character meant that codes, safe houses, agents, and such things would weigh lightly in their plans, which, in any case, were very short term.

On Sunday, New Year's Eve, Macintosh was working late at TAC HQ when Farran burst into his office, dressed in his best uniform. 'Hell, you can't work late tonight, let's bash the town,' he said.

Macintosh generally avoided Florence after dark, as it was a favourite place for those on leave from the front, and more often than not, he would meet up with some of the officers he had got to know well during the battle for Florence. Inevitably, they would insist on a celebration. 'Still,' he thought, 'it is New Year's Eve,' and gave in.

Sure enough, the pair soon ran into some 8th Indian Division officers, who wanted to talk with Macintosh about their recent experience of combat. Farran became bored and left the group. Sometime later, his companions realised that the band that they thought had stopped for an interval had vanished, together with their instruments.

A few minutes later, Farran reappeared: 'Follow me, Charles,' he said. 'This place is bloody boring and I've found a much better party. They had no band, so I have bribed the one that was here. Come on, we're going to have one hell of a good time.'

Charles Macintosh recalled that as week followed week at the TAC HQ, Farran 'was all impatience'. The squadron had been brought up to strength and they were fit and ready. Towards the end of February, the SAS commander decided that he would lead the next mission regardless of orders from the UK to remain in command in Florence and in spite of the objections that would be raised by Col. John Riepe, the American officer in charge of special operations at the Fifth Army HQ. To become operational without official approval, Farran decided that he would 'have to fake an accidental fall from an aircraft', making sure that he had a parachute.

The 2nd SAS Regiment carried out five operations between December 1944 and the end of the war in Italy in May 1945; they were codenamed Galia, Canuck, Cold Comfort, Tombola, and Blimey. Three chapters follow on the two major operations, Galia and Tombola, both of which were successful; in contrast, the last operation, codenamed Blimey, which was largely a failure, merits only a short description. In between these operations were Canuck and Cold Comfort, the first another success, and the second another failure.

The Canuck operation was tasked with disrupting enemy communications in Piedmont and assisting the Resistance in the imminent final offensive. There had always been a large number of Allied missions working alongside partisans in this region of north-western Italy. As well as the usual Communist formations and some from the Action Party (Justice and Liberty) and the Socialist Party (*Matteotti*), the rebels included many groups known as *Autonomi*, originally created by disbanded soldiers from the Italian 4th Army, which had been stationed inside France on the September 1943 Armistice.

The Commanding Officer of Operation Canuck was a Canadian, Capt. Robert MacDonald. He was born on 4 November 1920 in New Glasgow, Nova Scotia, and became a gifted amateur athlete. MacDonald attended the Royal Military College, Kingston, Ontario, in 1939, and two years later left for the UK with the Royal Canadian Dragoons, earning the nickname 'Buck' for his toughness.

On the afternoon of 26 April 1945, a partisan force, supported by the SAS parachutists, forced the surrender of the Fascist garrison in Alba, which is about 31 miles south-east of Turin, in the province of Cuneo. The town, which is situated on the right bank of the River Taro and is surrounded by vine-covered hills, is the historic and economic capital of the picturesque Langhe region, nowadays best known for its red wine and white truffles. Capt. MacDonald was credited with spurring on the partisans during the attack by his expert use of a 75-mm howitzer.

Alba had briefly been the location of one of the liberated zones (the so-called partisan republics) created in 1944 in a wide arc across the hills and mountains of the northern Apennines and the Alps. At the time, the town had a population of about 19,000, and it was the base for the last Fascist garrison in a large area controlled by the partisans. After being surrounded by around 2,000 men of Maj. Enrico Martini's autonomous formation, the Fascist garrison of 300 *Alpini* agreed a truce through the mediation of the church and marched out of the town on 10 October, though they were allowed to retain their weapons. A liberation committee (CLN) was established and Communist and Justice and Liberty partisans joined in the occupation, but overall control was always in the hands of Maj. Martini and his commanders. This created tensions between the various formations and weakened the response to the inevitable enemy counter-offensive, which was unique in Piedmont as the only one mounted by Fascist forces without the support of the Germans.

After offering the partisans mediation through the church, a deal which was quickly rejected, the Fascist commanders threatened to bombard the town with cannon fire, and the rebels were forced to make a fighting withdrawal on 2 November after only twenty-three days of freedom. They lost about 100 men during the campaign, and their forces only recovered and reorganised in the spring of 1945, when Allied missions came to their aid, including the parachutists of Operation Canuck.

One of Capt. MacDonald's men was NCO Jack Paley. He related that he came from the 1st Airborne Division: 'We joined the 2nd Special Air Service Regiment, which was formed after the 1st Special Air Service Regiment returned to England from the desert. I wouldn't say that we were fully trained like 1st SAS, but we did our bit in France [in Operation Rupert]'.

Paley recalled that a small advance party was sent in for Operation Canuck, consisting of Capt. MacDonald, his radio operator and two other parachutists. They landed safely, liaised with the partisans, and then prepared the reception for the main group, including Paley, which landed two or three weeks later. He noted that 'There were SOE guys down there too'. Only 12 miles to the north-west of Alba is the small commune of Cisterna d'Asti, then the base of the subversion and sabotage agency's surviving men from the Chariton Mission, which dropped to the Val Bormida on 4 February 1945 to a reception arranged by South African agent Capt. Hugh Ballard.

The mission commander Lt-Col. Max Salvadori left a few days later to provide liaison with the underground Liberation Committee for Occupied Italy, based in Milan. The second in command, Capt. John Keany, was killed on 8 March, when attempting to follow the Colonel together with radio operator William 'Bill' Pickering. Without orders and unable to reach Milan or to return to Allied lines, Pickering then joined a sub-mission led by the experienced Maj. Adrian Hope of the South African Staff Corps; it worked with the autonomous partisan brigade in Cisterna led by Giovanni Toselli (Otello), which developed into the 6th Alpine Division *Alpi* and stormed into Turin in the final offensive.

The back-up party for Operation Canuck landed in a valley about 20 miles south of Alba, near the little hill villages of Castino and San Donato, which then acted as bases for their work with the partisans. The SAS men roamed as far down as the suburbs of Alba in trucks or in any vehicle that they could lay their hands on. They also provided covering fire from the top of a hill to partisans who were attacking the town.

On 15 April, the SAS parachutists supported the united partisans of the zone in mounting what they thought would be the final push on Alba; the joint force penetrated the town's central core of ancient buildings and cobbled streets, but in the end, they were driven back to their base in the surrounding hills; five rebel fighters were killed and also two civilians.

Two days later, the SOE Chariton Mission suffered a second tragedy when the commander of the sub-mission Maj. Adrian Hope was accidentally shot by a partisan and killed.

Jack Paley recalled that the Fascist troops kept lobbing heavy mortar shells back in their direction, adding: 'We went down three times, and the last time, we took the town'. This was on the afternoon of 26 April. In the final phase of the attack, the SAS mopped up enemy snipers with machine-gun fire. Former partisans also recalled the presence during the action of the South African SOE agent Hugh Ballard; he was promoted to major and awarded the MC on 2 October 1945 'for gallant and distinguished services in the field' for his work with the partisans during this period.

Shortly after the conquest of Alba, the parachutists were deployed in a similar mopping-up role in the provincial capital of Cuneo, where there was also a lot of sniper fire, and they ended their time in Italy there. After the temporary disbandment of the SAS in October 1945, Jack Paley returned to his parent unit, the Parachute Regiment, and served with the 7th Parachute Battalion in Palestine for several months. At the end of the war, the town of Alba was awarded the Italian Gold Medal for Military Valour during the Liberation Struggle.

Operation Cold Comfort, also known as Zombie, was an ambitious attempt to block the Brenner Pass (1,370 metres), on the border between Italy and Austria, by causing a landslide. This would have immediately cut the road and rail links between Bolzano and Innsbruck, and disrupted the transit of German troop reinforcements to the south. The mission was led by Maj. Ross Robertson Littlejohn, aged twenty-three, a married man resident in Dunfermline, Fife, but born in Australia. A holder of the MC, he had served with the Black Watch (Royal Highland Regiment) and with 12 Commando and 4 Commando, before joining the SAS in 1944. The twelve-man SAS party, equipped with skis, was dropped north of Verona on 17 March 1945, but the parachutists and their supplies were scattered during the landing. Subsequently, they spent most of their time in hiding and found themselves among a hostile population, composed mainly of ethnic Germans.

Maj. Littlejohn and Cpl Joseph Patrick Crowley were captured by a German ski patrol in deep snow on 17 March and executed by a firing squad at Bolzano two days later under Hitler's notorious Commando Order. The corporal, aged twenty-seven, a Salford-born married man living in Manchester, enrolled in the King's Own Royal Regiment (Lancaster) and moved to 4 Commando before joining the SAS in 1944.

Roy Farran related that two Germans later found guilty of the killing of the SAS men 'paid an equivalent penalty' for their crime. He added that the major's mission 'failed, mainly because the weather was so terrible that it precluded resupply except at infrequent intervals. In a country which reminded me in a brief view from the air of a film called *Northwest Passage*, his hungry men fought against exposure and snow without fulfilling their main object of blocking the pass'.

On 31 March, the order was given for the exfiltration of the remaining men, as resupply and reinforcement were proving impossible. Once the war ended, the parachutists were sent on a sightseeing trip to Rome.

17

Operation Galia

At the end of December 1944, the SAS cooperated with SOE to disrupt enemy communications close to the front line in the mountains of the northern Apennines where the regions of Tuscany, Liguria, and Emilia meet, scene of the earlier ill-fated Speedwell mission.

The CO of Operation Galia was Capt. (later Lt-Col.) Robert 'Bob' Walker Brown. He was born in Sutton Coldfield on 9 April 1919, the only child of a Scottish surgeon and his wife, and educated privately at home. Walker Brown was commissioned in the Royal Engineer Territorial Army Reserve as a second-lieutenant on the outbreak of war at the age of twenty. He transferred to the Highland Light Infantry in 1941, and in June of the following year, he was wounded in action and captured by the Germans during the Battle of Bir el Tamar in Libya. After three months of treatment at the hospital for Allied POWs in Lucca, Tuscany (PG 202), Walker Brown was held in the officers' grim POW Camp 21 at Chieti in the Abruzzo region. Following the September 1943 Armistice, he was one of eight prisoners who hid in a tunnel (which they had excavated previously) as the camp was being emptied by the Germans and broke out at night. With two companions, he walked south towards the Allied lines. Briefly recaptured by German infantry troops, they escaped when the unit came under fire, and crossed Allied lines on 5 October.

Walker Brown was repatriated to the UK, appointed a Member of the Order of the British Empire (MBE) for his escape, and posted to the Infantry Training Centre at Aberdeen as an instructor. There he became rather restless, recalling: 'I saw a man in a pub who was covered with pistols, knives and goodness knows what else. He was a member of the Air Service Regiment and I thought this was the thing for me'. Walker Brown asked for the name and telephone number of the CO of 2nd SAS Regiment—by then Lt-Col. Brian Franks—went through the selection process and was accepted for training at Prestwick. His first parachute drop resulted in him landing on the roof of a double decker bus filled with a group of Wrens (members of the Women's Royal Naval Service).

After serving with the regiment in France, Walker Brown returned with the squadron to the United Kingdom, but less than forty hours later he and his men were ordered to Bari in southern Italy to undertake Operation Galia. A hasty briefing revealed that the situation on the Allied front was precarious and that there was a danger that the entire left flank of the position was liable to crumble. The only large-scale offensive operation of the war by the reconstituted Fascist Army had forced American troops from the segregated 92nd Infantry Division of the Fifth Army to retreat in the northern Apennines. On Boxing Day, the Italian *Monte Rosa* Division, supported by the German 16th SS Panzer Grenadiers, retook Barga and occupied both banks of the River Serchio, just north of Lucca. The local British Liaison Officer Maj. Anthony 'Tony' Oldham was forced to cross with his partisans into Allied territory to escape oblivion.

Reflecting the urgency of the situation, the officer chosen as second in command for the Galia mission had not even undertaken the SAS parachute course, and this would be his first jump from an aircraft. James Arthur Riccomini, born on 4 July 1917, spent his formative years as a pupil at the Henry Mellish Grammar School in Nottingham before the family moved to Maidstone in Kent. He enlisted in the Scots Guards on the outbreak of war, and in 1940 was commissioned in the Royal Army Service Corps. After operations in Palestine and Iraq, Riccomini served in North Africa and was captured at the Halfaya Pass on the Egyptian border with Libya on 16 June 1941. At the time of the September 1943 Armistice, the lieutenant was held in Italy's high security camp, PG 5 Gavi, the medieval Ligurian fortress, together with the SAS's creator, David Stirling, and over 200 other habitual escapers, nearly all officers.

As we have seen, on 9 September, the camp was seized from the Italians by a German SS detachment, and most of the POWs were entrained for camps in Greater Germany four days later. In contrast, Riccomini, together with David Stirling, Brig. George Clifton (who was the Senior Allied Officer), and fifty-five other captives, hid in an unused dungeon underneath the castle, but they were discovered after three days. The men were loaded on to buses on the morning of 17 September and driven away with a massive escort of German military police. The party stopped at a clearing centre for recaptured POWs at Mantua for the night; the next day, they were taken to a rail siding and loaded into cattle trucks to begin their journey towards the Italian border.

Sixteen other officers were locked in with Riccomini, and as soon as the train started, they began to cut a hole in the end of their truck. This was completed in about three hours, and they then drew lots as to who should jump first. From the evidence of another of the officers, Lt John Muir, they were fortunate in that this particular truck was made of wood, while the others were made of steel, preventing David Stirling and the other occupants in them from cutting their way out.

Lt Riccomini was paired with an Italian-speaking officer, Lt Harold Andrew Peterson of the Australian Imperial Force, and they jumped successfully from the train north of Rovereto at about 4.30 a.m. on 19 September, and fled into the hills above Trento. Around two weeks later, the pair made contact with a nascent rebel group led by disbanded Italian Army officers and they remained with them until January 1944, when the formation was scattered by enemy action. The two escapers narrowly avoided recapture and decided to carry the reports and information that they had compiled to neutral Switzerland, while they were still of value; they left the area on 8 January and crossed safely to the Confederation three days later. Together with approximately 4,900 other Allied escapers (and 270 evaders, mainly airmen), they were held there until the successful invasion of southern France in August 1944 by the 7th Army (Operation Anvil/Dragoon) created a land corridor, which allowed their gradual return to their homelands.

Walker Brown related that he drew 'enormous confidence' from the fact that his friend, Maj. Gordon Lett, would be manning the reception party at the drop zone for the Galia mission. The escaper partisan was born on 17 November 1910 to Australian parents in Port Moresby, Papua New Guinea. He was commissioned in the East Surrey Regiment in 1933 and was stationed in India and the Sudan before serving in North Africa, where he was captured at Tobruk in Libya in June 1942. After sharing the hardships of life in the Chieti POW camp with Walker Brown, the major was sent to Camp 29 Veano, in my family's home province of Piacenza. On 10 September 1943, following the armistice, information was received that the Germans were approaching the camp, and both the Allied prisoners and their Italian jailers scattered into the countryside. Maj. Lett left the area with Sgt Robert 'Bob' James Grierson Blackmore, of the 2/15th Australian Infantry Battalion, and Rifleman John Micallef, a Maltese serving in the Second Battalion of the Rifle Brigade (Prince Consort's Own).

The trio decided to go south-east across the hills in anticipation of Allied landings on the west coast, which in the event never materialised. By the end of the month, they had reached northern Tuscany and the valley of Rossano in the commune of Zeri, Province of Massa Carrara. The first house the escapers came upon in the little village of Chiesa was that of the Deluchi family, the beginning of a lifelong friendship. Dissident Italians in the cities gradually created liberation committees (CLNs) to coordinate the activities of Resistance groups in the mountains and to assist disbanded Italian soldiers and Allied escapers. The committee based in Genoa sent two Italian Army officers to contact Maj. Lett, and as a result of their discussions, he decided to form an international battalion of partisans.

On 27 July 1944, the major was promoted to British Liaison Officer (BLO) and head of the Blundell Violet Mission run by Special Force. Its duties were to collect and evacuate POWs, gather intelligence, support partisan attacks, obtain supplies for appropriate partisan groups, and aid operations by special forces. After the Allied advance across central Italy in the summer of 1944, most of the POWs were sent through the valley to begin the journey across the lines. A mission codenamed Vermouth, belonging to 'A' Force, the AFHQ deception and escape service, organised the journey in cooperation with Maj. Lett and local partisans, and it ran for the remainder of the year. The evacuees included the major's two companions from Veano, Sgt Bob Blackmore and Rifleman John Micallef, both of whom had done sterling service with the partisans.

On 13 November, Gen. Alexander issued his controversial proclamation to the Italian Resistance, which was broadcast over the Allied Force Headquarters radio service, *Italia Combatte*. The partisans were told that the Allies would launch no major attack until the spring, and that they should cease from engaging in any large-scale operations, conserve all stores of ammunition, and await further orders. Though designed to prevent unnecessary sacrifice, the order was a great setback for the Resistance and a tonic for the Germans and Fascists. With the guarantee that they would not face a major attack over the winter, they launched a series of offensives on the partisans in the mountains. It was against this challenging background that Operation Galia took place.

Local conditions were also difficult. Attacks had to be made over steep terrain and in harsh conditions of ice, snow and low cloud. Without motor transport, operations were conducted on foot, when the drawbacks of using standard issue British Army hobnail boots on icy tracks soon became apparent. Men from Maj. Lett's International Battalion acted as guides, and local civilians led teams of mules and donkeys to carry weapons and supplies, though the animals could not be taken within 800 yards of the fire position due to the noise that their hooves made on rocky paths. Resupply by air was also a constant problem, as we shall see.

Capt. Charles Macintosh, the CO at Special Force's TAC HQ in Florence, recalled that planning for an SAS mission to attack enemy communications near the front line began in early December and that it was put into effect once his headquarters agreed with base that Gordon Lett's area would be the best to receive No. 3 Squadron of the 2nd SAS Regiment under Capt. Walker Brown. He only required a safe drop zone to ensure an undisturbed arrival, time for his parachutists to get organised, and the ability to select appropriate targets with the help of local advice.

On 22 December, Special Force sent Maj. Lett this message: 'Reply if ready to receive bodies, repeat bodies, on 24th. Force standing by. Urgent'. The major eagerly accepted the offer, adding that the drop zone would be identified by the letter 'H' for Harry, and by British and Italian flags, but he also arranged a delay of three days, as it was first necessary to seal off the valley with partisan forces to ensure the safe arrival of the parachutists.

However, on the eve of drop on 27 December, a message was received by Special Force in Florence, which said that Maj. Lett had been murdered; at the same time, no wireless contact could be made with his mission. In fact, the message on 22 December had been sent over an American transmitter, as the major's apparatus had broken down. A state of alarm had been caused in the valley the day before when a column of eighteen uniformed and heavily-armed men had turned up asking for the major. The troops of Italian-American origin formed an Operational Group of the Office of Strategic Services (OSS), which had been parachuted in August on Mont Aiona in the Sixth Partisan Zone around Genoa. A savage enemy roundup had been launched across the region in December and the partisans had been forced to scatter after three days. As a result, the Americans had been ordered to withdraw to Allied lines.

After speaking with their commander, Capt. William Wheeler, Maj. Lett promised to help the men on their way and was delighted to be able to use their radio in the morning, when he received the news of the SAS mission. The OSS group crossed to forward elements of US 92nd Infantry Division at Azzano on 26 December.

Maj. Charles Macintosh of TAC HQ agreed with Capt. Walker Brown that the operation to Rossano would proceed on 27 December as planned, but that one of the aircraft would go ahead of the others, drop its cargo, and watch the reaction. If there was the normal response from a ground reception party, a Special Force officer, Lt (later Capt.) Christopher 'Chris' Anthony William Leng, would parachute before the SAS to check conditions on the ground. He had been commissioned in the 27th Lancers in 1942 after serving in the Senior Division of the Officers Training Corps at Oxford University. Together with five companions, Leng volunteered for 'a special job in the Middle East', but following specialist training in various centres, he was detached to Special Force in Italy for a mission over the Brenner Pass; six attempts were made, but on each occasion they were cancelled at the last minute, either because of cloud cover or aircraft failure.

The aerial operation over the Rossano Valley was the largest mounted so far in daylight. As well as a fighter escort, seven C-47 Dakotas carried men and supplies. The drop zone was in the centre of the SAS's operational area. Codenamed Huntsville, it was a large meadow above Chiesa, a village that had been burned by the Germans in a roundup during the previous August. Maj. Lett asked the neighbouring partisan leader to send twelve well-armed men to help close off the roads leading to the valley in order that the whole area would be under Allied control for forty-eight hours. Daniele 'Dani' Bucchioni, aged twenty-seven, from Calice al Cornoviglio, had served as an officer in the Italian Army, and after the September 1943 Armistice, he formed a group of partisans in the province of La Spezia, becoming commandant of the Val di Vara Battalion of the Justice and Liberty Brigade, with an operative zone south of Lett's International Battalion.

On the morning of 27 December, the partisans set up the flags and the identification letter (both using pieces of coloured parachutes sown together) and waited for the planes to arrive. Maj. Lett prepared some cards in English for the partisans to hand to the parachutists on their arrival, indicating that they were among friends and directing them to the assembly point.

As the hours passed and nothing happened, the men on the ground grew increasingly anxious, but during the late afternoon, the noise of an aircraft could be heard coming from the direction of the Magra Valley, and a C-47 Douglas Dakota soon came into view, hugging the contours of the Rossano Valley, circling twice, and dropping six silk parachutes carrying supplies. Also attached were letters to Maj. Lett from his fiancée in London and a message from Special Force HQ indicating that partisan Nello Sani has been awarded the Italian Bronze Medal for distinguished service with the mission, the first granted to a partisan in the field.

As the village clock began to chime five o'clock, the sound of more planes could be heard in the distance and it eventually grew to a mighty roar as six Dakotas circled overhead. A figure was seen to drop from the door of the leading plane and a parachute billowed above him as he floated down to the centre of the field and became enveloped in the cords as he landed. Gordon Lett reached the khaki-clad figure just as he had extricated himself from the last ropes, finding him to be a fair-haired young officer (he was twenty-two) with a calm outlook and dry sense of humour, which at once placed him in the category of 'typically English'.

'Are you Major Lett?' he asked.

'I am, and I'm very glad to see you.'

'My name is Chris Leng of Special Force,' he said, holding out his hand. Then he laughed. 'This is rather like the "Doctor Livingston, I presume," touch. I'll give the others the signal, as they are waiting to come down and join us.'

Chris Leng related that two SAS men jumped with him: a young radio operator, Ted Robinson, and the second in command, Lt James Arthur Riccomini, on his first parachute drop. The captain fired a green Very light signal and more figures began to emerge from the circling planes, until the sky was full of coloured parachutes. The moustachioed Bob Walker Brown was the first man out, making another perfect drop. He related that Gordon Lett looked strained and tired and immensely relieved to see friendly British faces; they had a typically military conversation, with the whole thing marked by a lack of emotion. Finally, all the men had landed: thirty-three in total. The parachutists carried their personal kit and collected around the flags, swopping their helmets for the SAS berets. The airdrop continued for another half hour, and afterwards, the partisans carried the supplies to a central store. More than 300 parachutes were dropped. The Dakotas circled for the last time, dipped their wings in salute and flew back south.

Once the troop was assembled on the field and a roll call was held, Maj. Lett gave a speech of welcome and explained that there was no possibility of danger for at least forty-eight hours; after that it would be as well to be prepared. In the meantime, the men would find food and shelter with the people of the valley, who were all friends. The major finally told them: 'Now if you go over to that hut which you see among the trees,' pointing to the temporary billet of the Deluchi family, 'you will find a very courageous old lady who has prepared some hot tea for you. There's no sugar in this part of the world, but otherwise it should be fairly drinkable.' The men were accommodated with families around the valley and in the evening were able to gather in the village of Valle for dinner.

Walker Brown recalled that he had no hesitation in placing his SAS troops in Gordon Lett's support, saying that he has done absolutely splendid spade work within the context of operating with groups of partisans: 'He was really in a position of great trust on the part of many, but not all, of the partisans. His influence was clearly substantial'. Their joint assessment was that the SAS should begin a series of attacks on the enemy lines of communication in the interests of a speedy impact on the situation, accepting whatever partisan support was available, and in the hope that it would encourage more involvement. Walker Brown added that Gordon Lett gave them a first-rate briefing to the effect that the enemy forces were in the deep valleys some four hours' march away; the mountain passes were covered in thick snow and ice; there were no roads suitable for motor transport; some partisan bands were well disposed, others, the Communist *Garibaldi* Brigades, were unreliable; news of the SAS arrival would reach the enemy rapidly via informers, suitably exaggerated.

The first priority was to attack the enemy lines of communication used by the 148th Infantry Division, with the intention of making them withdraw troops from the line. Prime targets would be the ancient Via Aurelia—the main coastal road between Genoa, La Spezia, and Sarzana—and the inland routes from the town of Aulla that run to the Emilian cities of Reggio and Modena.

The unit of thirty-three men split into six detachments: the Troop Headquarters of seven men, led by Walker Brown, four sticks of five men, and one stick of six men. The parachutists were equipped with Bren guns, Winchester Carbines, and side arms, and the Troop Headquarters also deployed a 3-inch mortar, which proved highly effective; two Vickers medium machine guns were dropped later.

Walker Brown related that the overall aim of the SAS mission was to make the enemy believe that units of the British 2nd Parachute Brigade, which had recently left Italy for service in Greece, had returned. He recalled: 'This, it was felt, might make the Germans think twice before making a very risky penetration down the extreme left flank of the Allied position'. For this deception to succeed, it was necessary to make the presence of the SAS known to the enemy as soon as possible.

18

Attacking Enemy Communications

On the second day of Operation Galia to northern Tuscany, 28 December 1944, three SAS parties fanned out across the area to cause panic among the enemy forces. Sgt Rookes' No. 3 Stick moved north-east to attack the road from Pontremoli to the Cisa Pass; Lt Gibbon and his No. 4 Stick left to cross the Due Santi Pass in the north-west, in order to target the road from Borgo Val di Taro to Parma in the region of Emilia; and Lt Shaughnessy led his men of No. 5 Stick in a south-easterly direction to attack the roads connecting Aulla and the cities of Reggio Emilia and Modena on the Via Emilia.

Capt. Walker Brown and the remaining men stayed in Rossano to hide the stores and to establish liaison with Maj. Lett and the partisans. Meanwhile, the SAS radio operators attached to the headquarters, Parachutist Ted Robinson and Cpl William Cunningham were unable to establish wireless communications because of difficulties in reception caused by the mountains or by enemy jamming. A third operator, Cpl Johnson, was attached to Sgt Wright's Stick. All the men worked to control sets located at the TAC HQ in Florence and the SOM (Special Operations Mediterranean) base at Monopoli.

On 29 December, Maj. Lett, accompanied by Lt Leng, led a party consisting of the SAS Troop HQ, No. 1 Stick under Sgt Wright, and the No. 2 Stick of Lt Riccomini, on a tortuous climb over the western mountains to Pieve, a small village in the commune of Zignago, where the partisans had set up a temporary headquarters. All formations in the area, including the International Battalion, were now part of the 4th Partisan Zone, commanded by a former Italian Army officer, Col. Mario Fontana. Aged forty-seven, he was a native of La Spezia and served with distinction in both world wars before throwing in his lot with the partisans. After a conference with the rebel leaders, which discussed future cooperation, the British spent the night in the nearby hamlet of Vezzola.

Meanwhile, the men of Lt Shaughnessy's No. 5 Stick were guided by partisan Leonardo Chella to the hamlet of Borseda, part of the commune of Calice al Cornoviglio, the base of the neighbouring partisan leader to the south, Daniele 'Dani' Bucchioni. After spending the night with the lieutenant, they began the march towards the River Magra and the village of Vecchietto, on the other bank, where they were to establish a base, but interrupted their advance to settle for the night in a farm shed at Montebello di Mezzo, perhaps due to deteriorating weather or because of security concerns.

On 30 December, Walker Brown's party left Vezzola to attack the coastal road. As they marched across the mountains, four Dakotas suddenly swooped low overhead, flying in the direction of the Rossano Valley. Chris Leng looked up at them and swore. The evening before, he had warned base that a further drop would be unwise owing to the deteriorating weather and to the other duties of the British personnel who would be required to arrange the reception. However, it seemed that the message had not been received. As the SAS troops were preparing to leave for a raid that evening, a messenger arrived with a message from one of Bucchioni's men who had remained in the valley to guard the supplies. He reported that a plane had got caught in an air pocket and crashed with the loss of all of those on board.

Dakota 42-92680, piloted by 1Lt Don Alan Ray, from Illinois, was part of the same unit that had carried out the supply drop three days earlier: No. 4 Troop Carrier Squadron of the 62nd Troop Carrier Group, based at Malignano, near Sienna. After dropping its supplies on the 'Huntsville' landing zone, the aircraft climbed over the ridge to the north, ran into severe turbulence, and began to lose height. The crew made a doomed effort to regain control and finally to land on another meadow, but a wing hit the branches of a giant oak and the plane crashed on a small ridge in deciduous woodland below the hamlet of La Dolce in the commune of Zeri, bursting into flames on impact.

There were five crew and two passengers. The other airmen were 2Lt Earl S. Hurlbut, co-pilot, also from Illinois, and Staff Sergeants William H. Close, Junior, radar operator, from Maryland; Israel Goodman, radio operator, from Connecticut; and Fred Reyther, from Texas. The remaining occupants of the plane were British dispatchers serving with the RASC: Cpl William Oldershaw, aged thirty-four, from Nottingham, and Driver James Wilfred Cox, aged twenty-one, from the 352nd Infantry Division Transport Company.

During the night, Walker Brown's group moved to be nearer the main coast road. They trekked to Serò, a hamlet of medieval origin in the commune of Zignago, situated at 575 metres above sea level and providing spectacular views of the Vara Valley, transport links and the Gulf of Spezia. The SAS established their local base here in the home of an Italian called Louis Siboldi, known as Pippo, aged about fifty, who spoke English as he had spent some time working in America before the war. Subsequently, he always accompanied the SAS on their raids and was praised by Walker Brown for his audacity and intimate knowledge of the unmapped approaches to German supply roads.

In the evening, a courier brought Maj. Lett a note from 'Dani' outlining events that had taken place earlier that day. Walker Brown's post-combat report summarised its content: 'Lieutenant Shaughnessy and the whole of his stick were reported captured in Montebello by a party of *Brigate Nere* who were said to have been dressed in Italian civilian clothes. The Italian guide was interrogated, tortured and then shot by the *Brigate Nere* while attempting to escape'. The young courier told Maj. Lett that an enemy drive had been launched nearby and that a spy brought men of the Black Brigades to Montebello during the night. They surrounded the British soldiers in a shed just before dawn. The parachutists were rounded up and loaded in a lorry for transport to the civilian jail in La Spezia, but their guide, Leonardo Chella, had been dragged into the village street. A Fascist lieutenant had seen the British and Italian flags that he was wearing on his battle dress and recognised it as the insignia of the Maj. Lett's International Battalion. The officer ordered his men to beat the guide with sticks and then he was shot.

Walker Brown's party had clambered down the mountainside from Serò and ambushed a German convoy on a quiet patch of the coastal road west of Brugnato. His report related: 'Three German vehicles were destroyed and one set on fire. An enemy armoured vehicle replied with heavy 20-mm machine gun fire. Three enemy were killed instantly and one died later of his injuries in Borghetto hospital. The number of wounded is unknown'.

On the SAS's return from the raid, Maj. Lett gave Capt. Walker Brown the news of the capture of his men, and they agreed to inform base in the morning. The major thought that it was unlikely that the prisoners would be shot, as the enemy commanders were aware that the Allies had radio contact with the La Spezia area and had already named several jailers as war criminals. Walker Brown said: 'I'm very sorry indeed about your courier. We certainly won't forget when we have a few of those swine in our hands'. The fate of the SAS parachutists remained unknown, until they emerged from a German POW camp in April 1945.

At dawn on New Year's Day, Walker Brown's party, supported by fourteen partisans from the Justice and Liberty Brigade, attacked German and Fascist soldiers in Borghetto di Vara, a small town on the plain, about 9 miles along the main road north-west of the city of La Spezia. The objects of the action were to make the presence of the SAS known to the enemy in the quickest possible time; to create uneasiness among the garrison troops on the Genoa–La Spezia road and to cause them to be reinforced, and to stop further enemy movement on the road.

The raiders deployed the 3-inch mortar at a range of 1,000 yards and fired thirty-four high-explosive bombs. Direct hits were obtained on several houses occupied by the troops and on an enemy car. Two German trucks drove down the road towards Borghetto and stopped on hearing the mortar fire. Bren gunners moved forward a few hundred yards and destroyed both vehicles. The number of casualties was not known, but the entire enemy garrison withdrew from Borghetto and did not return for twenty-four hours. On 2 January, the victims of the air crash were buried with full military honours in the small churchyard at Chiesa. At the end of the war, the Americans were repatriated to the US: 2Lt Hurlbut to the Lincoln Memorial Park, Oswego, Kendall County, Illinois, and his companions, 1Lt Ray and Staff Sergeants Close, Goodman, and Reyther, to the Zackary Taylor National Cemetery, Louisville, Jefferson County, Kentucky. The two Britons, Cpl Oldershaw and Driver Cox, rest in the Monumental Cemetery of Staglieno, Genoa, together with many other Allied servicemen.

On 3 January, wireless communication was re-established and a message was sent asking for resupply, but the request was rejected out of hand, with the instruction that the 'Huntsville' drop zone was no longer be used owing to the loss of the Dakota. On the same day, Capt. Walker Brown sent Lt Riccomini and his No. 2 Stick to target the main road south of Montebello di Mezzo (where the six SAS men had been captured). It was cold, with heavy snow on the ground and ice on the mountain tracks, which made movement difficult and tedious. The post-combat report noted that on the 4th: 'Lieutenant Riccomini mined the road on the bridge over the river at Valeriano. A mine denoted during the night of 4-5 January destroying a German truck, killing twelve and wounding another eight according to subsequent information obtained'.

On 6 January, Sgt Wright's No. 1 Stick attacked an enemy staff car on the Via Aurelia, killing a senior Fascist official and wounding three German officers. The vehicle was reported by the partisans to be carrying 125 million lire in a suitcase, which the SAS allowed them to retain.

Three days later, Lt Riccomini and Sgt Wright led their sticks to a new drop zone, which had been given the codename of Halifax. It was five hours' march away from 'Huntsville', to the south-west, near the village of Pieve. A single plane successfully dropped supplies at 3.30 p.m., but they were scattered over 4 square miles of the countryside. Walker Brown marched with his headquarters party to help in the recovery effort, but the operation lasted well into the following day, and 40 to 50 per cent of the cargo was stolen by local Justice and Liberty partisans. The captain was again at the drop zone on 15 January to receive an airdrop of two Vickers medium machine guns and other supplies, though the reception was almost disrupted by the presence of an unruly mob of partisans, which forced the SAS to fire shots over their heads to restore order.

On 11 January, Walker Brown led a reconnaissance party from Serò to survey the road bridge over the river at L'Ago as a possible target. When they returned, they took up a firing position 300 yards from the German and Fascist headquarters building in Borghetto di Vara, while a main ambush party under Lt Riccomini was sent on ahead. Walker Brown was about to open fire on two Fascists playing tennis in the road when he heard a column of vehicles moving towards the town. It was decided not to open fire and to allow them to reach the main ambush party, as they had five Brens, as contrasted with the reconnaissance party's one. The vehicles halted in Borghetto for five minutes and were under close observation. The column consisted of a captured British staff car, a 10-ton lorry, and a truck, which turned into a side street in Borghetto and halted. Both leading vehicles were pulling trailers, the one on the staff car carried six Germans, including an officer, and the one on the lorry was loaded with twenty-seven Germans, five women, and a collection of white canvas packages. The two remaining vehicles left the town and were engaged by the main ambush party. The official report related: 'Thirty-two Bren magazines were fired, both vehicles and trailers were totally destroyed, the 10-tonner and trailer being set on fire with incendiary rounds. Twenty-five were killed'.

On 12 January, the day after the attack, news was received from civilians that Blackshirts were burning houses in Brugnato, the village on the main road at the base of the mountain pathway from the SAS local base of Serò. Walker Brown's party scrambled to reach the scene and fired three high explosive bombs on the road leading out of Brugnato. The enemy immediately began withdrawing towards the bridge and the river and they were engaged with mortar fire. A German party of platoon strength took up firing positions on the southern side of the bridge and opened up with MG 42 machine guns. They were mortared and withdrew into the hills in disorder. Small enemy parties attempting to ford the river were also engaged.

A number of the troops were reported to have drowned, presumably after having been wounded by mortar splinters, as the river is only two foot deep. An enemy 20-mm machine-gun position sited in the cemetery in Borghetto was then engaged with three rounds of rapid fire from the mortar, one bomb landing directly on the machine gun, which was put out of action and the crew killed.

At 4 p.m., all the ammunition was expended except for the reserve, and the troops prepared to move. At that moment, four USAAF P-47 Thunderbolt fighter bombers arrived on the scene. Two dive-bombed the bridge between Borghetto and Brugnato and two strafed the road. The enemy then brought up a field gun from La Spezia and began to shell the surrounding countryside, but they seemed to be unaware of the mortar's position, allowing the SAS party to withdraw up the mountainside without loss.

Around this time, reports began to emerge from the partisan intelligence service that enemy forces were about to launch a large-scale anti-partisan drive in the mountains. As a result, Colonel Fontana and the *Comando Unico*, the partisan command, drew up a plan for a pre-emptive strike against the invaders at three different points on the night of 19 January.

The day before, Walker Brown's party, together with Maj. Lett and Lt Leng, had moved to the village of Codolo, west of the small town of Pontremoli, intending to carry out an attack with their new Vickers guns against an enemy garrison of 300 men at nearby Vignola. However, the action had to be abandoned as it was found that the enemy had the route under observation. As an alternative, it was decided to carry out ambushes on the roads north and south of Pontremoli, and the party accordingly marched to Arzelato, which is in in a commanding position south-west of the town. The journey was hard and slow 'because there was heavy cloud, ice and snow and it was pitch black'. However, it was found that it would be impossible to attack that night and then withdraw to a secure base by daylight, so the whole of 19 January was spent in Arzelato, where the men were forced to stay indoors, as the village was also under observation by the enemy garrison in Pontremoli.

During the day, a group of partisans who had been asked to volunteer for the mission by Maj. Lett arrived from the *Centocroci* Brigade and placed themselves under SAS command. The brigade, which operated north of Monte Gottero, was commanded by a junior *Carabiniere* officer called Federico Salvestri (Richetto). The detachment of twenty men he sent was led by Antonino 'Nino' Siligato, a native of Limina, near Messina, in Sicily, aged twenty-four. A junior naval officer and submariner, he was awarded the War Cross for Valour in 1942 and joined the *Decima Flottiglia MAS* after the September 1943 Armistice, but became a partisan in the Val di Taro in January 1944. Siligato, a flamboyant character with flowing, dark locks, willingly answered the major's call and led his men in a forced march over the mountains to take part in the raid, even though he was feverish and suffering from a bout of jaundice.

Once it was dark, a mixed party of SAS and partisans left Maj. Lett and Cpl Johnson with the wireless sets in Arzelato and carried out an attack at a point where the Pontremoli to Aulla road has a drop of 50 feet on the west flank and a steep cutting on the east flank. Lt Riccomini's stick deployed the two Vickers machine guns to fire on a single vehicle with headlights, which drove straight into a column of marching troops, who were also hit by machine gun fire. The casualties were not known, but German soldiers told Italian civilians on the following day that there were large numbers of dead on the road. The enemy responded with weak and ineffective fire.

The raiders then had to withdraw in haste from the ambush position at 12.30 a.m. on 20 January when they spotted enemy ski troops infiltrating the mountains. The group marched back to the village of Codolo; the partisans remained there, while the SAS party moved to the abandoned village of Noce for a planned rendezvous with Cpl Johnson and his mule train carrying supplies. However, a courier sent by Maj. Lett met them there and said that the column had clashed with an enemy patrol and had then been forced to return to Arzelato.

Walker Brown still expected the supply column to arrive and so his party marched the short distance south to the village of Coloretta to wait for them there, arriving at 7 a.m. They only had time to unpack their mules, when, as his report noted, 'At 07.15 hours, first light, a large force of Germans, estimated at battalion strength, were observed at 250 yards advancing in extended order'.

19

The Germans Strike Back

The Germans launched their operation against the Italian partisans and the British SAS on 20 January 1945 from several directions simultaneously: Bedonia, Borgo Val di Taro, Pontremoli, Varese, Borghetto di Vara, and Calice al Cornoviglio. Maj. Charles Macintosh at Special Force's TAC HQ in Florence identified their forces, firstly, as 'Mongol ski troops'—that is, legionaries from the 162nd German Infantry Division, often called the Turkoman Division, composed of captured Soviet POWs and refugees, mainly Turkmen and Azerbaijanis, with German officers; secondly, as German soldiers from the Massa and Parma military commands; and finally, as units of the 285th Grenadier Battalion, which was largely made up of conscripted men from the region of Alsace, which had been occupied by Germany in 1940.

Gordon Lett related that, on 20 January 1945, the enemy was pushing into the Rossano Valley from all directions. There was only time to collect three SAS personnel who had been receiving treatment at the makeshift partisan hospital, all of whom were able to walk: Parachutists Gargan, Hildage, and Rose. They were joined by three of their comrades sent by Lt Gibbon at Belforte to report and to receive fresh orders, Cpl Larley and Parachutists Dennie and Whittaker, and later also by two members of Walker Brown's composite party who became detached during a scouting mission: Parachutists Everett and Hann.

Maj. Lett then led a group made up of SAS troops and local partisans through snow drifts to the upper slopes of Monte Picchiara (1,158 metres). The men were equipped with two light machine guns, rifles, and as much ammunition as they could carry. However, by nightfall, it was apparent that the partisan counteroffensive had failed and that the enemy was moving into the main villages; Lett therefore made the decision to take his men to the last potential hideout, Monte Gottero, to the north, which separates the regions of Liguria and Emilia Romagna at a height of 1,639 metres.

However, once they reached the mountain, the major speedily came to the conclusion that there too 'all was lost'; he decided that the only hope of survival lay in retracing their steps and travelling the country trails that they knew well, but which were unfamiliar to the enemy. Lett related that his strategy was 'influenced to a great extent by the prospect of having with me a few well-trained soldiers of the SAS who could be relied upon to do the right thing in the moment of crisis'. The party he led was made up of eight parachutists and five partisans, including Louis 'Pippo' Siboldi, who acted as their guide. The mountain paths would eventually lead them as far south as Daniele Bucchioni's base of Borseda in the commune of Calice al Cornoviglio in the Vara Valley. The group came under enemy fire on three separate occasions and during the last of these, at Serò, Ivan, a Russian partisan, was captured and executed; two of the battalion's couriers were also shot during the enemy drive. Finally, on 26 January, after six days, the party was able to return to the Rossano Valley when the German forces withdrew.

Elsewhere under the hammer of the enemy offensive on 20 January, the main SAS party retreated under mortar and small arms fire from the village of Coloretta, but had to leave the Vickers guns and the other supplies on the ground, which were seized by the enemy. Cpl Johnson and his mules never did make contact, as he was fired on during the journey; most of the handlers deserted and the bulk of the equipment was lost, including the radios, rations, rucksacks, and sleeping bags—they had been unloaded before the alarm was given, and the mules were also captured by the enemy. The partisans of the *Centocroci* Brigade had remained at Codolo to rest and have some food, but they too were soon swept up in the enemy advance. Their commander, Antonino Siligato, was mown down by a machine-gun burst and six of his men were executed.

The SAS moved the short distance from Coloretta to the little village of Rio in the commune of Sesta Godano, arriving there at 5 p.m. Within thirty minutes, they came under enemy fire with a powerful 75-mm gun. Now, like the other Britons and the partisans, their only hope of survival lay in escaping the enemy's tightening grip by reaching higher ground; Walker Brown led his men to the foot of Monte Gottero, where they spent the night.

At first light on 21 January, the party crossed the summit of the mountain and halfway down met Lt Gibbon and Cpl Ford, from No. 4 Stick, together with a number of partisans, who all joined the main party, which reached the village of Montegroppo at 9 p.m. They were now in the region of Emilia, specifically in the upland Parmesan commune of Albareto in the valley of the Gotra torrent, a tributary of the River Taro. Two hours later, a detachment of 400 German infantry was reported to be one hour's march away. A force of 1,200 partisans drawn from a number of different bands, which had taken sanctuary in Montegroppo, 'immediately vanished into the mountains on hearing this intelligence'. In contrast, the SAS party moved north-east to the small village of Boschetto, lower down the valley, where information was received from partisans of the *Centocroci* Brigade that the same unit of enemy troops was still an hour's march behind; the German officers told Italian civilians that they were hunting British parachutists.

At 7 a.m. on 22 January, the SAS moved out of Boschetto, and an hour later, approximately 2,000 Germans attacked the village and captured the partisan leader Federico 'Richetto' Salvestri and sixteen of his men, though he managed to escape days later and many of the others were also eventually released as part of a prisoner exchange with the enemy. Lt Gibbon and Cpl Ford departed with their partisans to return to their base at Belforte. At 1 p.m., Walker Brown's party arrived in the village of Buzzò and made contact with Sgt Rookes and his No. 3 Stick. They were also joined by the remainder of Lt Gibbon's Stick, Cpl Ford and Parachutists Dennie and Whittaker, who had been with Maj. Lett. The official report noted: 'Captain Walker Brown's party by this time had completed fifty-nine hours of continuous marching without rations or rest through thick and exhausting snow'. The men marched for another hour and took shelter in a hut in the mountains near the Due Santi Pass (1,392 metres), which connects the territories of Albareto and Zeri, where they enjoyed twelve hours of rest and were fed by the locals.

The situation on 23 January was summarised succinctly: 'State of alarm. German troops in Buzzò. The SAS stood to'. Similarly, on the 24th: 'State of alarm. Lieutenant Leng joined the party'. He had been hiding in a cave on Monte Gottero with Colonel Mario Fontana and the partisan command, until it was safe to move.

The next day, 400 Mongol troops arrived in Buzzò. The SAS party accordingly moved to the abandoned village of Nola, two hours' march away. At night, Capt. Walker Brown and Lt Leng returned to Buzzò with an Italian guide to ascertain whether it was clear of the enemy or not. They got to within 20 yards of the village when they were fired upon by troops deploying a Schmeisser machine pistol, and an MG 42 machine gun, which fired a complete belt at 20 yards' range, but missed in the darkness; the trio were able to return unscathed to Nola.

On 26 January, Benito Mussolini braved the snows of the Cisa Pass to inspect troops of the Social Republic in Pontremoli and Aulla, who were bound for the Garfagnana front. He spent the night with a lady teacher and her mother in their splendid villa located in the square of the little village of Mocrone.

By 27 January, the anti-partisan drive was over and Capt. Walker Brown's party was able to return to Rossano, where the whole of the troop concentrated. They were joined later in the day by Maj. Lett and his group. There had been no British casualties, but the enemy offensive resulted in nineteen fatalities among civilians and 150 in the ranks of the partisans in the Zeri area, including three of Maj. Lett's men and those of the *Centocroci* Brigade under Antonino Siligato, slain at Codolo. The next day, Lt Leng left with an SAS party to dig up the buried rations and ammunition. A squad was also sent to Arzelato to recover a spare 'B' radio set buried by Cpl Johnson on 20 January.

It was only on 30 January that the SAS operators were able to re-establish wireless communication. An urgent request was sent blind for resupply of weapons and ammunition, rations, and medicine, also indicating that the drop zone would have to revert to 'Huntsville' as Germans were in the vicinity of other sites. On 2 February, thick clouds lay halfway down the mountains, but the American pilot of a lone Dakota was able to locate the field and then to carry out a series of precise supply drops, returning two hours later to parachute Capt. Milne, Royal Army Medical Corps, who was to provide urgent medical attention to a number of combatants. He immediately cared for Parachutist Gordon 'Lofty' Rose, mortar operator with the Troop Headquarters, who was ill from a bacterial infection; he was advised to remain in the Rossano Valley with Maj. Lett until he was well enough to make his way back through the lines.

Walker Brown's troop then moved south, accompanied by a mule train laden with their weapons and supplies. His report noted that contact was made on 7 February with Maj. Lett's ally, Daniele Bucchioni, 'who commanded a band 150 strong'. He added: 'This band had high morale and had done a considerable amount of damage in their area including raids on La Spezia'. Walker Brown once again attacked the Genoa–La Spezia road, destroying two enemy trucks and damaging a third; casualties were not known. The enemy burnt down three houses in two nearby villages as a reprisal. Meanwhile, Sgt Rookes and his No. 3 Stick carried out a successful attack on the road between Aulla and La Spezia, destroying eight German vehicles and causing a number of casualties among a detachment of German troops bivouacked at the side of the road.

The following day, the SAS held a conference with Daniele Bucchioni, who advised them against a planned mortar attack on the garrison in Padivarma, a village in the commune of Beverino, in the Vara Valley. He said that since the assault on Borghetto the enemy troops no longer lived in requisitioned billets, but in houses occupied by civilians, and that the action would undoubtedly cause casualties to the residents and thereby alienate the local population.

On 10 February, a B-25 Mitchell medium bomber, part of Special Force's TAC HQ's small private air force, dropped 'operational money and comforts'. During the day, Walker Brown made the decision to begin withdrawing toward the Allied lines, carrying out small attacks on the way. Medical Officer Capt. Milne had advised that several of the parachutists were still sick and that many more were very fatigued. In addition, after over six weeks of constant warfare, Walker Brown judged that the possibilities for further operations were limited. He related that German Intelligence had by that time established that they were really fewer in number than at first reported, and he thought that they had exhausted the potential of surprise and exaggerated rumours. It was therefore time to withdraw from that particular operation with a view to being deployed in another area, where once again they could exploit surprise and rumour. This proved to be Operation Tombola in the province of Reggio Emilia—the topic of the next three chapters.

Walker Brown recalled that they did things the SAS way, stating: 'Had we conformed to partisan ideas of tactical movement we could have been in trouble'. He described the rebels as an extraordinary mixture of quite remarkable courage, bravery and endurance, allied to what one can kindly call a certain lack of organisation, but this was not meant to be a harsh judgement, 'after all it takes a very brave man to decide that a very small force of British parachutists is a wise thing to back, when his home and his family are surrounded by some very hostile people'.

Once the decision had been made to return to Allied lines, the troop was split in two columns for the journey. Walker Brown led the largest group, consisting of his HQ, Sgt Rookes' No. 3 Stick, Lt Gibbon's No. 4 Stick, five partisans, including Louis 'Pippo' Siboldi, and a German deserter. The group left immediately and followed the well-established escape line south through the marble mountains of Carrara to the villages of Vinca and Forno and over Monte Altissimo (1,589 metres) in the Seravezza commune of the province of Lucca. On the final stage of the march, it was not possible for the men to carry much owing to their physical condition, and as result, they left their Bren guns with the partisans and only kept carbines and reserve ammunition.

Walker Brown described the march over Monte Altissimo as 'difficult and tiring'. It was pitch black and impossible to use the normal trails, as they were mined, so about 2,000 feet or more had to be climbed at an average slope of one in four. The pass at the top of the mountain was reached at about 11 p.m. on 14 February; at the same time, an enemy mortar fired on several sections of the track leading through their positions. Half an hour later, a German patrol of four men was seen moving up the path towards the SAS party. The point men got into fire position, but the enemy troops saw the troop, fled into a gully, and took no hostile action.

At 8 a.m. on 15 February, one of the SAS party sprang an enemy trip wire, which ignited a white phosphorous flare; it was feared that this was a signal that would trigger defensive fire, but nothing happened. 'At 04.00 hours,' Walker Brown, recorded modestly, 'the party passed the forward American platoon.'

Lt Riccomini led the smaller SAS group for the exfiltration, consisting of his No. 2 Stick, Sgt Wright's No. 1 Stick, and three foreign partisans. They left on 15 February, after a delay of four days owing to a move back to the Rossano Valley to support Maj. Lett, who wrote later that he was facing what he described as a 'political crisis resulting from the departure of the main SAS body'—that is, the threat of encroachment by rival partisan bands, which did not then materialise. The second SAS party crossed the lines without incident on 20 February. The mission was judged 'remarkably successful' by Maj. Roy Farran, commander of 3 Squadron in Italy.

In the Serchio Valley, the British Army's 8th Indian Division replaced the American 92nd Infantry Division, and the Ghurkhas soon expelled the Germans and Italians from Barga. The German Commander-in-Chief, Field Marshal Albert Kesselring, pulled the Italian divisions out of the line and thereafter deployed them in anti-partisan activity, where they were often more feared by their countrymen than the Germans engaged in similar operations.

As the Allied offensive was about to be resumed, Maj. Lett and Lt Leng were ordered to cross the lines to Florence for discussions to ensure that the partisan effort dovetailed with that of the Army. After the arrival of Special Force replacements, Maj. John Henderson and Capt. Frederick Williams, the officers left the valley on 13 March, together with a small number of companions, including Parachutist Gordon 'Lofty' Rose. Nine days later, they reached American forces in Barga. Following debriefings at Special Force TAC HQ in Florence, both officers were sent back into action.

Lt Leng witnessed the liberation of Turin by the Fifth Army and was mentioned in dispatches. Maj. Lett led the first of small Special Force forward parties chosen to liaise between the advancing Fifth Army and the partisans. He returned to the 4th Partisan Zone and late on 20 April was the first Allied officer to enter La Spezia, which was being held by a small force of partisans after the withdrawal of the enemy. He was accompanied by his driver, Harry Lewis, and Elio, a partisan commander. A patrol of American tanks arrived in the early hours of the morning, with the rest of the 92nd Infantry Division following next day; Col. Fontana and the main partisan force arrived on the 23rd, and the victory was complete.

Maj. Lett was attached to the Army HQ as Liaison Officer for Partisan Affairs and then became Allied Military Governor of Pontremoli. On 2 July 1945, he was granted the Freedom of the City. The major was also awarded the DSO for his services behind the lines, and the Italian Silver Medal for Military Valour. He remained in Italy until 1950, on attachment to the British Consulate in Bologna, and always maintained the links with the people of the Rossano Valley created in the dark days of war.

On 1 March 1945, Lt James Arthur Riccomini and his Australian former companion in enemy territory, Lt Harold Andrew Peterson, were appointed Members of the Military Division of the Most Excellent Order of the British Empire (MBE) for gallantry and distinguished service in the field. After citing their escape from the prison train on its way to the Italian border, the recommendation noted that the two officers remained with the partisans until January 1944 'helping to organise resistance, getting together dumps of ammunition, and obtaining intelligence reports'. In addition, on 5 July 1945, the award of a MC was gazetted to Lt Riccomini for 'gallant and distinguished services in Italy' during Operation Galia. Sadly, though, the honour was a posthumous one, as the lieutenant was killed in action at the end of March of the same year during Operation Tombola, as we shall see.

Sgt Leonard Wright (then living in Sheffield) was awarded the MM on 5 July 1945 for his part in the 11 January operation against the enemy convoy in Borghetto di Vara, being commended for accounting personally for at least three of the Germans killed or wounded and for his 'complete disregard for his own safety in the face of accurate enemy fire [when] he calmly stayed in position directing the fire of a machine gun'.

On 21 June 1945, Robert Walker Brown was awarded the DSO in recognition of gallant and distinguished services in Italy. He was then living in the little Welsh village of Llangurig, in Montgomeryshire (now Powys), in the upper Severn Valley. Walker Brown returned to the Highland Light Infantry in 1946, served with 21 SAS as a training major, with 22 SAS in Malaya in the 1950s, becoming second in command, and with 23 SAS as Commanding officer from 1960–1963, with the rank of lieutenant-colonel. He served briefly on the Defence Intelligence Staff of the Ministry of Defence before finally retiring from the Army in 1964 and settling in Wiltshire, where he enjoyed country pursuits.

In the last weeks of the Second World War, there was a strange postscript to the Galia Operation: the arrival of another party of SAS parachutists in the same area, with the same tasks. Codenamed Blimey, it was the service's final operation of the war in Italy and is generally judged to have achieved very little. Twenty-four men dropped safely to Rossano on 6 April, including a handful of veterans of the earlier mission. The troop was divided into three sticks, one led by CO Capt. Alan Scott, Royal Artillery, another by Lt John Wilmers, and the third by 'a very young and able officer', Lt Pepper. The operation is poorly documented in official files, and little is known about two of the officers, but John Wilmers was born in Munich to a German father and a Swiss mother and his real name is believed to have been Wilmersdorfer; he moved to the UK as a refugee and eventually served with 10 Commando as a corporal; his ability led to him being commissioned and given a leadership role in Operation Blimey, and after the war, he was a successful barrister and judge.

The troop carried out a few small-scale missions (with varying results) in the middle of the month, but on 20 April, Walker Brown was ordered by 15th Army Group to jump in and take command, owing to what he described as Capt. Scott's 'conspicuous lack of success ... in ideal operating conditions'. However, the need did not arise, as on 25 April, the troop was overrun by the advancing US 92nd Infantry Division and withdrawn to Florence. The end of the war came a few days later.

20

Operation Tombola

Towards the end of February 1945, Maj. Roy Farran decided to lead the next SAS operation regardless of clear orders from home to remain in command in Florence and the objections that would be raised by Col. John Riepe, the American in charge of Special Operations at 15th Army Group. The major recalled: 'If I could not go officially, I would have to fake an accidental fall from an aircraft, making sure, of course, that I had a parachute'. Capt. Walker Brown would take his place in liaising with Special Force and the Army Group.

As the time for the spring offensive approached, there were discussions at the highest military levels on how best to direct the partisan formations in front of the Fifth Army. It was decided that, as well as calling for all-out guerrilla warfare to coincide with the Army attack, they would try and create chaos in the German communication system by hitting enemy headquarters, telephone lines, and wireless stations, as well as roads, railways, and bridges. The Army insisted that the plans had to be prepared by Special Force's TAC HQ in Florence, and that the missions would only be informed much nearer the time. The commander Maj. Charles Macintosh recalled: 'This led to the only difficulty we were to experience with the SAS in all their Italian operations'.

Before agreeing on an operational area for the SAS, Macintosh and Farran asked three Special Force British Liaison Officers in Emilia for their reaction to receiving a regular British parachute force in their provinces. Macintosh recalled that he was mindful of the go-slow instructions still in force and the need to avoid an enemy response. Charles Holland (Parma) and Jim Davies (Modena) were guarded in their replies, fearing that the arrival of the SAS would provoke enemy reaction, but Mike Lees (Reggio) had no such reservations. 'Send as many as you can,' he signalled. Farran recalled: 'I heard that Lees had a wild reputation, but I felt from the tone of his message that if his deeds were as good as his words he was certainly the man for me. I later learned to admire him as the best partisan liaison officer in the whole of Italy'.

The parachute captain had dropped to the mountains at the head of the Secchia Valley on 2 January 1945 to relieve Maj. Vivian Johnston as commander of the Special Force Envelope Mission. Lees, aged twenty-three, was tall, burly, and outgoing. He had already worked with partisans in Yugoslavia and Piedmont, where his actions had led to him being labelled 'a wild man' by colleagues at headquarters. The captain brought with him his radio operator from his 'Flap' Mission to northern Italy, Bert Farrimond, a Lancashire miner in civilian life. Their tasks were to liaise with the Reggio partisans, organise sabotage, provide intelligence, and prepare for the coming spring offensive.

In retrospect, Mike Lees and the Italians laid the foundations for Operation Tombola since it was Farran's objective 'to use the partisan valley as a base from which to build an offensive force that would aim at German supply lines behind the main front, the last enemy defensive line before the open plains of the Po Valley'. Within days of Lees' arrival, the Germans launched a drive, and the agents and the partisan headquarters' staff were forced to seek refuge on the border with the province of Parma, only returning at the end of January. Lees was pleased that the attack had come so soon, as the enemy had deployed a full division and it was unlikely that they would be able to spare this number of troops a second time. He felt sure that the partisans could count on at least a month or two in which to gather their strength for the spring. It would have been difficult to revamp the old organisation, but now that the enemy had obliged by destroying it for them, they would be able to start afresh with ample raw material and reserves.

Capt. Lees set about organising a sabotage squad and a private intelligence service. He asked a twenty-one-year-old *Alpini* lieutenant in the intelligence section of the partisan provincial HQ (*Comando Unico*), Glauco Monducci (Gordon), to find the best forty men in the brigades to form a sabotage squad. The men were issued with camouflaged uniforms, automatic weapons and red berets and sent back to the brigades to lead teams for special operations. 'Gordon' chose the name of *Gufo Nero* (Black Owl) for his elite squad, reasoning that the nocturnal predator was the perfect symbol for the partisan, who also had to live and survive in the mountains. Lees located his headquarters in the village of Secchio, little more than a huddle of houses perched on the side of the valley, where the local priest, Don Pietro Rivi, had placed his house at Special Force's disposal. The *Gufo Nero* sabotage squad was based in school buildings next to the church and the rectory.

A partisan known as Kiss was appointed to lead the intelligence service. Giulio Davoli, in his mid-twenties, had escaped from the Germans twice.

He recruited a team of twenty-five young women to act as couriers. They carried orders, brought messages from a network of agents, and cycled into towns and villages to obtain information on the enemy's strength and dispositions. Lees recalled that the mass of intelligence was so plentiful that he was often up until dawn, checking the facts and preparing messages for Farrimond to dispatch in the morning. On 6 February, the partisan commander, Augusto Berti (Colonel Monti), entrusted the quartermaster at his headquarters, Maj. Annibale Alpi (Barbanera), with forming a new fighting detachment, which would be independent of the existing three *Garibaldi* and one Green Flame brigades. The thirty-three-year-old officer, from Parma, had served as an airman in the Royal Italian Airforce. To emphasise its apolitical nature, the new detachment was called the Military Formation.

By the middle of February, the division was on an active footing from its base in the village of Febbio, and Lees convened a conference of partisan commanders. He promised them arms, food, and clothing. Defensive positions would be dug, and in case of attack, they would retreat into the area and not flee or go underground. Partisans would be responsible to the *Comando Unico* as regards administrative matters, but for operational questions, sabotage, and tactical command, they would answer to him personally, and all intelligence would come direct to the mission. Political disturbances would not be tolerated, and all the brigades would be treated equally as purely military formations. Finally, material from supply drops would be stored centrally and distributed fairly. The partisan leaders were in total agreement.

Now that the operational area for the SAS mission had been chosen, it was clear to Macintosh that Farran would disobey his instructions and go with the squadron. The SOE commander could not quarrel with his friend, as he too was planning to leave his desk job as soon as he could, recalling: 'My main preoccupation was that once in the field he would outrank Lees, who was the most impatient and headstrong of the British Liaison Officers. Together they could be a bloody menace—I consoled myself with the thought that it was the Hun who should be worried'.

The squadron had arrived from Britain under strength, so Farran had permission to recruit a few officers and men from the infantry depot in Florence. After interviewing hundreds of volunteers, he chose two officers and ten men on a trial basis. Lieutenants Tysoe and Eyton-Jones would make their first parachute jump on the operation. The major chose Capt. Jock Easton as his second in command, describing him as a tough old Scot with a heart of gold, who had spent two years in an Italian POW camp and spoke with a broad Falkirk accent. Lt Riccomini, who had been Easton's companion on his escape from the Italian camp and had just completed

Operation Galia, was brought back for his ability to speak Italian, which he had learned during his months on the run behind enemy lines.

Three sergeants were selected: Reginald Godwin and Frank 'Taffy' Hughes, who were veteran SAS soldiers, and Sidney Guscott, who was still with his wireless set in the La Spezia area and was ordered to march across the mountains to join the group. He had been sent as head of a four-man mission codenamed Brake Two to find out what had happened to the SAS men engaged in Operation Galia when they lost contact with headquarters. Farran noted that the men in the troop were a good cross section of the whole regiment. They included three Spaniards, Rafael Ramos, who had accompanied Sgt Guscott to Rossano; Justo Balerdi (Robert Bruce) and Francisco Geronimo (Frank Williams); an Austrian Jew, known as Lt Stephens, who acted as interpreter; and a partisan who Farran described as 'the old sailor with a lion's heart called Louis' ('Pippo' Siboldi, from the Galia Mission), brought through the lines by Walker Brown. The major recalled: 'It was an odd collection of toughs. I loved every one of their cracked, leathery faces. There was not a single passenger in the whole crew and they marched with the same cocky roll to the end of the operation'.

Farran went down to their new billet at Cecina, near Leghorn, in Tuscany, to check on the administrative organisation for the first drop. Officially, an advance party of Capt. Jock Easton and five men would jump on 4 March, having been dispatched from the plane by Farran. In fact, he intended to go ahead of Easton, and his kit would be pushed out on a separate parachute by a dispatcher. The air crew were briefed to say that the major had accidentally fallen from the plane while attending to his duties; they told the tale so convincingly that he was reported as killed until his first wireless messages were received at base.

Roy Farran led the six men out of a Dakota over the Secchia Valley on 4 March in his eighteenth parachute drop. The Reggio partisans would come to know him only as Maj. Patrick McGinty. He recalled: 'For approximately the same reasons that the partisans did not carry their own names, any member of the Special Air Service who had been a prisoner of war carried false identity papers'.

Other Dakotas delivered supplies, while Thunderbolts acted as escorts. A circle of coloured parachutes was laid out in the snow as a ground signal on the small drop zone, codenamed Swell Crimson, which was situated on a steep slope above the hamlet of Case Balocchi in the Asta Valley. However, there was a strong wind and the parachutists were pushed down the valley. Farran hit the snow with tremendous force and rolled down the hill twice. While he was still on his back, trying to collapse his parachute, a youth in battledress ran towards him: '*Buongiorno*. I am Bruno,' he said, slinging the major's heavy kitbag over his shoulder and beginning to walk away.

The youngster was seventeen-year-old Bruno Gimpel, who was born in London. When Italy declared war on the UK in June 1940, his father, a banker, and his eldest brother were interned, while he and his second brother were sent to Italy with their mother. After completing his education, Bruno became a partisan courier in the winter of 1944, and he went on to assist Lees' mission; his brother, Franco, also joined the partisans. Bruno Gimpel recalled: 'My functions were to act as interpreter, as coding officer, and as a general dog's body'. He later described Farran as: 'A typical Irish soldier of fortune, multi-decorated, and a dare-devil'.

Farran and Bruno climbed up the hill to join several Italians on an icy track. The major dumped his kit and took off his smock. A tall Italian with a long, grey beard and an *Alpini* hat seemed to be in charge. He was known as Scalabrino, real name Ettore Scalabrini. Farran recalled: 'His green jacket, battledress trousers, white socks and long Italian carbine gave him a quaint Robinson Crusoe air, but at least he looked more of a soldier than the motley collection of long-haired youths around him'. The major asked Scalabrino to collect the containers in a central point, and he organised teams with mules and oxen to haul them to the village of Case Balocchi, which was about a quarter of a mile down the track. The Dakotas circled for the last time and the escort of Thunderbolts did a victory roll over the valley.

The other soldiers were safe, though most had fallen into the village streets. Parachutist Russell Kershaw, making his first drop, had slid down a roof into the arms of a buxom Italian woman, breaking his fall and probably saving his life. Capt. Easton was not so lucky: he had dislocated his shoulder and was in great pain.

A familiar figure, dressed in an American shirt and battledress, came up the track. Farran had met Lt Ian Smith, Lees' Scottish second in command, two months earlier in Florence. The lieutenant was excited by the arrival of British soldiers and the abundant supply drop. He told Farran that his main responsibility was to organise the reception of the cargoes and their distribution to the partisans. In addition, he had to ensure that the power station at Ligonchio, six hours' march away in the next valley, to the west, was not put out of action.

Easton came staggering up the track and fainted in the snow. His companions brought him round and found him a comfortable bed in the village. Bruno was sent to summon a doctor, who lived 12 miles away in Febbio. The rest of the SAS soldiers had a meal of fried eggs, chestnut bread, and red wine in the village café.

Mike Lees arrived on a large, brown mare. Farran recalled: 'He was a huge man, with excited, urgent eyes, who pumped my hand until I began to think my parachuting days were over. In all the time I knew him, he was never one to waste a minute'. For his part, Lees related: 'I enthusiastically welcomed the offer of SAS help by Roy Farran and subsequently I was absolutely delighted (perhaps even a little relieved) when he made a surprise personal appearance on stage and offered to take command'.

Farran recalled that Capt. Lees told him, 'I've lots of targets for you.' Chief among them was the HQ of the German Army in the hamlet of Botteghe in the Commune of Albinea, on the edge of the Reggio plain. In his official report, the major wrote: 'He had collected extremely accurate information on the dispositions of the enemy in this zone, information which convinced me of the possibility of carrying out an attack of this sort'. The HQ of the 51st Mountain Corps, the same unit that had executed men of the Speedwell Operation, was housed in two period dwellings taken over by the Germans, known as the Villa Rossi and the Villa Calvi. Through his intelligence service, Lees learned that they also acted as the forward headquarters of the German 14th Army. Austrian Gen. Valentin Feurstein, the sixty-year-old commander of the 51st Mountain Corps, lived there, and a week earlier, he had been visited by Marshal Rodolfo Graziani, the Fascist Defence Minister and commandant of the Army of Liguria.

Lees decided to assassinate the general, a devout Catholic, on his way to church and then to attack the Corps HQ. He carried out a personal reconnaissance from a farmhouse, which stood on a small hill overlooking the plain. Botteghe was in the foreground, consisting of a few cottages bunched around a crossroads, and the two large villas 300 yards farther on. Lees drew a careful map of the area and returned to Secchio. On 3 March, a German who had fallen into partisan hands revealed that he was the telephonist in Gen. Feurstein's private exchange, and he freely gave details of the internal layout of the buildings and the number and location of the guards. The HQ was designated 451 and controlled all the divisions from Bologna to the west coast. Lees recalled: 'Villa Rossi was more than a mere Corps HQ. Effectively it was Army Tactical Headquarters, and Villa Calvi contained the main communications centre and direct telephone and teleprinter link with the *Reich* for all German Forces on that front'. The captive related that Gen. Feurstein had been there when he was captured, but that he was leaving to be replaced by Gen. Friedrich Wilhelm Hauck. He was younger at forty-eight and a holder of the Iron Cross. Lees recalled ruefully that the new commander was apparently not as devout as his predecessor and did not go to church on the route chosen for his assassination.

After greeting Farran and his men on the drop zone at Case Balocchi, Lees left his horse and took the group on a three-hour climb to a village near enough to be visible on the hillside, but separated from them by tracks covered in thick ice. Farran recalled: 'We trudged off towards Secchio, my clumsy feet slipping and stumbling over the boulders, as I tried to keep up with the long stride of this dynamic, mountainous man'. Lees had arranged for the head of the Reggio Provincial Partisan Military Committee, Augusto Berti (Colonel Monti), to come to meet them. That evening, Farran, Lees and 'Monti' sat around a table in the priest's house at Secchio—drinking grappa and smoking German cigars—to discuss the 'startling proposal' that a new partisan formation with a nucleus of British parachutists should be formed under Farran's command, the *Battaglione Alleato*. The major was impressed by the commander, recalling: 'He looked like a soldier.... A clipped, black moustache, a fine upright carriage, a thin, handsome face, tightly drawn over his cheek bones, and a slick, dapper appearance, gave him the sort of look one associates with a Guards Sergeant-Major in civilian clothes'.

It was agreed that the battalion would consist of a British company, an Italian company, and a Russian company. It would also absorb the new Military Formation of Annibale Alpi (Barbanera), as well as twenty men from two *Garibaldi* brigades, ostensibly to receive training in the use of heavy machine guns, but really to maintain the political balance, which proved to be a sound move. Farran promised lavish supplies for the partisans, which were actually delivered.

Lees explained that the Battalion would not accept responsibility for any particular zone in the valley and would receive orders directly from Florence. The unit would only come under 'Monti' for administration, although the men would cooperate to the best of their ability if the valley were attacked. These proposals were difficult for the Colonel to accept, but he finally agreed, provided that other partisans were told that the Battalion was under the control of the Reggio *Comando Unico*.

Farran recalled that it was a departure from the traditional SAS technique of pin-prick raids with small parties, but the war was coming to a close and the last battle was imminent: 'Given time to equip and train the new men, I would have at my disposal 300 of all ranks—a respectable infantry force to use against German supply lines when the time was ripe'. He added that heavy weapons and large forces were used in the operation more than ever before: 'It can be regarded as the culmination of SAS experience in the last war. The beginnings were cautious until, in this last operation, the power of the gun was realised'.

Having sealed the deal over another bottle of grappa, the two Britons steered the colonel to his big, brown mare and waved him off down the track on the long ride back to his headquarters in Febbio.

The next day, by chance, Victor Pirogov (Modena) called on the headquarters at Secchio to plead with Lees for more arms for his men.

Described by Farran as 'A big, blonde Russian from Smolensk, with a charming smile on his face and a very captivating swashbuckler's air', the guerrilla leader was delighted to be appointed commander of the Russian Company. He said that he would immediately increase its size to 100 men by recruiting his countrymen scattered among other partisan formations. The Russian headquarters was higher up the valley in the village of Governara, near the drop zone at Case Balocchi.

In the afternoon, Annibale Alpi (Barbanera) called from Quara. He too impressed Farran—owing to his smart appearance and experience in partisan administration—and was appointed vice-commandant of the new battalion. The Italian was told to raise an Intendancy staff of fifteen men, which would be responsible for rationing and equipping the companies. 'Partisans did not receive any pay,' Farran noted.

The major then visited the SAS detachment in their billet at the deserted church at Tapignola. Capt. Easton had recovered a little from his injury sustained when landing and he had been appointed commander of the British company. The major found that he had commandeered a horse for him from an unwilling war widow. Easton also introduced members of his squad of runners, known as Arrows, who were recruited from the fittest members of the Italian company. They carried messages and acted as orderlies for Farran and the company commanders. The men wore battledress jackets with the design of an arrow and the word 'McGinty' embroidered in black on their pockets. The runners were sent to Florence about once a week and they only suffered two casualties during the period of the operation.

On 6 March, Farran rode down to Quara with Lees to address the Italian company, but he was badly shocked by what he found. About 100 men had formed up in two ragged lines across the square outside the local hotel. This is how he described them:

> It looked like a tableau of Wat Tyler's rebellion. The men were all young, but nearly all of them had some physical defect. Many had only one eye. Some had one shoulder higher than the other, and they all looked as though they were in the grips of some terrible disease.
>
> It appeared that Mike Lees' forebodings were correct. They were the worst partisans in the valley and had only arrived recently from the plains to avoid conscription for labour by the *Todt* Organisation. They were dressed in all sorts of bits of uniform. About half were armed with rusty old rifles, which I should have hated to have had to fire. The others had nothing. Some had not even shoes on their feet.[1]

Farran's stirring talk was greeted with a hesitant cheer. Over lunch with the officers and the newly-appointed commander, Remo Torlai (Tito),

Farran learned that they were prepared to go ahead with the plan, but were apprehensive about the future. In particular, he wrote, 'there was the suspicion that they were to be a shock force to carry out actual operations, instead of sitting in military splendour in the mountains like the majority of the partisans'. After the war, Annibale Alpi wrote a letter to Farran bitterly contesting his description of the scene in the 1948 book, *Winged Dagger*. However, in *Operation Tombola* (1960), Farran wrote: 'At least it was an accurate description of my impressions at the time'.

In fact, what Farran saw as the sorry appearance of the Italian company did not worry him unduly, as he planned to attach British officers and weapon instructors to the unit, who would become its leaders in practice if not in theory. He felt that with a little support, the company would serve its purpose: 'The young officers looked good and, though undoubtedly disappointed that my ceiling of a hundred men on their numbers precluded former ambitions to build right-wing partisan strength to the level of the *Garibaldini*, they knew better weapons would be some compensation'. The company wore green and yellow feathers in their hats and an embroidered badge on their pockets with the SAS motto, 'Who Dares Wins'. The Italian and the Russian companies both consisted of about 100 men, each one equipped with battledress, a khaki beret, good boots, and a weapon of some description.

The period from 7 to 24 March was spent in training and equipping the new battalion and in preparing defences against surprise attack. During this time, thirty-four more parachutists and plentiful supplies were dropped to the 'Swell Crimson' drop zone at Case Balocchi. Farran's first request was for personnel to help train the Italian and the Russian companies. The party landed safely at night on 7 March; it comprised three officers, an instructor and 'Pippo' Siboldi as interpreter, though in his first parachute drop he suffered the same fate as Capt. Easton and dislocated his collar-bone. Farran even asked for a piper, as he said, 'to stir the Italian mind and to gratify my own vanity'. Within three days, Company Piper David Kirkpatrick of the Highland Light Infantry dropped by day, kilt and all, with his pipes under his arm. He was from Girvan, a fishing town on the south Ayrshire coast, and it was his first parachute jump at the age of nineteen.

The major had conjured up the largest airdrop ever seen in the valley within three days of his arrival, and he noted that it engendered immediate confidence among the Italians and the Russians and ensured the success of the mission. On 9 March, twenty-three officers and men landed by day on the same zone. One officer and four British 'other ranks' were attached to each of the two local companies. The following day, Cpl Cunningham, who had already served with Farran in France, was dropped to share the duties of radio operator with Parachutist Green, and they were billeted with an Italian family.

In view of the difference British personnel had made to morale, the major decided to send out partisan detachments with heavy weapons under the command of British 'other ranks' as a first line of defence. These outposts were located at Gatta (on the River Secchia, the northern boundary of the area); at Civago, in the south; at Quara, in the east; and at Ligonchio, to the west, in the next valley. Civilian labour was also conscripted to build earthworks on the hills round the basin at the southern end of the valley. These main defensive positions were garrisoned by the various companies. The Russians were on Monte Penna, the Italians on Monte Torricella, and the British on Monte Cisa. Uniquely, this detachment fielded a 75-mm pack howitzer, which Walker-Brown had arranged to be dropped in pieces by parachute, together with shells in wicker baskets. The gun was nicknamed '*Molto Stanco*'—'Very Tired'—not to symbolise its work rate, but the labour required to haul it to the top of the Cisa Pass. Enough food for seven days was buried for all the defensive positions, with a similar amount hidden in thick snow behind Monte Cusna, which would be the final fall-back position if all the others collapsed.

In fact, the Germans only made one incursion during this period. They moved south across the River Secchia and attacked the Green Flame Brigade near Quara, but retreated after coming under fire from the heavy Browning machine gun manned by outpost commander Parachutist Wooding, leading ten of the Italian company. This first brush with the enemy hardened the resolve to attack whatever the situation.

Maj. Macintosh recalled that in mid-March he had a signal from Mike Lees to say that he and Farran had decided to attack the German 51st Corps HQ at Albinea, adding: 'The plan fitted well with the general scheme to destroy communications and, executed at the right moment, was what we were looking for'. Aerial photographs were dropped, the last on 18 March. Around two days later, the British mission received clearance to proceed with the attack, which was scheduled for the night of 26–27 March.

As regards the Allied Battalion, Farran decided that only the Russian and British companies could be relied upon because the Italian company was not sufficiently prepared. So Lees arranged that the group destined for the attack was reinforced with twenty *Garibaldini*, and with twenty of the *Gufo Nero* sabotage squad.

Farran recalled that the plan was simple enough. They would collect their force of around a hundred men—twenty-four British, thirty Russians, and forty Italians—at the extreme edge of partisan-controlled territory. The Communist contingent would be drawn from the 26th *Garibaldi*

Brigade, led by a young airman, Giovanni 'Gianni' Farri, who replaced its commandant, 'Luigi', owing to his ill health, and from the 145th Brigade, commanded by Nello Mattioli (Antonio).

On the night of 25 March, the men would infiltrate the German positions between Baiso and Carpineti and march to Casa del Lupo (the name of a hamlet, though the action centred on one farmhouse), located on the northern edge of the mountains overlooking the Po Valley. The force would stop during the day, while sending female couriers (*staffette)* to check on the German deployment. The men would approach the HQ during the night of 26 March, marching in three close columns.

During the attack, a group of ten SAS soldiers would force entry and be reinforced by twenty Italians at each of the villas. Meanwhile, the Russians would form a protective belt (from west to east) along the crossroads to the south of the Villa Rossi, in order to isolate the targets from any potential help from Botteghe, or from Puianello, where two anti-aircraft batteries were sited. Farran added: 'My orders were purely for destruction. No prisoners were to be taken because they would only hamper withdrawal. And the main object was to kill the German officers and to set fire to their headquarters'.

21

Attack on the Corps HQ

On the balmy weekend of 24–25 March 1945, the men of the Allied battalion created as part of Operation Tombola set out on the approach march for their attack on the German 51st Mountain Corps HQ at Botteghe, near Albinea, Reggio Emilia. The winding column of almost a hundred fighters crossed the River Secchia by the Cavola footbridge and climbed the heights beyond to Valestra. At this point, they found that the Germans had begun a drive in the area. They had advanced from the Po Valley towards the River Secchia, and their troops were clearly visible in the village of Baiso, only 5 miles to the north.

The enemy moves did not deter the attack on the headquarters. Both Farran and Lees were convinced that if they did not go ahead, having got so far, they never would. Security in the valley was so bad that rumours of an impending raid would soon reach German ears, and they would never have the same opportunity again. In addition, what would the Communists think if the much lauded *Battaglione Alleato* was so easily discouraged on its first operation? Farran decided that if the Germans did not attack them before the next night, they would march; he was superbly confident, saying that if he could not infiltrate a hundred men through a widely dispersed battalion at night, it was time he took a staff appointment.

Billets were found for the men in the partisan village of Valestra, more than half way on the approach march, and pickets were placed at good points for observation. The Russians marched in from Governara at dusk, and their exhausted condition finally dispelled any vague intention Farran might have had of carrying on that night. In the morning, the partisans told him they wanted to join local Green Flames in defending the valley against the German drive, rather than continuing with the raid. Farran dissuaded them and explained the plan of attack over the aerial photographs received from Florence. Every sentence was translated first into Italian and then into Russian.

As the men relaxed on the grass after the talk, a male runner arrived from Smith and Farrimond, who were manning the wireless set at Secchio, with a curt signal from 15th Army Group ordering Farran not to attack. The moment, they said, was inopportune. The major reacted instinctively: 'We would march at dusk on the morrow. Did those pen-pushing map-boys in Florence understand that if I did not attack now I would never attack at all? Did they understand that my prestige with the partisans would be nil?'

Bob Walker Brown recalled the events that led to the order. Gen. Mark Clark gave him the date of the Fifth Army offensive and said that it was most important that the planned attack should be delayed, so that the two events could be coordinated. Walker Brown told him that 'partisan morale, having been wound up to a pitch, could only be unwound at substantial risk to the success of the operation and its security'. This argument was not accepted by the general. Walker Brown found himself in a difficult position, but related that he sent a carefully worded signal to Farran with ample scope to read between the lines. He urged him if possible to postpone operations; as subsequent events proved, this was not possible.

Charles Macintosh related that Colonel Riepe at 15th Army Group shared Gen. Clark's concerns. It was thought that an isolated attack on a corps HQ would alert the Germans to the security needs of all the others near partisan areas, and might at the worst give them some idea of Allied plans. Messages were immediately sent to the field. Macintosh, while giving 'full approval of the plan', emphasised the necessity of delay to Lees. To maintain security, it was not possible for him to give the full reasons for the postponement or any indication of a future date for the operation; he could only make reference to 'important general considerations'. However, Macintosh recalled that both Lees and Farran were 'more than confident'. A message came back to the effect that the operation was already under way and could not be postponed. Macintosh replied immediately, again ordering a postponement. Bert Farrimond at Secchio answered that the message could not be delivered as 'the party had started down towards the foothills'. Lees later denied that a message had been received prior to their departure for the attack. He suspected that the decision to postpone the action was not taken until it was too late to stop them. What they did receive from Florence were warnings of roundups reported by neighbouring missions; they took little notice of these, as their dispositions, reinforced by the SAS, were such that that they could have held anything that the enemy were likely to be able to throw at them.

Following Farran's decision to proceed with the raid, the battalion sheltered behind the ox sheds of Valestra for most of 25 March. They left at 7 p.m. and moved to Montevrolo by making three trips on a captured

German diesel truck; the driver was a deserter from the German Army, a blonde Austrian parachute second-lieutenant called Hans Amoser, who specialised in holding up his former companions in vehicles on the highway. The attackers then proceeded on foot along the road in the direction of Viano. As they came to isolated farms and hamlets, the leading files would lie flat and everybody behind would follow suit. Two British scouts would then creep forward with an Italian guide, and once they saw that the coast was clear, they would whistle the others on. The raiders passed the flank of the German troops at Ca' de Pazzi, near Monte Duro, and marched across the countryside in the direction of Casa del Lupo.

The raiders reached the hamlet and the hill-top farm at 6 a.m. on 26 March. Here, they were reinforced by the arrival of Lt Kenneth Gordon Harvey and ten of his men. The 6-foot-tall, twenty-year-old officer was born on 7 December 1924 and came from Bulawayo in the British colony of Southern Rhodesia. He had served with the King's Royal Rifle Corps and the Seaforth Highlanders before moving to the SAS in 1944. Harvey joined the squadron on 18 February in Cecina after being interviewed by Roy Farran; six days later, he began four day's training at the nearby parachute school.

The lieutenant had landed at Case Balocchi with the main party on 9 March. His detachment was on guard duty near the Cisa Pass when he received orders to link up with Maj. Farran with all speed. He recalled that their journey took them over extremely rugged country, up mountains of considerable height and across rivers, the largest of which was the Secchia, which was quite flooded from the thawing snows: 'The fact that not one man had failed to make the journey spoke well for the general standard of physical fitness'.

The troops and the civilians were kept indoors on the farm all day, while two sentries manned Bren guns in the upper windows. Fortunately, a dense fog prevented anything from being seen by Germans based at Regnano. At midday, two women couriers were sent to visit Albinea and Botteghe; they returned in the evening, confirming that everything seemed normal. It was estimated that a total of about 500 enemy soldiers were in the area.

At the farm, Farran became very worried about Lees, who had suddenly developed malaria. The captain himself wrote later: 'Had there been a delay I would personally have been relieved because I was ill at the time and in bad shape to march and fight'.

An Italian from the farm volunteered to guide the force to the road, and at 11 p.m., they moved off in the following parties: Group Command: two British, one Italian guide, one Italian intelligence officer; Column One: thirty Russians; Column Two: ten British and twenty Italians; Column Three: ten British and twenty Italians; Total: ninety-four men. It was dark and misty as they descended the foothills on to the plain, but the going was much easier now and they made good time. There was no contact with the Germans, and the battalion reached the target zone at 2 a.m. without being seen.

After crossing a large field, the raiders suddenly came upon the Villa Calvi, the Chief of Staff's residence and operations room. Bathed in bright moonlight, it was a large, white mansion, perched on a small hill and surrounded by trees. No lights were showing and Farran began to wonder if the Germans were really there. Villa Rossi, the home of the corps commander, was situated on the other side of the north-south road. Each of the villas was guarded by four sentries, with six machine gun positions sited tactically around the camp. Various other buildings were located between the villas and the foothills to the south: namely, a telephone exchange, billets for the troops, a guardroom, and a prison.

The battalion moved on to the dispersal point, which was located behind a clump of trees (nicknamed 'Half-Moon Wood' by the troops) near Villa Calvi. The column, led by Lt Riccomini—which included Lees, 'Gordon' (Glauco Monducci), and his *Gufo Nero* squad—was sent towards Villa Rossi three minutes ahead of the others, as they had to cover a slightly longer distance. The Russians went to take up their positions, and finally the column of SAS parachutists and *Garibaldi* partisans left for the Villa Calvi, led by Lt Harvey. Farran established his Column HQ in a slit trench on the road between the two villas, accompanied by Piper Kirkpatrick, Parachutist Morbin, and partisan Giulio Davoli (Kiss). 'Unfortunately,' Farran recalled, 'I had not left the column making for Villa Rossi enough time, so the firing began at the Villa Calvi before the other column reached its objective.'

Kenneth Harvey related his experiences of that night at Villa Calvi to the Bologna conference on 'No. 1 Special Force and the Italian Resistance' in 1987 (he was then a retired colonel in the Rhodesian Army):

> We arrived on the large expense of lawn in front of the villa. I had dropped off my Bren gunners with orders to shoot anyone who appeared at any of the windows or came out of any of the doors, except the front door, which I arranged we would use.
>
> I set up the bazooka in front of the door, having tried it and finding it securely bolted, we made the necessary contact. No result—damn, now bad luck was with us. Again I tried, with no result. We gathered around to try to determine the cause of the failure. Then I heard the unmistakable crunching of boots on the gravel road between the two villas and then the deep guttural voices. Germans! Well, we must not be caught red-handed. From behind the masonry pier, I could see the

sentries now, only a few feet away—four of them, marching up the road. I stepped into the road and shot them. It was essential that this was all done at point blank range to ensure that they were killed immediately, for these shots would set the whole area off and we would have to act quickly to attain our desired results. And above all, I could not afford to have wounded Germans in the road while I engaged myself in getting into the house.

The men reacted immediately. As soon as the shots rang out they rushed the door and when I arrived I gave a burst of fire at the lock and shot our way in. The Germans were shooting at us from the windows, but our Bren gunners were doing a good job and taking a heavy toll of them, resulting in the easing of our job. One of my men was wounded in the leg. I gave the lock a final burst, pushed in the door, threw in a few hand grenades and ran into the dark interior. There were scuffling noises and bullets started to fly. The din was deafening in the enclosed space. I had to see the lie of the land, so holding my torch at arm's length so as not to attract fire to myself, I switched it on and had a quick look around. The firing increased. They could see me, so I dived under the table, torch still on. My sergeant [Reginald Godwin] opened up as I went to ground and killed the chief offender.[1]

From his headquarters on the road, Farran told Kirkpatrick to strike up 'Highland Laddie', just to let the Germans know that they had the British to contend with. The piper had only played a few bars when the phut-phut of a Spandau picked them out. Farran pushed him into a slit trench and he continued to play from his cramped position.

Meanwhile, at Villa Calvi, Ken Harvey recalled:

We rushed the staircase, but the Germans were firing over the balustrade from above, and it would have been impossible to get past the hail of bullets, we just did not have enough men for that sort of thing. As if to finalise this, someone rolled a hand grenade down the stairs and it went off between the three of us, one man being quite badly wounded. I had him taken outside and put with the other wounded man. However, on the ground floor things had gone well and we had taken it completely. Later we heard that one of those killed in the furious fighting in the room was Colonel Lemelson, the Chief of Staff. No enemy remained alive on this floor, and outside our Bren gunners were continuing their good work, and many Germans were killed when they tried to shoot from the windows or run out of the back doors.

We started a fire on the ground floor and helped it to get a good start with some explosives that we had brought. We added some furniture to

> keep it going and made our exit. Despite our accurate and determined Bren gun fire, grenades from above were being thrown on to the lawn and we had to run the gauntlet. Germans were now on the road where I had killed the sentries and were firing towards the house. Our exit, fully silhouetted against the fire, was not easy, and how we managed to get out without further casualties I do not know.[2]

The document and map rooms were set on fire and most of the contents destroyed. While the battalion was retreating, Villa Calvi was burning furiously and finally exploded. At least twenty Germans were killed inside the house and all the telephone links were destroyed.

At Villa Rossi, things had not gone so well. Before the attackers were in position, firing had already started at the Villa Calvi. The alarm was given by a sentry on the roof, a siren was sounded and all the lights were switched on. Mike Lees recalled that the attackers rushed forward, enemy machine guns opened up, and he heard the first wild skirl of the pipes. Then they went through the wood, across the road—the bullets cracking past their heads—and into a gateway. The villa was 10 yards in front of them. The four sentries were killed and the main door was found to be open. After a hard fight the ground floor was occupied, but the Germans resisted fiercely from the upper floors, firing guns and throwing grenades down a spiral staircase.

Mike Lees led a raid up the stairs, as he related:

> With 'Gordon' following on my heels, I raced through the doorway into a brightly-lit, stone-flagged hall. The crash of breaking furniture and the rattle of Tommy guns sounded as the SAS cleared the adjoining room. The General would be in his bedroom; I turned and ran for the stairs. The landing above was in darkness and, as I started up, I heard a shout of warning behind me. Unheeding, I went on; a flash broke the gloom above: a sharp pain burned in my chest and, rolling over backwards, I felt my head crack against the ground.[3]

Lt Riccomini led another attempt to storm the stairs, but this too was repulsed, and he was killed. So were six Germans, who tried to come down. The lights on the ground floor were extinguished and the wounded were carried out. Meanwhile, the raiders set fire to the kitchen. After the twenty minutes allowed for the attack, the group retreated towards the west through intense fire and carrying their wounded.

In his official report, Farran wrote that there were seventeen casualties among the ranks of the Allied Battalion: SAS: one officer missing, believed killed, one soldier missing, believed killed, one soldier killed; one officer and two soldiers wounded; Russians: six missing, believed to have been taken prisoner, two soldiers wounded; *Gufo Nero*: one soldier wounded; *Garibaldini*: two soldiers wounded. The British losses were Lt James Arthur Riccomini, aged twenty-seven, and two twenty-four year olds—Sgt Sidney Elliott Guscott and Cpl Samuel Bolden. As we have seen, the first two men had come to Tombola from the Galia operation. Cpl Bolden landed at Case Balocchi with the third SAS group on 9 March. He was from Giffnock, in Renfrewshire, and had been awarded the MM for the courage and leadership he displayed in 1943 during duty in Norway with the Special Service Brigade.

Mike Lees and Glauco Monducci were both seriously wounded. At least twelve Germans were killed inside the Villa Rossi, but they did not include Gen. Hauck; by chance, he was away on the night. This was not immediately apparent, as is clear from Farran's official report and his first book, *Winged Dagger* (1948), but it was confirmed in *Operation Tombola* (1960).

The Germans had many automatic weapons and attacked repeatedly from the direction of Botteghe. The Russians responded to the firing with great precision and their defence was never breached during the attack. Several enemy machine guns were silenced, and their troops sustained many fatalities, especially around the telephone exchange. Towards the end of the action, the anti-aircraft guns at Puianello began firing in the direction of Villa Calvi, and some bright star shells were launched from Botteghe, Modena, and Reggio. At 2.25 a.m., Farran fired his red Very light as the signal to withdraw. The men moved in twos and threes, in a westerly direction, towards the rendezvous on the far bank of the Crostolo torrent, and then went south into the mountains.

It took an extra fifteen minutes for Lt Harvey and his men to disengage. He led them in the opposite direction to the one which they would ultimately take, believing that this would deceive the enemy, who would try and cut them off on the direct route to the mountains. The column walked straight through a German post unchallenged and cut the electricity wires strung along a hedge, though Harvey received a severe shock in the process. The two injured men—Cpl Layburn (wounded by a grenade) and Parachutist Mulvey (hit in the knee by a bullet)—were carried by their comrades in turn. Lt Harvey's column was reunited with Maj. Farran and most of the British and *Garibaldini* at Casa del Lupo.

Meanwhile, Parachutist Burke and Parachutist Ramos, one of the Spaniards, refused to leave Lees, who was in great pain. They hoisted his fifteen stone body on to a ladder and carried him for four days, deeper into the plains towards Reggio, rather than into the foothills that were combed by the Germans, and found him a safe hiding place. Having assured themselves that he would be well looked after, they returned to the mountains. The two soldiers were awarded the MM for this action. SOE and the partisans organised the escape of Lees and 'Gordon', who were flown to Florence from different airstrips in the province of Parma in Special Force's Fieseler Storch, piloted by Furio Lauri. Charles Macintosh related that Lees bore his serious wounds extremely well: 'In the circumstances there was no question of any disciplinary action against him'.

Parachutist Mulvey was left on a farm after arrangements had been made for him to be smuggled up to the mountains in a bullock cart later. A horse was requisitioned for Cpl Layburn. The animal was blind and stumbled frequently. Finally, it had to be abandoned and the corporal was hoisted on to a stretcher made out of saplings and an army blanket. He volunteered to stay behind, but his companions refused to hear of it and carried him ever onwards in teams of four.

Roy Farran recalled that there were no halts during the return journey, which lasted for the rest of the night and all next day. The whole countryside seemed to be buzzing with Germans and it was often necessary to make a detour to avoid them. The mist was still thick, which was to the raiders' advantage, but rain had made the mountain tracks slippery under foot. They were all exhausted and Benzedrine tablets were swallowed freely.

The battalion marched in step through the village of Valestra 'for pure show' in a column of threes behind the pipes, with Layburn on his stretcher leading the way. No Germans were encountered and the group successfully passed through their lines near Carpineti without contact. After marching non-stop for twenty-two hours, the men were forced to make a 5-mile detour and cross the flooded River Secchia at the Cavola footbridge. The old wounds in Farran's legs gave way and he had to finish the journey on horseback. The Battalion arrived in Secchio at 10 p.m. on the night of 27 March and received a rousing welcome from the Green Flame partisans. Fried eggs, bread, and wine by the gallon were produced at houses all over the village, but most of the men were too tired for merry-making. Farran was soon asleep in the local schoolmistress's bed and did not wake up for fourteen hours.

After the war, Mike Lees sought to put the record straight on the significance of the raid:

> This was an attack on a Corps Headquarters in a highly defended zone and it must rate as one of the most ambitious, organised and daring operations carried out by the Resistance forces. One hundred men were infiltrated more than 30 miles down towards the plains and right inside a Headquarters directly defended by 300 troops. What is more, after the action, apart from the three SAS heroes killed in the Villa Rossi, the entire party was got out again, sooner or later, without one single prisoner being

> taken by the Germans, thanks to the superb leadership of Roy Farran. It was a remarkable feat of arms, of organisation at every level, and above all of cooperation between the SAS under Roy Farran, the British Mission, the partisans from Reggio, and the patriotic action groups and squads.... I had the good fortune to interview General Hauck in a prisoner of war camp near Riccione in 1947 and I know that the attack caused a serious disruption to German control and morale, apart from giving a very well deserved boost to the confidence of the Resistance.[4]

Because it was carried out by regular British soldiers in uniform, the attack did not provoke a reprisal by the Germans against the people of the area. Instead, the troops already carrying out a drive in the foothills (who were by-passed by the Allied Battalion twice) were sent to attack the partisan-held territory south of the River Secchia which was hosting the SOE and the SAS.

The Allied battalion's outpost on the flooded river came under attack on 28 March. It was manned by a detachment of partisans from the 26th *Garibaldi* Brigade, with Lt Michael Eld and ten other SAS troops in the centre; Farran and Luigi, the partisan leader, made a tour of inspection next day. The defenders were well dug in on high ground overlooking the blown bridge at the junction of the Secchiello torrent with the River Secchia; the German-held village of Gatta was just across the water. The men were equipped with Brens and Stens, a water-cooled Vickers machine gun and a 3-inch mortar; Sgt Godwin, who had been with Farran at Botteghe (as had two more of parachutists), commanded the Vickers post, while Lt Eld deployed the mortar at the other end of a deep trench in the sandy soil.

The enemy battalion consisted of 400 Germans and Russians in four understrength companies, equipped with two field guns, mortars, and horse-drawn transport. There was to be a week-long exchange of fire across the river and, according to Farran, on the whole, the British and Italians had the best of the contest.

However, at 3 a.m. on Easter Sunday, 1 April, the major was awoken by a runner with the alarming news that 200 enemy troops, in two companies, had crossed the river over the Cavola footbridge 5 miles farther downstream. The partisans stationed in the zone were taken by surprise and retreated in disorder, including Green Flames, who went to their base at Quara. Parachutist Wooding, based nearby with ten of the Italian company, 'fired his thirty-seven-millimetre cannon to some effect and had succeeded in extricating both himself and his weapon'.

The Germans penetrated the valley as far as Monte della Castagna (879 metres), south of the village of Ca' Marastoni in the commune of Toano. The commandant of the Green Flames, the partisan priest Don Domenico Orlandini, had been awoken by the arrival of a courier with a note from

Gianni Farri, adjutant to the 26th *Garibaldi* Brigade, requesting urgent reinforcements for his men on the mountain. Don Domenico immediately ordered a battalion of the Green Flames based at Monte Croce, near Manno, to go to the aid of the Communists. A first detachment of twenty-one men left at 6.30 a.m. and arrived at 9 a.m. Someone from the summit called to them in local dialect: 'Come on up, so that we can talk'. However, when they approached, they were hit by machine-gun fire. Instead of *Garibaldini* there were only Germans there. The young partisan commander, Vito Caluzzi (Taylor), was killed, together with three of his men.

At first light, it became apparent that a force of about 150 Russians with German officers had occupied the mountain and set-up machine gun posts among the trees and piles of hay. At 11 a.m., the survivors from the Green Flames, some wounded, disengaged, full of suspicion of the motives of the Communists, who had not alerted them to the changed situation.

Shortly afterwards, Farran rode to Quara with Morbin, his batman. Accounts differ as to whether the major actually met Don Domenico Orlandini in the village, but in any event, the Green Flames were able to reorganise after the return of their surviving men from the mountain. Some of the headquarters staff and two detachments joined the fight, one led by Gottardo Bottarelli (Colonel Bassi), a former vice-admiral in the Italian Navy, and the other by the brigade's vice-commandant, Capt. William Manfredi (Elio), who was to die in the fighting.

Farran sent Capt. Easton an order to take the British and Italian companies north, so as to create a strong defensive position around Villa Minozzo on the left bank of the Secchiello torrent, which would block any potential advance by the enemy in that sector.

The major left his horse with Morbin in Quara and walked 2 miles to the scene of the battle. At least for the moment, men of the *Gufo Nero* squad were keeping the two enemy companies at bay from a position on Croce del Fornello, a mountain to the south-east of Monte della Castagna, and similar in size at 820 metres. The sabotage squad was led by Vice-Commandant Mario Giberti (Rubens), who was deputising for the wounded 'Gordon'. In overall charge was a new British Liaison Officer, Capt. John Lees (no relation to Michael), who had been parachuted three days earlier; he was being assisted by Capt. Neil Oughtred, another SOE officer in the zone.

Farran discussed the options with the officers in a secluded cottage. They thought that the enemy would outflank the northern outpost at Gatta during the night and then move swiftly to attack the British and partisan bases in the west of the valley. The only hope lay in an immediate counterattack by the 100 men of Victor Pirogov (Modena) and his Russians, which should then allow the invaders to be driven back across the river.

The major sent a *staffetta* to Governara to tell 'Modena' to march down with all speed, while his own motley collection of men held off the enemy for three hours, all the time fearing that they might charge. It was hot on the exposed mountainside and bullets ricocheted on the hard gravel all around them. The Russians arrived at 4 p.m., after a three-hour forced march over the rough tracks from Governara. The situation was quickly explained to 'Modena' by Lt Stephens, the Austrian interpreter, and by Parachutist Taylor, who was attached to the company.

The force on the ridge facing the enemy eventually grew to 200 men. As well as the SAS, the British SOE Mission, the *Gufo Nero* squad, a growing number of Green Flames, and the Russians of 'Modena', there were two detachments of *Garibaldini*, commanded by Gianni Farri, fresh from his role in in the attack on the German HQ. At 4.30 p.m., the Allied battalion began to lay down covering fire with Brens and Stens, and with a mortar targeted by 'Modena' himself, as the men approached the enemy positions; bombs were scattered across the 4 square miles between the battalion and the river, but two Green Flames were killed during the bombardment.

Half an hour later, a brief halt in the firing signalled the start of the main attack, as Farran related:

> I got up, waved my pistol and ran five paces down the hill. Not a soul moved. I ran back to the ridge with bullets whistling by my ears. I tried three times, once succeeding in getting them to their knees, before the whole mob followed me down the slope. It was all very exciting. Stephens and Taylor had got them moving on the right and, with loud cheers, we charged the German positions. It was too much for the enemy. One or two forlorn distress signals were fired into the air, then, throwing away their weapons, they bolted for the Secchia. We did not stop until we got to the river, where we had great fun picking off the Germans on their way across. The Vickers gun from Gatta did a lot of execution in the water. By nightfall, not a single German remained on our side of the river, except their twenty dead and twenty-five prisoners they had left behind.[5]

For the first time, the Reggio partisans had defeated a German battalion. In a message sent to the *Garibaldi* and Green Flame brigades by the Reggio *Comando Unico* three days later, the counter-attack was described as 'timely, decisive and brilliant'.

The moment was now fast approaching for the SAS to play its role in the final offensive.

22

Victory in Italy

On Easter Monday, 2 April 1945, the day after the German counterattack had been repulsed at Ca' Marastoni, the men of SAS Operation Tombola received a big supply drop at Case Balocchi. Two days later, Maj. Roy Farran met Maj. James 'Jim' Thomas Mann Davies, the British Liaison Officer for the neighbouring province of Modena, which was nearer the front and on the main path of German withdrawal. Subject to approval from 15th Army Group in Florence, they agreed that the Allied battalion would move to the province as soon as possible and sever its connections with the Reggio partisan command.

The proposal was approved and Farran was ordered to attack Route 12, the main road running through the mountains towards the plains and the city of Modena, as soon as the main offensive began. The highway provided the supply channel to the 114th and the 232nd German divisions on the US 4th Corps front.

The major set only three days for the men of the battalion to assemble at Quara prior to their departure, with all the detachments being required to withdraw from their outposts. In the meantime, Annibale Alpi (Barbanera) scrambled to obtain 100 bullock carts and their handlers to provide bulk transport. Four jeeps were also parachuted from Halifaxes, together with plentiful supplies, especially mortar bombs and shells for the howitzer.

On 7 April, the battalion moved off in four groups: Sun Column, led by Victor Pirogov (Modena), consisting of 100 Russians, with five SAS attached; Moon Column, led by Capt. Easton, consisting of twenty-five SAS and thirty *Garibaldini*; Star Column, led by Remo Torlai (Tito), consisting of sixty Italians; and Eclipse Column, led by Lt Eyton-Jones, consisting of 10 SAS, and equipped with four jeeps. Each of the other three columns had six mules for transport. As they left the high ground for the plains, the battalion suffered what proved to be the only German attack in the valley, but it was beaten off, and the whole unit was able to assemble unscathed in the village of Vitriola, inside Modena Province, on 11 and 12 April. At this time, as there seemed to be clash of personality between Lt Tysoe and the leader of his group of partisans, Remo Torlai (Tito), command of the Star Column was given to Lt Eyton-Jones, while Lt Tysoe went to Eclipse Column and the jeeps.

Two days later, 15th Army Group ordered offensive action to begin; but early results were disappointing. Farran related that it was easy to ambush a road running through a valley, because safe cover positions existed from which it was simple to withdraw, but Route 12 ran along a ridge and it was necessary to get right up to the road to attack it. Also, the Germans were less exposed, as they were now billeted in small farms along the road to avoid Allied bombing of all the villages behind the front.

The major decided to take command of the Eclipse Column and to lead it into the plains, accompanied by Lt Tysoe. The jeeps were all equipped with rapid-firing machine guns (the aircraft version of the Vickers) mounted in pairs, and the three-man crews also carried Brens. One jeep was detached to target a company of German infantry, which had moved into the village of Moncerrato. After making a successful attack, the vehicle returned to the base at Vitriola. The other three jeeps reached the plain, but found that they were in the middle of an enemy divisional area. They successfully extricated themselves, but in several near misses during contact with enemy forces, Farran lost touch with the other two vehicles at a crossroads. He learned later that, led by Lt Tysoe, the jeeps had run the gauntlet of a stationary enemy convoy and eventually found sanctuary in a partisan-held enclave around Torre Maina. Over the next fortnight, they attacked German posts and transport on Route 12 and made a frontal assault on a supply dump. One of the Spaniards serving with the battalion, Justo Balerdi, known as Robert Bruce, was killed during the fighting. The detachment finally returned to the plain and was the first to occupy Modena on the heels of the retreating Germans. The Russians were soon involved in an orthodox infantry attack against the Germans on Monte Mocogno and so they were not able to be used for ambushes on the road.

On 16 April, Farran called a conference of the column commanders and gave them a reprimand, stating that 'no concrete results' had been obtained. He ordered an all-out effort to inflict casualties on enemy traffic on the road. Leading by example, the major decided to launch a sally into the plain with the object of shelling German positions with the 75-mm pack howitzer, 'Molto Stanco'. Another jeep had been dropped while he was in enemy-held territory, so he was able to field fifteen men in three vehicles; they crossed the flooded River Secchia at a ford, and took up positions on a hill farm near the village of Montegibbio. Ten shells were unleashed on each of six towns occupied by the Germans, with an extra ten directed on the bridge at Sassuolo for luck. As soon as this was done, the men drove back safely to Vitriola. The technique of moving to the edge of the mountainous area and shelling the enemy positions on the roads below proved so effective that Farran used it as the model for all subsequent attacks, making good use of mortars and Brens, as well as the pack howitzer, and so avoiding most of the problems of approaching Route 12 up an exposed embankment.

On 18 April, there was a final airdrop by four Dakotas at Vitriola. The abundant supplies included spares and shells for the gun, petrol for the jeeps, and cigarettes for the men, and now they could be collected in the jeeps, rather than relying on mules and ox-carts; the whole village was busy with unpacking and storing containers. Two days later, Maj. Jim Davies again met Farran and told him that he believed that the German withdrawal was imminent. Davies was better informed, as he was able to maintain a twenty-four-hour-a-day wireless schedule with Florence, as opposed to the battalion's two hours a day. Farran summoned the column leaders and gave his orders for the general offensive. The Russians would launch an infantry attack to capture the village of Lama Mocogno on Route 12; Lt Harvey was to continue operating with his British column at the point where the highway runs into the plain; Lt Tysoe, still based at Torre Maina, would carry out raids on German transport on the plain around Modena; Lt David Eyton-Jones and his Italians were to target Route 12 around Montefestino.

The lieutenant, aged twenty-two, served in the Royal Sussex Regiment as an infantry officer and arrived in Italy in 1944; in early 1945, he volunteered for special duties and 'a chance to employ knowledge of weaponry in a more unorthodox way', and on 7 March, he parachuted to Farran's mission in order to provide small arms training to the partisans. Once he took charge of the Star Column, Eyton-Jones was detailed to accompany the Italians under Remo Torlai (Tito) to attack German convoys on Route 12. From a base near Monteforco they marched under cover of darkness to reach a vantage point above the highway. It was an arduous trek over very rough ground for a column of men and mules and any noise started the farm dogs barking. They did not find a target every night, and so the lieutenant decided to divide the column into two parts for greater agility and better results. The next night, a small party under Cpl Ford, equipped with four Thompson sub-machine guns and a Bren, attacked a column of ten armoured half-tracks and fifteen trucks, setting five vehicles on fire and making a fighting withdrawal. The corporal was later awarded the MM for this action. He reported that there appeared to be a German staging post in the village of Montebonello, and a *staffetta* also suggested that there was also a signals station there, which was confirmed by questioning a German prisoner.

Eyton-Jones related that once he received Maj. Farran's order to mount an attack to coordinate with the American Fifth Army offensive, a short meeting was held with the Italian commander, which was sufficient to decide to attack the German HQ in the village. All hands started cleaning their weapons and loading the mules with ammunition, cheered with a ration of grappa. Then they began the advance:

> The column by-passed a farm at Monteforco in the evening light, crossed two valleys, and we found a knoll about 400 yards from Montebonello without being detected by the German sentries in the bell tower. With the aid of the moon, which had conveniently risen above our target, we were able to site the Browning heavy machine guns and mortars. All the partisans had just found good firing positions when we heard the unmistakable sound of a convoy starting up.
>
> Immediately our Browning heavy machine gun started firing with tracer bullets to point out the target for the mortars to range upon. The accuracy of the shooting was confirmed by a conflagration, followed by a series of explosions in Montebonello. A small party sent forward to cover the German exit on the far side of the village shot up the few vehicles that tried to escape, while our main party rapidly evacuated their firing positions, which were becoming the subject of German return fire.
>
> The next morning we heard that the Germans had evacuated Montebonello on foot, leaving heavy casualties and a wrecked convoy of vehicles.
>
> There was no need to call '*Avanti!*' ['Forward!'] to 'Tito's' column as they strode down the hills into the valley near Sassuolo—they were singing as they marched towards their homes in the Reggio Emilia area. The only sign of the Germans was a cloud of dust subsiding northwards.[1]

The remainder of the battalion was grouped into a new mobile unit under Farran's command. Codenamed Victory Column, it consisted of twenty British and thirty Italians, with three jeeps, the 75-mm howitzer, and twenty-three bullock carts. Shortly after the convoy moved off, a motor cyclist arrived from Maj. Jim Davies with the news that the German retreat had finally begun. Farran decided to assault the City of Reggio without delay, as it was directly on the German line of retreat to the River Po. He went ahead with the jeeps and the gun, leaving Easton to lead the bullock train with the ammunition; the captain was far from happy at the prospect, but as a peace offering, Farran left him his horse.

The major's little convoy took up positions on a hill farm at a crossroads only 2 miles from Reggio. The first shots hit the main square, and a plume of smoke rose from the foot of the cathedral; Farran ordered the firing of five quick rounds, and the smoke increased. A siren sounded, and within two hours, the Germans and Fascists had abandoned the city, believing that the SAS troops were the advance guard of an American armoured division.

Farran's men had fired twenty-four shells and were coming to the end of the volley when one of the projectiles jammed in the breech and had to be released by a crowbar. When firing a final replacement, the gun recoiled, there was a loud explosion, and the shell hit a tree. The crew commander, Sgt Frank 'Taffy' Hughes, staggered back, hands to his head, blood streaming from a shrapnel wound to one eye. The unit doctor, Jock Milne, treated him and took him to the Convent of Santa Maria back at Baiso, where they were assured that he would be looked after by trained sisters. The force returned to Vignola by the same route and no Germans were encountered. Once back in the village, Farran was surprised to meet Easton with the ox-carts; he had made the journey from the mountains in record time by marching day and night.

Two days later, a jeep sent down into Castellarano returned with the news that the Germans were withdrawing headlong through Sassuolo in the direction of the River Po. The Allies had broken through near Bologna, and the whole German Army was in full retreat. Farran sent a section under Lt Eld to mortar Scandiano, the nearest large town on the plain, while he took the remainder of the column into the foothills overlooking a ford over the River Secchia and the Sassuolo Bridge, which was about a mile to the south. Two Vickers guns were sited on the forward slopes of the last hill before the town, and the howitzer was placed just behind it. Farran recalled that his Armoured Corps commands were not to the liking of the artilleryman Jock Easton, who shouted back down the walkie-talkie: 'Why the hell don't you use the proper fire orders?'

'Don't argue, just fire where I tell you, you understand, fire five shells now,' Farran screamed back.

Easton seemed to pay little attention to him, but rained shell after shell in the middle of the enemy column. About twelve trucks in the river and five more on the road were set on fire. A flight of passing Spitfires with Brazilian pilots was attracted by the smoke, and, seeing the jammed column in the ford, they dived down to make their contribution to the carnage. Farran recalled: 'The excitement was greater than anything I had experienced since the Battle of Crete'. The SAS next targeted the Sassuolo Bridge; the one-sided battle went on all day, with very little retaliation from the enemy. Towards evening, after they had fired over 150 rounds, the men withdrew into the foothills.

The next morning, the SAS used their last twenty-five shells on Sassuolo, after hearing that it was full of fleeing Germans. Farran moved the rest of the column under cover, while he went off in a jeep for a reconnaissance. During the day, Easton destroyed or captured a large number of the enemy's horses and carts. When driving down the Montegibbio road towards the plain, Farran passed huge bands of partisans marching on the City of Modena. They turned their happy faces towards him and screamed '*Viva McGinty*'. He recalled: 'Tears came to my eyes, I was so happy: These were my people. Maybe I had cursed them, had kicked them, had despised them, had driven them into danger, but they bore no resentment....They were men of peace and to them I was McGinty, a partisan chief. "*Viva McGinty*"'. On the main Sassuolo road through the plains, Farran came upon a tiny band of dusty figures resting in a ditch. They were the parachutists led by Lt Harvey, who reported that they had seen the Americans in their tanks, though they had not yet taken the town. At around the same time, Lt Eyton-Jones had a similar encounter, as he recalled:

> Suddenly there was a rumble of transport behind us and so we vacated the road, thinking that this was a straggling German convoy. Round the corner came the leading scout car and I recognised the American white star marking. The partisans had not seen this before, so only the British Corporal Ford and I stepped out into the roadway to greet them.
>
> '*Dove tedeschi?*' ['Where are the Germans?'] the American asked.
>
> 'Gone away,' I replied in English.
>
> 'You speak English?' came the surprised query.
>
> 'I am English, been with the partisans here for months.'
>
> I then gave the American my opinion that it had been the partisans, with a little bit of help from the British that had dislodged the enemy. It did not seem many months since I had joined the partisans, but in good company time passes fast. I had learned, in the time in 1945 when a winter turned to spring in Italy, that the spirit of the Resistance, unknown to many people in the world, albeit for reasons of security, had been so widespread that the date of our victory in Italy had been considerably advanced.[2]

By the next day, all the SAS men were together in Modena. The Americans had passed by and left a small amount of mopping up to the partisans. The British helped a little in the street fighting, but Farran soon realised that the Italians were best left to complete the task on their own.

A wireless message came through ordering the SAS back to Florence and telling Farran to disarm the Russians immediately. He related: 'I am afraid to say that I had not the moral courage for what seemed to us at the time to be such a cruel, unfair and premature act'. Farran left orders with a rear party to disarm the men after the victory parade in Reggio in four days and slipped off quietly with the rest of the British towards Florence. He recalled that it was a brave little convoy of four jeeps, two civilian cars, two captured lorries, a German ambulance, and the gun: 'We were all covered with the grime of months in the mountains, and our shabbiness was in sharp contrast to the huge armoured columns we passed on the road. They must have wondered who on earth we could be'.

In his official report, Farran stated that the actions of his small force contributed very largely to the panic of some three or four German divisions. One estimate was that the Allied Battalion killed 300 German soldiers and destroyed twenty vehicles, as well as taking 158 POWs; in return, the unit had sustained twenty-eight casualties.

In the aftermath of Operation Tombola, Charles Macintosh of TAC HQ recalled that consideration was given to disciplining Farran, but Col. Riepe 'quite rightly' decided against it and allowed him to defend the area against the attacks he had provoked and then, when the order was given on 4 April, to attack German communications in the hills and finally in the plains.

Roy Farran concluded his second book on the war, *Operation Tombola* (1960), on a suitably triumphant note:

> Fortunately I did not receive a trial by court-martial as I expected. The British faction that wanted to try me on two counts—for parachuting behind the lines when forbidden to do so and for attacking the German headquarters at Albinea in contravention of orders—was narrowly defeated, largely through support I received from Colonel Riepe, the US officer at 15th Army Group in charge of special operations. He even went so far as to recommend me for a US Legion of Merit—an ace in the hole because I could hardly be court martialled for something for which I had been decorated.
>
> His citation concerning Operation Tombola said that our operations against enemy rear units south of Modena materially assisted the attack of the United States 4th Corps and contributed significantly to the success of 15th Army Group.
>
> Who dares wins.[3]

The final victory came quickly in Italy as the 5th and 8th Armies swept north after breaching the Gothic Line, supported by a partisan rising, and against the background of months of secret talks in Switzerland on the surrender of German Forces. The negotiations were conducted by the Allied secret services and a group of senior German officers led by Gen. Karl Wolff, Highest SS and Police Leader and Plenipotentiary Gen. of the Armed Forces for the Rear Combat Areas of Italy.

At two in the afternoon on 29 April 1945, the document was signed in secret by German and Allied representatives in the Allied Force HQ in the Royal Palace of Caserta. Article one read: 'The German Commander-in-Chief Southwest hereby surrenders unconditionally all the forces under his command or control on land, at sea and in the air, and places himself and these forces unconditionally at the disposal of the Supreme Allied Commander, Mediterranean Theatre of Operations'.

The terms provided for the ending of hostilities at two in the afternoon on 2 May. The German delegates also had a written proxy from Marshal Rodolfo Graziani, Minister of Defence of the Italian Social Republic, providing for an equivalent surrender by the Fascist Armed Forces. On the 2nd, the agreement was duly made public and the ceasefire came into effect across the country; enemy forces surrendered unconditionally, either on that day or, in a few cases, the next day. The war in Europe ended officially on 8 May.

Within days of the surrender in Italy, victory parades were held, speeches were made, honours were awarded, and the partisans were demobilised. The same fate was to meet the SAS a few months later.

On his return from Colditz, Col. David Stirling was made Deputy Commander of the SAS Brigade and he began to develop plans for its possible deployment in the Far East. However, in the weeks following the Japanese surrender on 2 September, it was decided that the SAS was no longer needed and that it would be stood down.

A final parade was held on 8 October, and the men who had once ridden the slipstream returned to civilian life to enjoy the peace that their bravery had helped make possible.

Endnotes

Chapter 1

1. King's College London Archives: McLeod, Gen., Sir R. W. (1905–1980) papers; Stirling, DSO, OBE, Col. D., *Memorandum on the Origins of the Special Air Service* (8 November 1948).

Chapter 5

1. The National Archives (TNA): WO 373, 'Recommendations for Honours and Awards for Gallant and Distinguished Service (Army)'.

Chapter 7

1. TNA: WO 373, 'Recommendations for Honours and Awards for Gallant and Distinguished Service (Army)'.
2. *Ibid.*
3. Quoted in Dillon, M., and Bradford, R., *Rogue Warrior of the SAS, The Blair Mayne Legend* (Edinburgh: Mainstream Publishing, 2005), p. 90.

Chapter 8

1. Translated by the author from *Come si giunse all'armistizio dell' 8 settembre* 1943 (Piacenza: ANPI, 1977), pp. 89-90.
2. TNA: WO 218/177, 'Operation Speedwell, Report'.
3. TNA: WO 373, 'Recommendations for Honours and Awards for Gallant and Distinguished Service (Army)'.
4. Quoted in 'Lord Ashcroft's Hero of the Month: Major Tony Greville-Bell, DSO' in *Britain at War*, July 2014.
5. TNA: WO 373, *op. cit.*
6. TNA: WO 218/177, 'Operation Speedwell, Report'.
7. *Ibid.*

Chapter 9

1. Challenor, H., with Draper, A., *Tanky Challenor, SAS and the Met* (London: Leo Cooper, 1990), p. 59.
2. TNA: WO 373, 'Recommendations for Honours and Awards for Gallant and Distinguished Service (Army)'.

Chapter 10

1. A copy of the original letter was emailed by Victor Schmit's grandson, Rodrigo Quiroga Schmit, to teacher Michael Downes after he had written about the life and sad end of former pupil at Oundle School, Northamptonshire, Capt. Patrick Dudgeon, MC.
2. The United Nations War Crimes Commission, *Law Reports of Trials of War Criminals, Volume XII* (1949).
3. Cassese, A., (General Editor), *The Oxford Companion to International Criminal Justice* (Oxford University Press, 2009), pp. 670-671.

Chapter 11

1. TNA: WO 218/180, 'Operation Candytuft, Report'.

Chapter 13

1. TNA: ADM 1/13397, 'Evacuation of Escaped Allied Prisoners of War from Termoli, Italy'.
2. Farran, R., *Winged Dagger, Adventures on Special Service* (London: Cassell, 1998), pp. 199-200.

Chapter 14

1. TNA: WO 218/183, 'Operation Maple, Report'.
2. *Ibid.*

Chapter 15

1. TNA: WO 218/185, 'Operation Pomegranate, Report'.
2. *Ibid.*
3. The Imperial War Museum, Department of Documents, papers of Captain J. Q. Hughes.
4. *Ibid.*

Chapter 20

1. Farran, R., *Winged Dagger, Adventures on Special Service* (London: Cassell, 1998), p. 284.

Chapter 21

1. Harvey, K. G., 'The Attack on the Villa Calvi: Operation Tombola' in *No. 1 Special Force and Italian Resistance* (Bologna: University of Bologna, 1990), pp. 204-205.
2. *Ibid.*, p. 205.
3. Quoted in Lewis, L., *Echoes of Resistance, British Involvement with the Italian Partisans* (Tunbridge Wells: Costello, 1985), p. 105.
4. Lees, M., 'The Attack on the Villa Rossi' in *No. 1 Special Force and Italian Resistance* (Bologna: University of Bologna, 1990), pp. 217-218.
5. Farran, *op. cit.*, p. 308.

Chapter 22

1. Eyton-Jones, D., 'The Attack on the German Command at Montebonello,' in *No. 1 Special Force and Italian Resistance* (1990), pp. 248.
2. *Ibid.*, pp. 248-249.
3. Farran, R., *Operation Tombola* (London: Arms and Armour Press, 1986), pp. 255-256.

Bibliography

Ashcroft, M., *Special Ops Heroes* (London: Headline Publishing Group, 2015)

Cassese, A., (General Editor), *The Oxford Companion to International Criminal Justice* (Oxford University Press, 2009)

Challenor, H., with Draper, A., *Tanky Challenor, SAS and the Met* (London: Leo Cooper, 1990)

Churchill, W. S., *The Second World War: Volume V, Closing the Ring* (London: Book Club Associates, 1985)

Collotti, E., Sandri, R., and Sessi, F., *Dizionario della Resistenza* (Turin: Giulio Einaudi, 2006)

Come si giunse all'armistizio dell' 8 settembre 1943 (Piacenza: ANPI, 1977)

Dillon, M., and Bradford, R., *Rogue Warrior of the SAS, The Blair Mayne Legend* (Edinburgh: Mainstream Publishing, 2005)

Eyton-Jones, D., 'The Attack on the German Command at Montebonello,' in *No. 1 Special Force and Italian Resistance* (1990)

Farran, R., *Operation Tombola* (London: Arms and Armour Press, 1986); *Winged Dagger, Adventures on Special Service* (London: Cassell, 1998)

Harvey, K. G., 'The Attack on the Villa Calvi: Operation Tombola' in *No. 1 Special Force and Italian Resistance* (1990)

King's College London Archives: McLeod, Gen., Sir R. W. (1905–1980) papers

Kirby, D., *The Scourge of Soho, the Controversial Career of SAS Hero Detective Sergeant Harry Challenor, MM* (Barnsley: Pen and Sword, 2013)

Law Reports of Trials of War Criminals, The United Nations War Crimes Commission, Volume XII (London: HMSO, 1949)

Lees, M., 'The Attack on the Villa Rossi' in *No. 1 Special Force and Italian Resistance* (1990)

Lett, B., *S.A.S. in Tuscany 1943–1945* (Barnsley: Pen and Sword, 2011)

Lett. G., *Rossano* (London: Panther Books, 1956)

Lewes, J., *Jock Lewes: Co-Founder of the SAS* (Barnsley: Leo Cooper, 2000)

Lewis, L., *Echoes of Resistance, British Involvement with the Italian Partisans* (Tunbridge Wells: Costello, 1985)

'Lord Ashcroft's Hero of the Month: Major Tony Greville-Bell, DSO' in *Britain at War*, July 2014

Macintosh, C., DSO, *From Cloak to Dagger: An SOE Agent in Italy 1943–1945* (London: William Kimber, 1982)

Mather, C., *When the Grass Stops Growing, A War Memoir* (Barnsley: Leo Cooper, 1997)

McClean, S., *SAS, The History of the Special Raiding Squadron, 'Paddy's Men'* (Stroud: Spellmount, 2006)

Mortimer, G., *The SAS in World War II* (Oxford: Osprey Publishing, 2011); *The SBS in World War II* (Oxford: Osprey Publishing, 2013)

No. 1 Special Force and Italian Resistance (Bologna: University of Bologna, 1990)

SAS War Diary 1941–1945 (London: Extraordinary Editions, 2011)

Stirling, DSO, OBE, Col. D., *Memorandum on the Origins of the Special Air Service* (8 November 1948)

The Imperial War Museum, Department of Documents, papers of Captain J. Q. Hughes

TNA: ADM 1/13397, 'Evacuation of Escaped Allied Prisoners of War from Termoli, Italy'.

TNA: WO 218/177, 'Operation Speedwell, Report'

TNA: WO 218/180, 'Operation Candytuft, Report'

TNA: WO 218/183, 'Operation Maple, Report'

TNA: WO 218/185, 'Operation Pomegranate, Report'

TNA: WO 373, 'Recommendations for Honours and Awards for Gallant and Distinguished Service (Army)'

Tudor, M., *SOE in Italy 1940–1945: The Real Story* (Newtown: Emilia Publishing, 2011); *Among the Italian Partisans: The Allied Contribution to the Resistance* (Stroud: Fonthill Media, 2016)